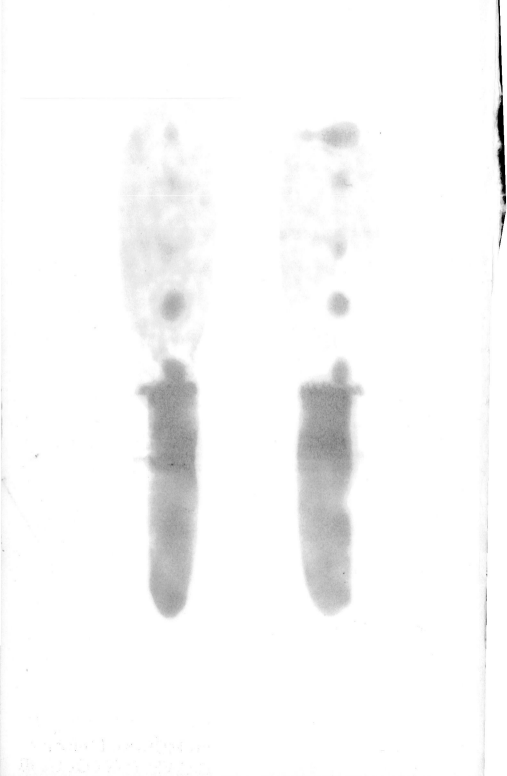

# Oscar Wilde
## Interviews and Recollections

### Volume 2

*Also by E. H. Mikhail*

The Social and Cultural Setting of the 1890s
John Galsworthy the Dramatist
Comedy and Tragedy
Sean O'Casey: A Bibliography of Criticism
A Bibliography of Modern Irish Drama 1899–1970
Dissertations on Anglo-Irish Drama
The Sting and the Twinkle: Conversations with Sean O'Casey
(*co-editor with John O'Riordan*)
J. M. Synge: A Bibliography of Criticism
Contemporary British Drama 1950–1976
J. M. Synge: Interviews and Recollections (*editor*)
W. B. Yeats: Interviews and Recollections (two volumes) (*editor*)
English Drama 1900–1950
Lady Gregory: Interviews and Recollections (*editor*)
Oscar Wilde: An Annotated Bibliography of Criticism
A Research Guide to Modern Irish Dramatists

# OSCAR WILDE

## Interviews and Recollections

## Volume 2

*Edited by*

## E. H. Mikhail

BOOKS
10 East 53d St., New York 10022
(a division of Harper & Row Publishers, Inc.)

*First published 1979 by*
THE MACMILLAN PRESS LTD
*London and Basingstoke*

Published in the U.S.A. 1979 by
HARPER & ROW PUBLISHERS, INC.
BARNES & NOBLE IMPORT DIVISION

*Printed in Great Britain*

**Library of Congress Cataloging in Publication Data**
Main entry under title:

Oscar Wilde: interviews and recollections.

  Bibliography: p.
  Includes index.
  1. Wilde, Oscar, 1854–1900—Interviews.  2. Wilde,
Oscar, 1854–1900—Anecdotes.  3. Authors, Irish—19th
century—Biography—Addresses, essays, lectures.
I. Mikhail, E. H.
PR5823.066  1978    828'.8'09    [B]       77–16829
ISBN 0–06–494815–3 (v. 1)
ISBN 0–06–494816–1 (v. 2)

# Contents

vi          ·    CONTENTS

# Acknowledgements

The editor and publishers wish to thank the following who have kindly given permission for the use of copyright material:

Adam International Review for the extracts 'The Causeur' by Sir Max Beerbohm and 'Some Unpublished Recollections of Oscar Wilde' by Stuart Merrill, published in Vols. 241–243, 1954;

Edward Arnold (Publishers) Ltd for the extract 'I Won a Bet' by Lady Randolph Churchill from *Reminiscences*;

Associated Book Publishers Ltd for the extract from *Contemporary Portraits* by Frank Harris, published by Methuen & Co. Ltd;

Associated Newspapers Group Ltd for the extracts from 'In the Depths' from the *Evening News* (1 March 1905) and *Evening Mail* (London) (2 March 1905);

B.B.C. Publications for the extract from 'Mark this Man' by Richard Best from *Irish Literary Portraits*;

The Bodley Head for the extract 'Oscar Wilde' by Coulson Kernahan from *In Good Company: Some Personal Recollections*;

The Bodley Head for the extracts from 'The Poet in Prison' by Thomas Martin and 'Wilde's God' by Robert Harborough Sherard from *The Life of Oscar Wilde* by Robert Harborough Sherard published by T. Werner Laurie Ltd;

The Bodley Head and Dodd, Mead & Co. for the extracts 'My Last Meeting with Oscar Wilde' by Robert Harborough Sherard and 'Oscar Wilde Worked All Night Long' by Jean Dupoirier from *The Real Oscar Wilde* by Robert Harborough Sherard;

Jonathan Cape Ltd on behalf of the Executors of the Augustus John Estate for the extract from *Chiaroscuro, Fragments of Autobiography*;

Jonathan Cape Ltd on behalf of the Executors of the Laurence Housman Estate for the extract from *Echo de Paris: A Study of Life*;

Chatto & Windus Ltd for the extract 'The Latter Days of Oscar Wilde' from *Confessions of a Journalist* by Chris Healy;

Chatto & Windus Ltd on behalf of the Literary Estate of Norman Douglas for the extract from *Looking Back: An Autobiographical Excursion*;

Edward Colman, Literary Executor of Lord Alfred Douglas, for the extract from *Without Apology* by Lord Alfred Douglas;

Constable & Co. Ltd for the extract from *Aspects of Wilde* by Vincent O'Sullivan;

Curtis Brown Ltd, on behalf of the Executors for Gertrude Atherton and Liveright Publishing Corporation, for the extract from *Adventures of a Novelist*, by Gertrude Atherton; US copyright renewed 1959 by Muriel Atherton Russell.

J. M. Dent & Sons Ltd and Coward McCann & Geoghegan Inc., for the extract 'Oscar Wilde in Dieppe' by Jacques-Émile Blanche from *Portraits of a Lifetime*, translated and edited by Walter Clement;

Eyre and Spottiswoode (Publishers) Ltd for the extract from *Melodies and Memories* by Nellie Melba, published by Thornton Butterworth Ltd;

Faber & Faber Ltd for the extract from *My Fill of Days* by Sir Peter Chalmore Mitchell;

A. M. Heath & Co. Ltd on behalf of S. N. Behrman and Brandt and Brandt Inc., for the extract 'A Rumour' by Sir Max Beerbohm from *Conversation with Max* by S. N. Behrman;

David Higham Associates Ltd and Liveright Publishing Corporation for the extract from *Return to Yesterday* by Ford Madox Ford, published by Victor Gollancz Ltd. US copyright renewed 1959 by Janice Ford Biala;

Hodder & Stoughton Ltd for the extract from *An Autobiography* by Richard Burdon Haldane;

William Hodge & Co. Ltd for the extracts from *The Trials of Oscar Wilde* edited by H. Montgomery Hyde;

Mrs Thelma Holland for an extract from *Time Remembered after Père Lachaise* by Vyvyan Holland;

Hutchinson Publishing Group Ltd for the extracts from *To Tell My Story* by Irene Vanbrugh and *As I Knew Them: Sketches of People I Have Met On The Way* by Ella Hepworth Dixon;

Mills & Boon Ltd for the extract from *The Great Reign*;

The Society of Authors as the literary representative of the Estate of Richard Le Gallienne for the extract from *The Romantic 90's*;

The Society of Authors on behalf of the Bernard Shaw Estate for the extract from 'My Memories of Oscar Wilde' by Bernard Shaw from *Oscar Wilde: His Life and Confessions* by Frank Harris;

A. P. Watt & Son on behalf of Michael Holroyd for the extract from *The Life of Oscar Wilde* by Hesketh Pearson, published by Macdonald & Jane's Ltd;

Every effort has been made to trace all the copyright holders but if any have been inadvertently overlooked the publishers will be pleased to make the necessary arrangement at the first opportunity.

# The Oscar I Knew*

Lillie Langtry

Vividly I recall the first meeting with Oscar Wilde in the studio of Frank Miles,[1] and how astonished I was at his strange appearance. Then he must have been not more than twenty-two. He had a profusion of brown hair, brushed back from his forehead, and worn rather longer than was conventional, though not with the exaggeration which he afterwards affected. His face was large, and so colourless that a few pale freckles of good size were oddly conspicuous. He had a well-shaped mouth, with somewhat coarse lips and greenish-hued teeth. The plainness of his face, however, was redeemed by the splendour of his great, eager eyes.

In height he was about six feet, and broad in proportion. His hands were large and indolent, with pointed fingers and perfectly-shaped filbert nails, indicative of his artistic disposition. The nails, I regretfully record, rarely receiving the attention they deserved. To me he was always grotesque in appearance, although I have seen him described by a French writer as 'beautiful' and 'Apollo-like.' That he possessed a remarkably fascinating and compelling personality, and what in an actor would be termed wonderful 'stage presence,' is beyond question and there was about him an enthusiasm singularly captivating. He had one of the most alluring voices that I have ever listened to, round and soft, and full of variety and expression, and the cleverness of his remarks received added value from his manner of delivering them.

His customary apparel consisted of light-coloured trousers, a black frock coat, only the lower button fastened, a brightly flowered waistcoat blossoming underneath, and a white silk cravat, held together by an old intaglio amethyst set as a pin. I do not think I ever met him wearing gloves, but he always carried a pale lavender pair, using them to give point to his gestures, which were many and varied. Apropos of his dress, I recall seeing him (after he had become celebrated and prosperous), at the first night of one of his plays, come before the curtain, in response to the applause of the audience, wearing a black velvet jacket, lavender trousers, and a variegated waistcoat, a white straw hat in one hand and a lighted cigarette in the other.

In the early part of our acquaintance Wilde was *really* ingenuous. His

---

* *The Days I Knew* (London: Hutchinson, 1925) pp. 86–97. Editor's title.

mannerisms and eccentricities were then but the natural outcome of a young fellow bubbling over with temperament, and were not at all assumed. Later, when he began to rise as a figure in the life of London, and his unconscious peculiarities had become a target for the humorous columns of the newspapers, he was quick to realise that they could be turned to advantage, and he proceeded forthwith to develop them so audaciously that it became impossible to ignore them.

He was ridiculed and he was imitated. When he wore a daisy in his buttonhole, thousands of young men did likewise. When he proclaimed the sunflower 'adorable,' it was to be found adorning every drawing-room. His edict that severely plain and flowing garments were the only becoming covering for the female form sent every young woman, and many elderly ones, scampering off to their *modistes* with delirious suggestions for Grecian draperies.

In the queer jargon of the day, he was the 'Apostle of the Lily,' the 'Apostle of the Transcendental,' and, among the revilers, the 'Apostle of the Utterly-Utter and Too-Too.' His affectations, I may say, were mainly for the benefit of the general public. To his friends he always remained the same, and both friends and enemies were forced to confess his brilliancy in spite of his shams. His vogue spread rapidly, and soon he was lionised by both artistic and social sets of London. It seemed to me, however, that he gradually grew less spontaneous and more laboured in his conversation as he became the fashion, which was not to be wondered at when he was counted on to be the life of every afternoon tea, and was expected to supply a *bon mot*[2] between every mouthful at dinner.

His mother, Lady Wilde, lived a retired life in Onslow Square, sometimes emerging from her seclusion to give an afternoon at-home to guests invited by her two sons. On these occasions she used to pull down the blinds and light the lamps, even on summer days. She was a poetess, and wrote verses under the *nom de plume* of Esperanza [*sic*], so perhaps her son partly inherited his poetic gift from his mother. Some said his elder brother, Willie, was as clever in his way, but I found him quite uninteresting.

When I met Oscar he had come down from Oxford fresh from winning the prize for the best poem of the year, called 'Ravenna,' but he was very modest about his success, and I heard the fact only from others. Presently, other and beautiful verses from his pen began to attract unusual attention and admiration, and it was then that I became the inspiration for one of his happiest efforts. The poem, which, with a dedication to me, originally appeared in *The World*[3] (a society paper edited by Edmund Yates), is included in Oscar's first volume. He presented me with a white vellum-bound copy bearing the following charming inscription:

'To Helen, formerly of Troy, now of London.'

I append this poem:

## THE NEW HELEN

Where hast thou been since round the walls of Troy
   The sons of God fought in the great emprise?
     Why dost thou walk our common earth again?
Hast thou forgotten that impassioned boy,
   His purple galley and his Tyrian men,
     And treacherous Aphrodite's mocking eyes?
For surely it was thou, who, like a star
   Hung in the silver silence of the night,
     Didst bear the Old World's chivalry and might
Into the clamorous crimson waves of war!

Or didst thou rule the fire-laden moon?
   In amorous Sidon was thy temple built,
     Over the light and laughter of the sea?
Where behind lattice, scarlet-wrought and gilt,
   Some brown-limbed girl did weave thee tapestry,
All through the waste and wearied hours of noon;
   Till her wan cheek with flame of passion burned,
And she rose up the sea-washed lips to kiss
   Of some glad Cyprian sailor, safe returned
From Calpe and the cliffs of Herackles?

No! thou art Helen and none other one!
   It was for thee that young Sarpedon died,
And Memmon's manhood was untimely spent;
   It was for thee gold-crested Hector tried
With Thetis' child that evil race to run,
   In the last year of thy beleaguerment;
Ay, even now the glory of thy fame
   Burns in those fields of trampled asphodel,
Where the high lords whom Ilion knew so well
   Clash ghostly shields, and call upon thy name.

Where hast thou been? In that enchanted land
Whose slumbering vales forlorn Calypso knew,
Where never mower rose at break of day,
But all unswathed the tramelling grasses grew,
   And the sad shepherd saw the tall corn stand
Till summer's red had changed to withered grey?
   Didst thou lie there by some Lethean stream
Deep brooding on thine ancient memory,

The crash of broken spears, the fiery gleam
From shivered helm, the Grecian battle-cry?

Nay, thou wert hidden in that hollow hill
    With one who is forgotten utterly,
The discrowned Queen men call the Erycine;
    Hidden away, that never mightst thou see
The face of Her, before whose mouldering shrine
    To-day at Rome the silent nations kneel;
Who gat from Love no joyous gladdening,
    But only Love's intolerable pain,
Only a sword to pierce her heart in twain,
    Only the bitterness of child-bearing.

The lotus leaves which heal the wounds of Death
    Lie in thy hand; O, be thou kind to me,
While yet I know the summer of my days;
    For hardly can my tremulous lips draw breath
To fill the silver trumpet with thy praise,
    So bowed am I before thy mystery,
So bowed and broken on Love's terrible wheel,
    That I have lost all hope and heart to sing,
Yet care I not what ruin Time may bring,
    If in thy temple thou wilt let me kneel.

Alas, alas, thou wilt not tarry here,
    But, like that bird, the servant of the sun,
Who flies before the north wind and the night,
    So wilt thou fly our evil land and drear,
Back to the sower of thine old delight,
    And the red lips of young Euphorion;
Nor shall I ever see thy face again,
    But in this poisoned garden-close must stay,
Crowning my brows with the thorn-crown of pain,
    Till all my loveless life shall pass away.

O Helen! Helen! Helen! yet a while,
    Yet for a little while, O tarry here,
Till the dawn cometh and the shadows flee!
    For in the gladsome sunlight of thy smile
Of heaven or hell I have no thought or fear,
    Seeing I know no other God but thee;
No other God save him before whose feet

In nets of gold the tired planets move;
The incarnate spirit of spiritual love,
Who in thy body holds his joyous seat.

Thou wert not born as common women are!
    But, girt with splendour of the foam,
Didst from depths of sapphire seas arise!
And at thy coming some immortal star,
Bearded with flame, blazed in the Eastern skies
    And waked the shepherds on thine island home.
Thou shalt not die: no asps of Egypt creep
    Close at thy heels to taint the delicate air;
No sullen poppies stain thy hair,
    Those scarlet heralds of eternal sleep.

Lily of love, pure and inviolate!
    Tower of ivory! Red rose of fire!
Thou hast come down our darkness to illume.
For we, close caught in the wide nets of Fate,
    Wearied with waiting for the World's Desire,
Aimlessly wandered in this House of Gloom,
    Aimlessly sought some slumberous anodyne
For wasted lives, for lingering wretchedness,
    Till we beheld thy re-arisen shrine,
And the white glory of thy loveliness.

In the heyday of his popularity Oscar and his fads were utilised by Gilbert
and Sullivan as their motive of *Patience*, and one of the former's best lyrics
ended with these lines:

> Though the Philistines may jostle
> You will rank as an apostle
>     In the high æsthetic band,
> As you walk down Piccadilly
> With a poppy or a lily
>     In your mediaeval hand.

Before Oscar had achieved celebrity, and was unconsciously on the verge
of it, he always made a point of bringing me flowers, but he was not in
circumstances to afford great posies, so, in coming to call, he would drop
into Covent Garden flower market, buy me a single gorgeous amaryllis (all
his slender purse would allow), and stroll down Piccadilly carefully
carrying the solitary flower. The scribblers construed his act of homage as a
pose, and thus I innocently conferred on him the title 'Apostle of the Lily.'

On my first visit to America[4] he was likewise touring under Henry
Abbey's management, and I was amused to find him 'dressed for the part.'

He was wearing a black velvet suit with knickerbockers, silk stockings, and black shoes with silver buckles, his neck embellished by a Byronic collar, and was lecturing on Greek art. Being asked by the U.S. Customs on his arrival the usual question: 'Have you anything contraband?' he replied superbly, 'No, I have nothing to declare but my genius.' His success was only moderate, probably due to the fact that the Press agent sought to impress the public with Oscar's personal eccentricities rather than with his genuine culture.

He was lecturing and I was playing at Buffalo at the same time that season, so we visited Niagara in a party, and in an interview he gave a reporter on his impressions of these mighty waters, he announced, 'that Mrs. Langtry was photographed with Niagara Falls as an unpretentious background!' A year later, when I was presenting the play (adapted from Sardou's *Nos Intimes*) called *Peril* in the States, Oscar became engaged to a beautiful Irish girl, and he sent me the following letter announcing the fact:

'I am really delighted at your immense success; the most brilliant telegrams have appeared in the papers here on your performance in *Peril*.[5] You have done what no other artist of your day has done, invaded America a second time and carried off new victories. But then, you are made for victory. It has always flashed in your eyes and rung in your voice.

'And so I write to tell you how glad I am at your triumphs – you – Venus Victrix of our age – and the other half to tell you that I am going to be married to a beautiful girl called Constance Lloyd – a grave, slight, violet-eyed little Artemis, with great coils of heavy brown hair which makes her flower-like head droop like a blossom, and wonderful ivory hands which draw music from the piano so sweet that the birds stop singing to listen to her. We are to be married in April.[6] I hope so much that you will be over then. I am so anxious for you to know and to like her.

'I am hard at work lecturing and getting rich, though it is horrid being so much away from her, but we telegraph to each other twice a day, and I rush back suddenly from the uttermost parts of the earth to see her for an hour, and do all the foolish things that wise lovers do.

'Will you write me and wish me all happiness, and
'Believe me,

'Ever your devoted and affectionate,
'OSCAR WILDE.'

Oscar's contemplated marriage did not surprise me, as I knew that he had for some time admired the girl who afterwards became his wife, and of whom he had often talked rapturously to me. I did not see him again for several years, as I remained in the States, and when we next met in London he had become a successful dramatist.

When his play *The Importance of Being Earnest* was in rehearsal at the St. James's, everyone concerned was bound to secrecy by George Alexander.[7] Oscar was adamant, and rather irritating one afternoon when I tried to worm the plot out of him. Next day he came to tea, and I thought I would get my own back, so I said: 'Arthur Bourchier lunched here and told me all about it!' (He was playing an important part.)[8] 'Who else was there?' gasped Oscar. I said casually, 'Only Smalley.'[9] (Exit the author hurriedly, moaning.) Two hours later, enter A. B.,[10] almost crying with annoyance: 'What's all this?' 'Only my joke. I'll write to Alexander.' I did, and got a freezing reply saying he 'did not understand jokes in business.' In the evening Tree heard the story at the Garrick. 'I am sure the Lily did that,' he said.

Oscar was a great student, and even during the whirl of my first season he induced me to improve my mind by attending Newton's lectures on Greek art at the British Museum, to the manifest delight of the students, who used to gather outside the door to receive us with cheers.

Oscar's wild worship of beauty, animate and inanimate, made him dreadfully intolerant of ugliness in any form, and he instinctively disliked and avoided unattractive people, using the most exaggerated language to express this repugnance, and being sometimes merciless in his attitude towards them, while, on the other hand, idealising those he admired, and placing some on pinnacles of his imagination who were unworthy, for his likes were as strong as his dislikes. Except in the case of a sacred few, he made fun of friend and foe alike, and he could be bitter as well. He was annoyed with old Lady C. on account of an ill-natured remark she was supposed to have made about me, and I heard him allude to her thus: 'Oh! that old woman who keeps the artificial roses in place on her bald head with tin tacks.'

When he was writing 'The New Helen' he became so obsessed with the subject that he would walk round and round the streets in which our little house was situated for hours at a time, probably investing me with every quality I never possessed, and, although Wilde had a keen sense of the ridiculous, he sometimes unconsciously bordered thereon himself. For instance, one night he curled up to sleep on my doorstep, and Mr. Langtry, returning unusually late, put an end to his poetic dreams by tripping over him.

There were times when I found him too persistent in hanging round the house or running about after me elsewhere, and I am afraid that often I said things which hurt his feelings in order to get rid of him. After a frank remark I made on one occasion, I happened to go to the theatre, and, as I sat in my box, I noticed a commotion in the stalls – it was Oscar, who, having perceived me suddenly, was being led away in tears by his friend Frank Miles.

It was for me that he wrote *Lady Windermere's Fan*. Why he ever supposed that it would have been at the time a suitable play for me, I cannot imagine, and I had never contemplated him as a possible dramatist. Besides, knowing him as well as I did, and listening by the hour to his rather affected, amusing chatter, was not an effective prelude to taking him seriously, nor had he even hinted that he was engaged on any work. He called one afternoon, with an important air and a roll of manuscript, placed it on the table, pointed to it with a sweeping gesture, and said:

'There is a play which I have written for you.'

'What is my part?' I asked, not at all sure if he was joking or not.

'A woman,' he replied, 'with a grown-up illegitimate daughter.'

'My dear Oscar,' I remonstrated, 'am I old enough to have a grown-up daughter of any description? Don't open the manuscript – don't attempt to read it. Put it away for twenty years.' And, in spite of his entreaties, I refused to hear the play.

In some of his many epigrams people declared they recognised clever inversions of the maxims of La Rochefoucauld, La Bruyère, and other French writers. Perhaps so; it is difficult even for a genius to be constantly original.

Wilde was genuinely romantic, and always poetic in thought and speech. As Sir Herbert Tree remarked to me one day: 'Oscar turned his words into gems and flung them to the moon!'

## NOTES

Lillie Langtry (1852–1929), famed English beauty and actress who became a leading figure in Society and a friend of the Prince of Wales. Vincent O'Sullivan records Wilde as saying in 1899: 'The three women I have most admired are Queen Victoria, Sarah Bernhardt and Lily [sic] Langtry. I would have married any of them with pleasure.'

1. Frank Miles, the artist and Wilde's friend, did many drawings of Lillie Langtry. She was also painted by Whistler, Poynter, Watts, Burne-Jones, Leighton, and particularly Millais, whose portrait of her, called 'The Jersey Lily', was the origin of her nick-name.

2. Witticism.

3. Wilde's poem to Lillie Langtry, entitled 'The New Helen', did not appear in The World as she says, but in Time (London), I, no. 4 (July 1879) 400–2. It was reprinted, with revisions, in his Poems (London: David Bogue, 1881) pp. 54–9.

4. Lillie Langtry made her first appearance in America in the part of Hester Grazebrook in An Unequal Match by Tom Taylor at Wallack's Theatre on 6 November 1882. Wilde reviewed this play favourably under the title 'Mrs. Langtry', The World (New York) (7 November 1882) p. 5. On Wilde's meeting with Lillie Langtry see also 'Mrs. Langtry on the Hudson', New York Herald (30 October 1882) p. 5.

5. Lillie Langtry played the part of Lady Ormonde in this play.

6. Wilde married Constance Lloyd on 29 May 1884.

7. Stage name of George Alexander Gibb Samson (1858–1918), English actor and manager. His tenacy of the St James's Theatre lasted from 1891 until his death. He was knighted in 1911.

8. Arthur Bourchier did not play a part in the first production of The Importance of Being Earnest.

9. G. W. Smalley.

10. Arthur Bourchier.

# The Importance of Being Earnest*

Irene Vanbrugh

Another first night at the St. James's which marked an epoch in the theatre was that of *The Importance of Being Earnest*.[1] I was cast as the Hon. Gwendolen Fairfax, and I started rehearsals full of zeal and confidence. But alas! I soon found out how inadequate I was. The style of writing was entirely different from that of anything I had ever appeared in. The atmosphere was strange and I was terrified at my task. George Alexander was very kind but I think occasionally nervous as to whether he had been wise to trust this important part to me.

I pointed out my doubts and misgivings to Violet[2] who said, 'Perhaps the lines will seem natural to you if you think them first. Try that way.' I tried it and the black veil of despair was lifted. I found myself getting into the author's train of thought and I rejoiced in the sparkling wit when I had learnt to speak it as though coming from myself. The play went with a delightful ripple of laughter from start to finish and we appeared to be in for a long run. A great personal success was made by that famous old actress Rose Leclercq – the natural *grande dame* of the stage with all the true polish and innate dignity of the unmistakeable 'lady'.[3] Her walk, her voice, her carriage, her every detail was marvellous. The handkerchief she used, the long bottle of eau-de-Cologne, the way she sat – such details marked her as the lady of rank and blue blood that she portrayed; she was never stagey or exaggerated. She held a position which has never been filled, to my mind, by any other actress.

When the curtain fell on the last act its success was assured. When Wilde came forward to make a speech he received an ovation. There followed a little buzz of whispering as he began to speak. He stepped from the wings with a cigarette and stood there smoking as he waited for the applause to subside. In those days people were great sticklers for convention.

A shadow passed over the brilliant horizon of that opening. We were playing to capacity and to a delighted public when the libel case which Oscar Wilde brought against Lord Queensberry resulted in the now historic end to his dazzling career.[4] During his trial the play seemed to

* *To Tell My Story* (London: Hutchinson, 1948) pp. 33–5. Editor's title.

benefit by the publicity, but after the verdict it was killed stone dead. His name was obliterated on all the playbills and it was hoped all would be speedily forgotten. But it was not to be; the case was too widely discussed and the play was withdrawn. Some time later it was revived by George Alexander and ran for nearly a year and will always remain a scintillating masterpiece.

I shall always be glad to have met Oscar Wilde and to have realized his charm of manner and his elegance. No one was too insignificant for him to take trouble to please and I felt tremendously flattered when he congratulated me at one of the rehearsals – and very glad that that particular morning I had borrowed my mother's sealskin jacket in which I fancied myself enormously.

It is interesting to note how important Wilde's plays have become. Constant revivals, some resulting in long runs, show what a hold they still have on the public. They certainly mark a definite 'period', and I doubt whether anyone has ever so revolutionized taste in furniture, decorations, colouring, the arrangement of flowers, women's dresses, as he did. W. S. Gilbert realized his influence by making him the central figure of *Patience*.

Wilde was very tall, with longish straight hair, compelling eyes and a rather badly shaped mouth of which he appeared to be conscious because in conversation he covered it with his eloquent, finely shaped hands which he would also use a good deal in gesticulation. He vanished from society but spent the final few years of his life in Paris.

## NOTES

Irene Vanbrugh (1872–1949), English actress.

1. *The Importance of Being Earnest* started its career at the St James's Theatre on the evening of St Valentine's Day, 14 February 1895, with George Alexander as John Worthing, Allan Aynesworth as Algernon Moncrieff, Irene Vanbrugh as Gwendolen Fairfax, and Rose Leclercq as Lady Bracknell. For further information on the first production of this play see Joseph W. Donohue, Jr., 'Wilde, George Alexander, and "The Importance of Being Earnest" ', *Notes and Queries*, XVII, no. 5 (May 1970) 182–3; Barry Duncan, *The St. James's Theatre; Its Strange & Complete History 1835–1957* (London: Barrie & Rockliff, 1964) pp. 242–4; W. Macqueen-Pope, *St. James's; Theatre of Distinction* (London: W. H. Allen, 1958) pp. 139–41; A. E. W. Mason, *Sir George Alexander and the St. James's Theatre* (London: Macmillan, 1935) pp. 72–90; and Paul C. Wadleigh, '*Earnest* at St. James's Theatre', *Quarterly Journal of Speech*, LII, no. 1 (Feb 1966), 58–62.

2. Violet Vanbrugh (1867–1942), Irene's sister, who was also an actress.

3. Rose Leclercq played the part of Lady Bracknell.

4. Lord Queensberry, Lord Alfred Douglas's father, had been planning to create a disturbance during the first night of *The Importance of Being Earnest*, but when he was unable to get a seat in the theatre he contented himself with having a bouquet of vegetables, addressed to Wilde, delivered at the stage door. In a letter to R. V. Shone, the business manager of the St. James's Theatre, Wilde said: 'Lord

Queensberry is at Carter's Hotel, Albemarle Street. Write to him from Mr. Alexander that you regret to find that the seat given to him was already sold, and return him his money. This will prevent trouble.'

# The Last First Night*

### Ada Leverson

On Valentine's day, the 14th February, 1895, there was a snowstorm more severe than had been remembered in London for years. A black, bitter, threatening wind blew the drifting snow. On the dark, sinister winter's night, when the first representation of *The Importance of Being Earnest* was produced at the St. James's Theatre, it was with difficulty that one drove there at all, and one had to go very slowly on account of the horses. Crowds of hansoms, smart broughams, carriages of all kinds blocked Little King Street.

When at last we took refuge in the playhouse, how grateful was the contrast! Outside, a *frost;* inside the very breath of success; perfumed atmosphere, of gaiety, fashion and, apparently, everlasting popularity. The author of the play was fertile, inventive, brilliant and with such encouragement how could one realise his gaiety was not to last? That his life was to become dark, cold, sinister as the outside evening.

Perfumed, for had not the word gone forth from Oscar that the lily of the valley was to be the flower of the evening as a souvenir of an absent friend? Flowers meant much in those days, and nearly all the pretty women wore sprays of lilies against their large puffed sleeves, while rows and rows of young elegants had buttonholes of the delicate bloom of lilies of the valley. Most of the smart young men held tall canes of ebony with ivory tops; they wore white gloves with rows of black stitching and very pointed shoes.

It was a distinguished audience such as is rarely seen nowadays, either at the Opera or even at a first night of a Revue. The street just outside was crowded, not only with the conveyances and the usual crowd of waiting people, but with other Wilde fanatics who appeared to regard the arrivals as part of the performance; many of them shouted and cheered the best-known people; and the loudest cheers were for the author, who was as well-known as the Bank of England, as he got out of his carriage with his pretty wife, who afterwards joined friends, when the author himself went behind the scenes.

* *The New Criterion* (London), (Jan 1926) 148–53.

What a rippling, glittering, chattering crowd was that. They were certain of some amusement for, if, by exception, they did not care for the play, was not Oscar himself sure to do something to amuse them? Would he perhaps walk on after the play smoking a cigarette, with a green carnation blooming in his coat, and saying, in his slow way, with a slight smile (emphasizing certain words in the tradition of Swinburne) 'The play is delightful, I've enjoyed myself *so* much.' Or, as on another occasion, would he bow from a box and state in clear tones, heard all over the theatre, that Mr. Wilde was not in the house.

If he played to the Gallery, he got the Stalls.

There had been rumours for weeks that at Worthing[1] Oscar was writing a farce, and how each day he wrote a part of it and each evening he read it to the Elect, his wife, children and a few friends. He himself said it was a delicate bubble of fancy, but in truth he cared little for any of his plays excepting only *Salomé*.

Influenced as he had been at the time by Maeterlinck, Flaubert and Huysmans, yet *Salomé* expressed *himself* in his innate love of the gorgeous and the unique. He said it was indeed unique, for it was written by an Irishman in French and done into English by a young Scotch friend.[2] . . . !

But to return to the first night – to be the last—

For months before, Lewis Waller had been tender and manly in *The Ideal Husband*,[3] Sir George Alexander superb as *Lord Windermere* and Beerbohm Tree had been elegant, witty and amusing in the favourite *Woman of No Importance*.[4] Oscar was, therefore, no novice, but he had not yet written a farce.

Everyone was repeating his 'mots'. Society at the moment was enthusiastic about that rarest of human creatures, a celebrity with good manners.

It is really difficult to convey now in words the strange popularity, the craze there was at this moment for the subject of my essay; 'To meet Mr. Oscar Wilde' was put on the most exclusive of invitation cards. And every omnibus-conductor knew his latest jokes. If Caviare to the general, he was Gentleman's relish to the particular. He adored amusing the mob and annoying the burgess and fascinating the aristocrat.

With his extraordinary high spirits and love of fun he appealed to the lower class; his higher gifts enchanted the artistic and such of the great world as love to amuse themselves, indeed with sincere artists he was most himself. But the lower middle-class never liked him, always distrusted him and disliked his success.

People as a rule do not object to a man deserving success, only to his getting it.

Whoever still lives who was present that night will remember the continual ripple of laughter from the very first moment – the excitement, the strange almost hysterical joy with which was accepted this 'Trivial Comedy for Serious People.'[5] In some ways it was almost childish fun.

For a long time Oscar had been criticised for his continual use of paradox and epigram; witty and apt and cynical as the fashion of that period, it still was, at times, wearying in the other plays.

*'Men marry because they are tired, women because they are curious.'*

*' The cynic is a person who knows the price of everything and the value of nothing.'*

*' The good American goes to Paris when he dies. Where do the bad Americans go? They go to America.'*

Oscar's style of wit lent itself only too dangerously to imitators: and for very many years we suffered from a plethora of half-witted epigrams and feeble paradoxes by the mimics of his manner.

However he had resolved to have nothing of this formula of wit in the farce. There was even a rollicking pun in the title! He intended it should be all Pure Nonsense. There is not a *mot*, not a paradox in the play, but the unexpectedness of this pleased all the more, and when the curtain went down on the first act – which seemed to be principally about cucumber sandwiches – on the pathetic wail, so well cried by Allan Aynesworth,[6] the childlike simplicity of the phrase 'But I haven't quite finished my tea!' it was indeed a triumph. Oscar had been right in replying to a friend who said that the farce should be like a piece of mosaic, 'No, it must be like a pistol shot.' And that was how it went. It came off.

And how they laughed when dignified George Alexander arrived on the stage in the deepest mourning – for the imaginary funeral of Bunbury, who had now become a nuisance to his creator and had to die. Even black-tipped cigarettes were suggested – but Alexander drew the line there.

After the next act Robert Ross and Oscar came to my box in which were the Beardsleys, Mabel and Aubrey, and one or two other friends.

Before I first met Oscar, several years before, I had been told that he was rather like a giant with the wings of a Brazilian butterfly. I was not disappointed, but I thought him far more like a Roman emperor who should have lived at the Pavilion at Brighton with George IV.

He was on this evening at the zenith of his careless, genial popularity, beaming with that *euphoria*[7] that was characteristic of him when he was not in actual grief or pain. He had a low, wide brow, with straight, heavy hair – in which the iron had entered giving him the look of a Roman bust. His face was a clear red-brown from a long stay at Worthing. He had blue-grey eyes and a well-formed mouth on which was a perpetual smile and often a laugh of sincere humorous enjoyment of life. He had a superb vitality, a short-sighted joy in living for the moment. All genius has its *naif* side, and he, a spectacular genius, greater perhaps as an improviser in conversation than as a writer, had it in excess. But I am not here intending to criticise the work or the man, merely to give an impression of a period, and specially of one evening that has remained in my memory.

Oscar bore no trace, in 1895, of the pale slender long-haired youth who met Sarah Bernhardt on her first arrival in England; his arms full of Madonna lilies; and who introduced the new 'Helen', the Jersey Lily,

Mrs. Langtry,[8] to Millais[9] who painted her portrait, and which led to her introduction to Royalty. He had written reams of verse to her, and was so much in love with her that he insisted on lying on her doorstep half the night until Mr. Langtry – that legendary but real figure – stumbled over him on returning from the club.

He was no longer wan – 'alone and palely loitering' like the victim of the Belle Dame sans Merci.

That evening he was dressed with elaborate dandyism and a sort of florid sobriety. His coat had a black velvet collar. He held white gloves in his small pointed hands. On one finger he wore a large scarab ring. A green carnation – echo in colour of the ring – bloomed savagely in his buttonhole, and a large bunch of seals on a black moiré ribbon watch chain hung from his white waistcoat. This costume, which on another man might have appeared perilously like fancy dress, and on his imitators was nothing less, seemed perfectly to suit him; he seemed at ease and to have a great look of the first gentleman in Europe.

'Don't sit on the same chair as Aubrey. It's not compromising' was his first remark. Aubrey Beardsley had a habit of folding up his long, lank figure and perching on the arms of chairs.

'What a contrast the two are,' Oscar continued, 'Mabel like a daisy, Aubrey like the most monstrous of orchids.'

Well the piece went splendidly and we went after to supper at Willis's, a small restaurant then the mode, only a few doors from the theatre. As we walked there in the mud and blinding sleet, what a shock, what a horrible contrast, from the warmth, the perfume within! Oscar did not join us at supper as he usually did. Some dark forecast perhaps – some chill presentiment—

One of the great hits of the evening was when Alexander says of Bunbury, 'He expressed a desire to be buried in Paris,' and the clergyman: 'I fear that does not show a very desirable frame of mind at the last.'

Oscar is buried in Paris under the magnificent monument of Epstein,[10] given by a lady whose friendship for the poet remained steadfast to the end.


## NOTES

Ada Leverson (1862–1933), English writer who contributed witty pieces to *Punch* and other periodicals, and later published successful novels. She was one of Wilde's closest friends and he always called her 'The Sphinx'. On 17 April 1895 he wrote to her from Holloway Prison expressing his gratitude for her kindness and that of her husband in arranging bail; and on 12 May he moved to the Leverson's house in Courtfield Gardens, where he stayed until 20 May. See *Letters to the Sphinx from Oscar Wilde* (London: Duckworth, 1930); Charles Burkhart, 'Ada Leverson and Oscar Wilde', *English Literature in Transition*, XIII (1970) 193–200; Colin MacInnes, 'The Heart of a Legend: The Writings of Ada Leverson', *Encounter*, XVI (May 1961) 45–56; Horace Wyndham, 'Ada Leverson', *The Cornhill Magazine*, CLXXIII (spring

1963) 147–63. and Osbert Stiwell, 'Ada Leverson, Wilde & "Max"', *The National and English Review* (London), CXXXV (Sept 1950) 286–90.

1. In September 1894, Wilde went with his family to Worthing, where at The Haven, 5 Esplanade, he began to work on *The Importance of Being Earnest*. 'Worthing is a place in Sussex', says Jack Worthing in the play, explaining the origin of his name. 'It is a seaside resort' (Act I).

2. Lord Alfred Douglas.

3. Lewis Waller played the part of Sir Robert Chiltern in *An Ideal Husband*.

4. Herbert Beerbohm Tree played the role of Lord Illingworth in *A Woman of No Importance*.

5. The sub-title of *The Importance of Being Earnest*.

6. Allan Aynesworth created the part of Algernon Moncrieff in *The Importance of Being Earnest*.

7. Feeling of well-being.

8. For a note on Lillie Langtry see p. 264.

9. Sir John Everett Millais (1829–96), English painter. In a letter to Norman Forbes-Robertson sent from San Francisco and dated 27 March 1882, Wilde said: 'Pray remember me to all at home, also to that splendid fellow Millais and his stately and beautiful wife.'

10. For a note on Epstein see p. 477.

# A Rumour*

## Max Beerbohm

One day, Sickert[1] said to me, 'Your caricatures of dear Will[2] and of Oscar Wilde were so deadly. I know how Oscar feels about them – he can't bear them – but doesn't Will resent them? Isn't he angry?' 'More frightened,' I said to Walter, 'than angry.' But I loved Will; he was so kind. No one took such trouble over young artists, to help them; there was nothing he wouldn't do. But Oscar—'

Max leaned over the parapet, looking across the gulf. I encouraged him to say what he was thinking of Oscar.

'Well, in the beginning he was the most enchanting company, don't you know. His conversation was so simple and natural and flowing—not at all epigrammatic, which would have been unbearable. He saved that for his plays, thank heaven.'

As an illustration of Wilde's imperturbability at the beginning of his terrible debacle, Max repeated a story told him many years before by

* Extracted from S. N. Behrman, *Conversation with Max* (London: Hamish Hamilton, 1960) pp. 66–7. Editor's title.

Lewis Waller, a matinée idol of the time. Waller was walking down Piccadilly with Allan Aynesworth, another accomplished actor. Waller was playing Sir Robert Chiltern in *An Ideal Husband* and Aynesworth Algernon in *The Importance of Being Earnest*. The Wilde scandal looked like closing both plays. The two actors were deep in talk about the source of their imminent unemployment when, to their horror, they were hailed cheerily by their disemployer, riding blithely down Piccadilly in a hansom cab. They returned his greeting pallidly, hoping Wilde would ride on, but he didn't. He got out and came up to them. 'Have you heard,' he inquired, 'what that swine Queensberry has had the effrontery to say?' Writhing with embarrassment, they both protested that no rumour of the Marquess's allegation had reached their chaste ears. 'Since you haven't heard it, I'll tell you,' said Wilde, with the eagerness of a tutor avid to fill in a gap in folklore. 'He actually had the effrontery to say' – and he fixed his eye on Waller – 'that *The Importance of Being Earnest* was a better-acted play than *An Ideal Husband!*' He smiled radiantly, waved, got back into his hansom, and rode off down Piccadilly, leaving his victims gasping.

## NOTES

Sir Max Beerbohm (1872–1956), English critic, essayist, and caricaturist; half-brother of Sir Herbert Beerbohm Tree. His writings on Wilde include a gently satirical portrait, 'A Peep into the Past', for *The Yellow Book* of 16 April 1894; and a review of *De Profundis*, 'A Lord of Language', for *Vanity Fair* of 2 March 1905. He was a close friend of Wilde, whom he met at the rehearsals of *A Woman of No Importance*. On 8 December 1900 he received a letter from Reginald Turner in which Turner described Wilde's death and said: 'I got your wreath.' See David Cecil, *Max: A Biography* (London: Constable, 1964) *passim*; J. G. Riewald (ed.), 'Max Beerbohm and Oscar Wilde', in *The Surprise of Excellence; Modern Essays on Max Beerbohm* (Hamden, Connecticut: Archon Books/The Shoe String Press, 1974) pp. 47–64; Max Beerbohm, *Letters to Reggie Turner*, ed. Rupert Hart-Davis (London: Rupert Hart-Davis, 1964) *passim*; and Max Beerbohm, 'A Satire on Romantic Drama', *The Saturday Review* (London), xc (8 Dec 1900) 719–20 [evaluation of Wilde as a dramatist].

1. Walter Sickert (1860–1942), British painter and etcher.
2. William Rothenstein (1872–1945), English painter.

# The Causeur*

## Sir Max Beerbohm

I have always retained great admiration for Oscar Wilde's essays and his fancy stories and his plays. And I deem myself very fortunate in having often heard his surpassingly brilliant conversation.

I suppose there are now few survivors among the people who had the delight of hearing Oscar Wilde talk. Of these I am one.

I have had the privilege of listening also to many other masters of table-talk – Meredith and Swinburne, Edmund Gosse and Henry James, Augustine Birrell and Arthur Balfour, Gilbert Chesterton and Desmond MacCarthy and Hilaire Belloc – all of them splendid in their own way. But assuredly Oscar in *his* own way was the greatest of them all – the most spontaneous and yet the most polished, the most soothing and yet the most surprising.

That his talk was mostly a monologue was not his own fault. His manners were very good; he was careful to give his guests or his fellow-guests many a conversational opening; but seldom did anyone respond with more than a very few words. Nobody was willing to interrupt the music of so magnificent a virtuoso. To have heard him consoles me for not having heard Dr. Johnson or Edmund Burke, Lord Brougham or Sydney Smith.

* *Adam International Review*, XXII, nos 241–3 (1954) viii–ix.

## NOTE

In 1954, the centenary of Wilde's birth was commemorated and a plaque was affixed to his Chelsea house, 16 Tite Street. See 'Plaque for Oscar Wilde's House', *The Times* (London), (30 July 1953) p. 10; Irene Pengilly, 'Chelsea Week', *The Times* (London), (24 May 1954) p. 5; 'Centenary of the Birth of Oscar Wilde', *The Times* (London), (12 Aug 1954) p. 8; 'Commemoration of Oscar Wilde: Chelsea Ceremony', *The Times* (London), (18 October 1954) p. 8; 'Wilde Centenary', *Plays and Players* (London), II, no. 2 (Nov 1954) 21; 'Special Exhibitions at British Museum', *The Times* (London), (12 Oct 1954) p. 10; Compton Mackenzie, 'Sidelight', *The Spectator* (London), CXCIII (29 Oct 1954) 523; 'Sir Max Beerbohm Tribute to Wilde', *The Times* (London), (15 Oct 1954) p. 5; and 'Tributes from France and Belgium', *Adam International Review*, XXII, nos 241–3 (1954) viii–ix. For a note on Sir Max Beerbohm see p. 272.

# I Won a Bet*

## Lady Randolph Churchill

At a particularly pleasant luncheon-party given by Lady de Grey I remember once meeting, among others, M. Jules Claretie of the Français, Mlle. Bartet, the gifted actress, Lord Riddlesdale, and Mr. Oscar Wilde, than whom a more brilliant talker did not exist – that is, when he was in the mood for it. An argument arose between him and Lord Ribblesdale on after-dinner speeches, Mr. Wilde declaring that there was no subject on which he could not speak at a moment's notice. Taking him at his word, Lord Ribblesdale, holding up his glass, said 'The Queen.' 'She is not a subject,' answered Wilde, as quick as lightning. Once, having been accused of misquoting from 'The Importance of Being Earnest,' I appealed to Mr. Wilde, telling him I had made a bet on my accuracy, and that if I found I was right, he should receive from me a beautiful penholder. This was his answer:

THE COTTAGE, GORING-ON-THAMES.

'DEAR LADY RANDOLPH' –

"The only difference between the saint and the sinner is that every saint has a past and that every sinner has a future!" That, of course, is the quotation.[1] How dull men are! They should listen to brilliant women, and look at beautiful ones – and when, as in the present case, a woman is both beautiful and brilliant, they might have the ordinary common sense to admit that she is verbally inspired.

'I trust your bet will be promptly paid, as I want to begin writing my new comedy, and have no pen!

'Believe me,
'Yours sincerely,
'OSCAR WILDE'

As I had won, the pen was duly sent him.

* Extracted from *Reminiscences* (London: Edward Arnold, 1908) pp. 216–17. Editor's title.

## NOTES

Jennie Jerome (1854–1921) married (1874) Lord Randolph Churchill, the third son of the seventh Duke of Marlborough; mother of Sir Winston Churchill.

1. *A Woman of No Importance*, Act III.

# Oscar Wilde*

I first met Oscar Wilde when I was on a visit to a friend at Magdalen College, Oxford, he being then an undergraduate there.

He exhibited a certain affectation of manner, but he was manifestly a man of wide reading and scholarship. He talked well, and was extremely humorous and diverting.

Later on I had occasion to see him frequently, as he shared with me the reviewing of books on one of the London papers.

I myself undertook the task of reviewing because I wished to combine a congenial occupation with the acquisition of a good standard library, the latter object being achieved by the exchange with booksellers of masses of new books, sent me from the paper, for old standard works.

An amusing incident in our joint reviewing occurred when we reviewed each other's books. I hope the public were duly impressed with the charming things we said of each other. I fear we were unblushing adepts at the gentle art of 'log rolling.'

In those days he was a genial, happy fellow, bubbling over with kindly fun, and as far as I could see with nothing abnormal, much less repulsive, about him.

His good nature and also his personal courage were displayed very finely on one occasion in defence of a friend. He was at the time sharing his rooms looking over the Thames with a young gentleman who was an artist[1] of some repute and whose father was a dignitary of the Church.

This young artist, as has happened before and will happen again, got into trouble with a woman, who, by pretending that certain things were so that were not so in truth, induced the silly boy to commit an act of extreme folly. Then began the usual black-mail, entailing the terror and misery of its ingenuous victim. He revealed his trouble to his fellow tenant, and Wilde immediately volunteered to do his best to rescue him from his persecutor.

The lady was invited to come to the flat for a conference on a certain day, and the young artist was sent to his home, leaving Wilde alone for the interview.

The lady duly arrived, and Wilde explained that his friend had gone out for a few minutes but would be back directly, and proceeded to express

* *The Great Reign* (London: Mills & Boon, 1922) pp. 94–9. Anonymous recollections.

reluctant sympathy. with his visitor and listened with shocked surprise to the tale recited by the lady.

Presently Wilde appeared to be entirely won over to an endorsement of the lady's charges, and even showed an inclination to assist her in the righting of her wrongs. But before he could do anything to assist her, he explained that he must see the evidence upon which she relied.

The lady, completely deceived by Wilde's admirable acting, produced from her bag the incriminating document and handed it to Wilde, who affected to inspect it with conviction of his friend's guilt.

'This is, I suppose,' he said, 'the only evidence you have?'

'It is,' she replied.

'You ought to have taken a copy of it,' he went on, 'in case you should lose it. Have you done so?'

'No,' she replied, 'but I will do so.'

'I am afraid it is too late,' said Wilde, placing the document in the fire and pressing it into the flames with the poker.

The lady, in a fury, went to the door and called up the bully who was waiting below, but when he arrived and saw Wilde, who was a big, poweful man, quite prepared to throw him down the stairs, he departed, after some volcanic language, with his accomplice, and they were heard of no more.

It is not everyone who would with kindliness, courage, and skill, thus come to his friend's help when in dire trouble. These were Wilde's happy and prosperous days, before he fell into the abyss from which he only emerged to die.

Some of his writings have nothing but the most exquisite purity and beauty in them. The volume written for children, *The Happy Prince and Other Stories*, has a story in it entitled 'The Selfish Giant' which it is impossible to imagine as having come from a man with a foul mind. There must have been in this man a dual personality ever contending for the mastery of his soul.

I remember on one occasion desiring to take a young girl-relative to a theatre, and finding that the only play then being performed in London that was entirely and unquestionably fit for the enjoyment of an innocent little girl was *The Importance of Being Earnest*.

It should be remembered that abnormal tendencies are admittedly heritable, that his mother was eccentric even to the margin of personal irresponsibility, and that his father was reputed to be without adequate self-control in certain fields of human activity. These, his antecedents, open up questions deep, dark, and obscure, as to personal responsibility in such a man who did deeds inconceivable to ordinary healthy people.

I remember reading many years ago in a little play published in Blackwood's a dialogue which I can only now quote from an imperfect memory, but I think it ran thus:

*A.* Do you blame the oak for being stunted that is planted on a rock?
*B.* No, I blame the husbandman who planted it there.
*A.* But what if the husbandman be God? It will take another world to explain the injustices of this one.

No one will ever see the other face of the moon till, having climbed heaven, he looks back.

There I must leave this dreadful matter, hoping and believing that there is infinite mercy for the worst of sinners that truly repents.

NOTE

1. Frank Miles.


# Oscar Wilde Laughed Heartily*

Hesketh Pearson


Two nights before the trial[1] began Wilde dined with his wife and Douglas at a restaurant, and then the three of them went on to a box at the St. James's Theatre, where *Earnest* was running to packed houses. Constance could scarcely have enjoyed herself. 'She was very much agitated', Douglas writes, 'and when I said good-night to her at the door of the theatre she had tears in her eyes.' They never met again. Oscar was in an airy mood. Between the acts he paid a visit to George Alexander, who told me what passed between them.

'I don't think you ought to have come to the theatre at such a time', said Alexander. 'People will consider it in bad taste.'

'Are you going to accuse everyone in the theatre of bad taste for seeing my play at such a time?' asked Wilde laughing. 'I would consider it in bad taste if they went to anyone else's play.'

'Do be serious.'

'Then you mustn't be funny.'

'Will you take a bit of advice?'

'Certainly . . . if it is advice that I wish to take.'

'Why don't you withdraw from the case and go abroad?'

'Everyone wants me to go abroad. I have just been abroad.[2] And now I

* *The Life of Oscar Wilde* (London: Methuen, 1946), p. 288. Editor's title.

have come home again. One can't keep on going abroad, unless one is a missionary, or, what comes to the same thing, a commercial traveller. But make your mind easy, my dear Alec. I have consulted Mrs. Robinson, the palmist, and she assures me that I shall win.'

'Do you really believe in palmists?'

'Always . . . when they prophesy nice things.'

'When do they ever prophesy anything else?'

'Never. If they did no one would believe in them, and the poor creatures must earn a living somehow.'

'Oh, you're impossible!'

'No, not impossible, my dear fellow . . . Improbable . . . yes . . . I grant you improbable.'

Alexander gave it up, and Wilde returned to his box, where he laughed heartily all through the last act.

## NOTES

1. The Queensberry trial commenced at the Old Bailey on 3 April 1895. Lord Queensberry, Lord Alfred Douglas's father, had called at Wilde's club, the Albemarle Club, on 18 February and left a card with the porter on which he had written 'To Oscar Wilde posing as a somdomite' [sic] (his rage no doubt being responsible for the misspelling). The porter put the card in an envelope and handed it to Wilde when he next came to the club, which was on 28 February. On 1 March Wilde obtained a warrant for the arrest of Queensberry, who on the following day was arrested and charged with criminal libel. A turning-point in Queensberry's case took place on 5 April when the prosecution collapsed, Queensberry was acquitted, and it was agreed that a warrant for Wilde's arrest should be applied for. Wilde was arrested the same day at 6.30 p.m. at the Cadogan Hotel, driven to Scotland Yard, and at 8.00 p.m. taken to Bow Street Police Court, where he was charged with committing acts of gross indecency with other male persons. See 'Oscar Wilde at Bow Street', *Sunday Times* (London), (7 Apr 1895) p. 5; 'Lord Alfred Douglas Appeals for Fair Play', *The Star* (London), (20 Apr 1895) p. 3; 'Entre Nous', *Truth* (London), xxxvii (11 Apr 1895) 887; 'London, Friday, April 5', *Daily Telegraph* (London), (5 Apr 1895) p. 4; 'Lord Queensberry', *The Echo* (London), (5 Apr 1895) p. 3; 'Queensberry-Wilde Case', *Daily Telegraph* (London), (6 Apr 1895) p. 3; 'Wilde Case', *The Star* (London), (19 Apr – 1 May 1895); 'The Wilde-Queensberry Libel Case', *Westminster Gazette* (London), 3 Apr – 7 May 1895); and 'Central Criminal Court', *The Times* (London), (6 Apr – 27 May 1895).

2. After Wilde had obtained a warrant for the arrest of Queensberry, he and Douglas went to Monte Carlo for a short holiday.

# The Trials*

Hesketh Pearson

Wilde's novel[1] did him a great deal of harm. Hating the book, especially when they had not read it, people hated the author, and the journalists almost to a man were thenceforward among his bitterest enemies.[2] In the Queensberry case it was used in evidence against him, and there are no more instructive passages in forensic records than his cross-examination on the subject by Edward Carson,[3] a contemporary of his at Trinity College, Dublin.

*Carson:* You are of opinion, I believe, that there is no such thing as an immoral book?

*Wilde:* Yes.

*Carson:* Am I right in saying that you do not consider the effect in creating morality or immorality?

*Wilde:* Certainly I do not.

*Carson:* So far as your works are concerned, you pose as not being concerned about morality or immorality?

*Wilde:* I do not know whether you use the word 'pose' in any particular sense.

*Carson:* It is a favourite word of your own.

*Wilde:* Is it? I have no pose in this matter. In writing a play or a book I am concerned entirely with literature: that is, with art. I aim not at doing good or evil, but in trying to make a thing that will have some quality or form of beauty or wit.

*Carson:* After the criticisms that were passed on *Dorian Gray*, was it modified a good deal?

*Wilde:* No. Additions were made. In one case it was pointed out to me – not in a newspaper or anything of that sort, but by the only critic of the century whose opinion I set high, Mr. Walter Pater – that a certain passage was liable to misconstruction, and I made one addition.

(Wilde admitted the following day, on re-examination by Sir Edward Clarke,[4] that Walter Pater had written several letters to him about *Dorian Gray*, 'and in consequence of what he said I modified one passage.')

*Carson:* This is in your introduction to *Dorian Gray:* 'There is no such

* Extracted from *The Trials of Oscar Wilde*, ed. H. Montgomery Hyde (London: William Hodge, 1948).

thing as a moral or an immoral book. Books are well written or badly written. That is all.' That expresses your view?

*Wilde:* My view on art, yes.

*Carson:* Then I take it that no matter how immoral a book may be, if it is well written it is, in your opinion, a good book?

*Wilde:* Yes; if it were well written so as to produce a sense of beauty, which is the highest sense of which a human being can be capable. If it were badly written it would produce a sense of disgust.

*Carson:* Then a well-written book putting forward perverted moral views may be a good book?

*Wilde:* No work of art ever puts forward views. Views belong to people who are not artists.

*Carson:* A perverted novel might be a good book?

*Wilde:* I do not know what you mean by a perverted novel.

*Carson:* Then I will suggest *Dorian Gray* as open to the interpretation of being such a novel.

*Wilde:* That could only be to brutes and illiterates. The views of Philistines on art are incalculably stupid.

*Carson:* An illiterate person reading *Dorian Gray* might consider it such a novel?

*Wilde:* The views of illiterates on art are unaccountable. I am concerned only with my view of art. I don't care twopence what other people think of it.

*Carson:* The majority of persons would come under your definition of Philistines and illiterates?

*Wilde:* I have found wonderful exceptions.

*Carson:* Do you think the majority of people live up to the position you are giving us?

*Wilde:* I am afraid they are not cultivated enough.

*Carson:* Not cultivated enough to draw the distinction between a good book and a bad book?

*Wilde:* Certainly not.

*Carson:* The affection and love of the artist for Dorian Gray might lead an ordinary individual to believe that it might have a certain tendency?

*Wilde:* I have no knowledge of the views of ordinary individuals.

*Carson:* You did not prevent the ordinary individual from buying your book?

*Wilde:* I have never discouraged him.

(Counsel then read a long extract from *Dorian Gray*, using the Lippincott version,[5] which describes the meeting between Dorian and the artist, Basil Hallward.)

*Carson:* Now I ask you, Mr. Wilde, do you consider that description of the feeling of one man towards another, a youth just grown up, was a proper or an improper feeling?

*Wilde:* I think it is the most perfect description of what an artist would feel on meeting a beautiful personality that was in some way necessary to his art and his life.

*Carson:* You think that is a feeling a young man should have towards another?

*Wilde:* Yes, as an artist.

(Counsel read another extract. Wilde asked for a copy, and was given one of the complete edition in book form. Carson, in calling his attention to the place, remarked 'I believe it was left out in the purged edition.')

*Wilde:* I do not call it purged.

*Carson:* Yes, I know that; but we will see. (Counsel read a further extract.) Do you mean to say that that passage describes the natural feeling of one man towards another?

*Wilde:* It would be the influence produced on an artist by a beautiful personality.

*Carson:* A beautiful person?

*Wilde:* I said 'a beautiful personality.' You can describe it as you like. Dorian Gray was a most remarkable personality.

*Carson:* May I take it that you, as an artist, have never known the feeling described here?

*Wilde:* I have never allowed any personality to dominate my art.

*Carson:* Then you have never known the feeling you describe?

*Wilde:* No; it is a work of fiction.

*Carson:* So far as you are concerned you have no experience as to its being a natural feeling?

*Wilde:* I think it is perfectly natural for any artist to admire intensely and love a young man. It is an incident in the life of almost every artist.

*Carson:* But let us go over it phrase by phrase. 'I quite admit that I adored you madly.' What do you say to that? Have you ever adored a young man madly?

*Wilde:* No; not madly. I prefer love; that is a higher form.

*Carson:* Never mind about that. Let us keep down to the level we are at now.

*Wilde:* I have never given adoration to anybody except myself.

*Carson:* I suppose you think that a very smart thing?

*Wilde:* Not at all.

*Carson:* Then you never had that feeling?

*Wilde:* No; the whole idea was borrowed from Shakespeare, I regret to say; yes, from Shakespeare's sonnets.

*Carson:* I believe you have written an article[6] to show that Shakespeare's sonnets were suggestive of unnatural vice?

*Wilde:* On the contrary, I have written an article to show that they are not. I objected to such a perversion being put upon Shakespeare.

*Carson* (continuing to read): 'I adored you extravagantly –'

*Wilde:* Do you mean financially?

*Carson:* Oh, yes, financially. Do you think we are talking about finance?

*Wilde:* I do not think you know what you are talking about.

*Carson:* Don't you? Well, I hope I shall make myself very plain before I have done. 'I was jealous of everyone to whom you spoke.' Have you ever been jealous of a young man?

*Wilde:* Never in my life.

*Carson:* 'I wanted to have you all to myself.' Did you ever have that feeling?

*Wilde:* No; I should consider it an intense nuisance, an intense bore.

*Carson:* 'I grew afraid that the world would know of my idolatry.' Why should you grow afraid that the world should know of it?

*Wilde:* Because there are people in the world who cannot understand the intense devotion, affection and admiration that an artist can feel for a wonderful and beautiful personality. These are the conditions under which we live. I regret them.

*Carson:* These unfortunate people, that have not the high understanding that you have, might put it down to something wrong?

*Wilde:* Undoubtedly; to any point they chose. I am not concerned with the ignorance of others. I have a great passion to civilise the community.

*Carson:* In another passage Dorian Gray received a book. Was the book to which you refer a moral book?

*Wilde:* Not well written; but it gave me an idea.

(Pressed as to whether the book concerned had a certain tendency, Wilde declined with some warmth to be cross-examined upon the work of another artist. It was, he said 'an impertinence and a vulgarity.' He admitted that he had had in mind *A Rebours* by Huysmans. Counsel wanted to elicit Wilde's view as to the morality of that book, but Sir Edward Clarke succeeded, on appeal to the judge, in stopping further reference to it. Counsel then quoted yet another extract from the Lippincott version of *Dorian Gray*, in which the artist tells Dorian of the scandals about him and asks him 'Why is your friendship so fateful to young men?' In reply to the question as to whether the passage in its ordinary meaning did not suggest a certain charge, Wilde said that it described Dorian Gray as a man of very corrupt influence, though there was no statement as to the nature of his influence. 'But as a matter of fact', he added, 'I do not think that one person influences another, nor do I think there is any bad influence in the world.')

*Carson:* A man never corrupts a youth?

*Wilde:* I think not.

*Carson:* Nothing he could do would corrupt him?

*Wilde:* If you are talking of separate ages—

*Carson:* No, sir, I am talking common sense.

*Wilde:* I do not think one person influences another.

*Carson:* You do not think that flattering a young man, making love to him in fact, would be likely to corrupt him?

*Wilde:* No.

\*     \*     \*

[Carson began by cross-examining Wilde on *Dorian Gray* and the *Phrases and Philosophies for the Use of the Young*,[7] their interchanges having been given in previous chapters. Next there was a passage between them relating to the letter, already quoted, that Wilde had written to Douglas.] 'I think it is a beautiful letter', said Wilde. 'It is a poem. I was not writing an ordinary letter. You might as well cross-examine me as to whether *King Lear* or a sonnet of Shakespeare was proper.'

'Apart from art, Mr. Wilde?'

'I cannot answer apart from art.'

'Suppose a man who was not an artist had written this letter, would you say it was a proper letter?'

'A man who was not an artist could not have written that letter.'

'Why?'

'Because nobody but an artist could write it. He certainly could not write the language unless he were a man of letters.'

'I can suggest, for the sake of your reputation, that there is nothing very wonderful in this "red rose-leaf lips of yours".'

'A great deal depends upon the way it is read.'

' "Your slim gilt soul walks between passion and poetry." Is that a beautiful phrase?'

'Not as you read it, Mr. Carson. You read it very badly.'

'Have you often written in the same style as this?'

'I don't repeat myself in style.'

After reading another letter from Wilde to Douglas, Carson asked: 'Is that an ordinary letter?'

'Everything I write is extraordinary', Wilde retorted. 'I do not pose as being ordinary, great heavens!'

Then there were questions about a young man named Alphonse Conway, whom Wilde had met at Worthing.

'He sold newspapers at the kiosque on the pier?' queried Carson.

'No, I never heard that up to that time his only occupation was selling newspapers. It is the first I have heard of his connection with literature.'

'Was his conversation literary?'

'On the contrary, quite simple and easily understood. He had been to school, where naturally he had not learned much.'

## NOTES

1. *The Picture of Dorian Gray.*

2. Much of the bitterness manifested against Wilde in the press was caused by his contemptuous and unfair remarks about the profession of journalism. In *The Soul of Man Under Socialism* he says, 'In the old days men had the rack, now they have the Press.' 'Literary criticism is not your forte, my dear fellow,' says Algernon to Jack in *The Importance of Being Earnest.* 'Don't try it. You should leave that to people who haven't been at a University.' In *A Woman of No Importance*, when Lady Hunstanton asks Lord Illingworth if he believes all that is written in the newspapers, he says, 'I do. Nowadays it is only the unreadable that occurs.' And in

*An Ideal Husband* Sir Robert Chiltern says, 'Oh, spies are of no use nowadays. Their profession is over. The newspapers do their work instead.' On Wilde's dislike of journalism see Earnest Benz, *Oscar Wilde: A Retrospect* (Vienna: Alfred Hölder, 1921) p. 40; 'Mr. Oscar Wilde on Mr. Oscar Wilde', *St. James's Gazette* (London), (18 Jan 1895) p. 4; and G. J. Renier, *Oscar Wilde* (London: Peter Davies, 1933) pp. 43–4.

3. Sir Edward (later Lord) Carson (1854–1935), British advocate and politician. The cross-examination did not worry Wilde, who was never at a loss for a reply, but his adversary, Carson, was an upright and subtle barrister who had never been able to stand Wilde, and whose professional zeal therefore was reinforced by personal antipathy. Carson and Wilde had been fellow-students at Trinity College, Dublin, where Wilde easily outshone his later antagonist. Carson, it is said, disliked Wilde's flippant approach to life and envied him his early academic success. See H. Montgomery Hyde, *Carson: The Life of Sir Edward Carson, Lord Carson of Duncairn* (London: Constable, 1974) pp. 127–43.

4. Sir Edward George Clarke (1841–1931), English lawyer, politician, and writer. He was leading counsel throughout Wilde's three trials. On these trials see H. Montgomery Hyde (ed.), *The Trials of Oscar Wilde* (London: William Hodge, 1948); Hilary Pacq, *Le Procès d'Oscar Wilde* (Paris: Nouvelle Revue Française, 1933); Albert Crew, *The Old Bailey* (London: Ivor Nicholson & Watson, 1933) pp. 46–7; Edward Marjoribanks, 'The Oscar Wilde Case', *The Life of Lord Carson*, vol. 1 (London: Gollancz, 1932) chap. xiv; Percival Pollard, 'Oscar Wilde', *Their Day in Court* (New York: Neale, 1909) pp. 340–73; Arthur D. Austin, 'Regina v. Queensberry', *University Review* (Kansas City, Missouri), XXXII (Mar 1966) 179–86; Joseph O. Baylen, 'Oscar Wilde Redividus', *University of Mississippi Studies in English*, VI (1965) 77–86; Alfred L. Bush, 'Wilde v. Queensberry', *Manuscripts*, XVIII (spring 1966) 33–5; F. K. Kaul, 'Der Prozess gegen Oscar Wilde: April–May 1895', *Die Weltbühne*, XVI (1961) 463–7, 504–7; Robert Merle, 'Le Procès d'Oscar Wilde', *Les Temps modernes*, VI (1950–51) 1206–24; W. T. Stead, 'The Conviction of Oscar Wilde', *The Review of Reviews*, XI (15 June 1895) 491–2; and Mieczyslaw Szerer, 'Dramat Oskara Wilde'a', *Prawo i Życie*, no. 13 (1957) 8; and no. 14 (1957) 8.

5. The novel was first published in *Lippincott's Monthly Magazine*, XLVI, no. 271 (July 1890) 3–100. It was published in book form by Ward Lock in 1891.

6. Oscar Wilde, 'The Portrait of Mr. W. H.', *Blackwood's Edinburgh Magazine*, CXLVI, no. 885 (July 1889) 1–21.

7. Oscar Wilde, 'Phrases and Philosophies for the Use of the Young', *The Chameleon* (Oxford), I, no. 1 (Dec 1894) 1–3. Much play was also made at the trial with two other items in this magazine: a poem by Alfred Douglas called 'Two Loves' and an anonymous story called 'The Priest and the Acolyte', which was attributed to Wilde but was in fact written by the magazine's editor, John Francis Bloxam. Wilde's 'Phrases' were reprinted in *Miscellanies* (London: Methuen, 1908) pp. 176–8.

# Unbreakable Spirit*

### Seymour Hicks

IT was about this time that I first met Oscar Wilde, a man generous to a fault and witty past belief. I have of him only pleasant memories. What happened in the years that followed, when his friends and admirers saw with the greatest pain the downfall of a man of genius, is not for me to write of or to criticize. We all have our faults, and as Father Bernard Vaughan once said to me: 'Don't let us ever blame anyone for what they do, but instead kneel down and thank God that it is only through His goodness we are free from the things we might be tempted to condemn in others.' Oscar Wilde had to pay for the perversion of his genius[1] in bitter agony and bloody sweat. I knew him as a charming companion from whose lips I never heard fall anything but the most delightful sentiments and the finest thoughts. So I prefer to remember him as I knew him, and to those who never enjoyed the privilege of being in his company, and read of him only when he had ceased to be the real Wilde we all admired, I would venture to recall a speech in 'The Merchant of Venice,' which, I believe, begins with a line to the effect that 'The quality of mercy is not strained.'

Innumerable are the witticisms of which he was the father. What could be more delightful than his remark to the gushing female admirer who, shaking him warmly by the hand, said: 'Oh, but Mr. Wilde, don't you remember me? My name is Smith.' "Oh, yes," said Wilde, 'I remember your name perfectly, but I can never think of your face.' It was this great writer who, on being asked on returning from a fashionable premiere[2] how he liked the piece, replied: 'My dear friend, it is the best play I ever slept through.' And again, nothing could be neater than his remark to a well-known London manager who had bought a comedy in Paris called 'His Wife.' 'I've got it, and I'm glad I have it,' said the manager. 'Do you know, Wilde, I've kept "His Wife" for three years.' 'Really?' replied the poet. 'Isn't it about time you married her?'

I sat with him once at a music-hall, the entertainment of which he looked upon with good-humoured tolerance. During the evening a man came on the stage whose speciality was mimicry. 'Perfectly splendid!' said Wilde, putting his bent forefinger over his mouth, which was a great trick of his.

* *Me and My Missus; Fifty Years on the Stage* (London: Cassell, 1939) pp. 97–9. Editor's title.

'And I do think it so kind of him to tell us who he is imitating. It avoids discussion, doesn't it?'

Sitting in a box opposite to us that evening was a Hebrew dealer in 70 per cent. young men, curios and precious stones, accompanied by a very beautiful lady whose hair matched her dress. I drew Wilde's attention to the couple, and looking up leisurely he said: 'Yes, a charming woman, no doubt, and really Hogheimer never looks so well as when he is among his "objet Tarts"!'

It was of moneylenders he made one of his most famous remarks, alluding to them as 'Gentlemen who breathe through *their* noses and make you pay through *yours*.'

Wilde's was a wonderful personality, and the sad ending of his career just as he had turned his mind seriously to the stage was a calamity for my profession.

I went to the Old Bailey to see the last day of this great genius's trial.[3] I went for one reason, and for one reason only. I knew that he was doomed, and I thought to myself, if by chance he should catch sight of me he would see at least one sympathetic and sorrowing friend.

As an instance of his fortitude while serving his sentence, surely no better example can be given of his unbreakable spirit than the brilliant epigram he made to a warder, when standing handcuffed to two felons in the pouring rain on a suburban railway station. It was:

'Sir, if this is the way Queen Victoria treats her convicts, she doesn't deserve to have any.'

## NOTES

Sir Seymour Hicks (1871–1949), English actor, playwright, and manager.

1. See Clifford Allen, 'Homosexuality and Oscar Wilde: A Psychological Study', *Homosexuality and Creative Genius*, ed. Hendrik M. Ruitenbeek (New York: Astor-Honor, 1967) pp. 60–83; Marc-André Raffalovich, 'L'Affaire Oscar Wilde', *Uranisme et Unisexualité: Étude sur Différentes Manifestations de l'Instinct* (Lyon: Storck, 1896) pp. 241–78; and Robert André, 'Oscar Wilde et Lucifer', *Nouvelle Revue Française*, XIV (June 1966) 1072–7.

2. By Arthur Pinero.

3. The last day of Wilde's trials at the Old Bailey was 25 May 1895. The jury having found him guilty, Mr Justice Wills sentenced him to two years' hard labour in prison.

# A Man of Genius Disappears*

John Boon

A few days after my return to work – I could only get about with a couple of sticks – I received a visit from one of my closest friends, the late Charles H. E. Brookfield, a distinguished actor and a brilliant wit.[1] He told me that a fracas had taken place in the Burlington Arcade, in which the principal actors were the Marquis of Queensberry and one of his sons, and that the cause of the trouble was the association of the latter with Oscar Wilde. There is no need to go into any details of the unhappy business. On April 5th the Marquis of Queensberry was tried on a charge of libel brought by Wilde, and acquitted. The acquittal was immediately followed by Wilde's arrest. I knew the Marquis of Queensberry slightly – he was prominent in the world of sport and an avowed Freethinker. He once protested against certain lines of a play, causing some uproar in the theatre, and now I remember having some conversation with him while I was in the company of Mr. John Morley at Bradlaugh's funeral. Wilde I had known for a number of years; the first time I saw him he was the head of the cult so delightfully satirised by W. S. Gilbert in *Patience*. He was weirdly attired, and I particularly remember that he wore dark green small clothes and silk stockings. At that time his performances were harmless enough, and years must have elapsed before the very unpleasant stories which led to his arrest and downfall began to be freely circulated in the West End of London. This was after his plays had achieved immense success, and they were undoubtedly the work of a man of genius. It was the publication of *Dorian Grey* which precipitated matters, and not long after this work made its appearance I found Wilde a frequent visitor to one of my clubs. He was a sort of god in a circle composed of young men newly down from the Universities. Two of these young men were sons of two of my personal friends. They had not known Wilde for long and one had indeed introduced Wilde to the family circle. I took the risk of warning both boys of their dangerous situation. Both resented the interference and I think both mentioned it to Wilde. I warned the father of one of the young men, a big figure in the City and a man universally respected, and was saved the

* *Victorians, Edwardians and Georgians; The Impressions of a Veteran Journalist Extending over Forty Years*, vol. 1 (London: Hutchinson, 1928) pp. 199–204. Editor's title.

necessity of communicating with the very stern father of the other boy owing to the action taken by the young man himself. He promised me he would leave the set altogether, and he kept his promise. I went a step further. On the next occasion that I saw Wilde at the club I chose a favourable opportunity of telling him that I should be glad if he would cease his visits altogether. By this time I think he must have been aware that his life was attracting a great deal of grave criticism. He made no reply, but was not seen in the club again. Another young gentleman who was fascinated by Wilde's conversation was the son of a well-known Scottish divine and litterateur. He achieved some small distinction later in life, but his main object when he came south was to secure employment in a secretarial or literary capacity. He had met Wilde and had been completely swept off his feet by the association. He used to tire us to death with his never-ending hymn of praise. Brookfield took him in hand first, and I had occasion to act very firmly at a later date. I do not for one moment suggest, nor do I believe, that any of these three young men were corrupted by Wilde; but the sequel showed that the risk was a very real one indeed. The young Scotsman came to me one day and told me he had taken the bold step of writing to a very famous statesman indeed, asking for an appointment, mentioning his father's name. The distinguished states-man received him with his habitual courtesy and pointed out to him that secretaryships to ministers were provided by the departments of which they were the head, and that his personal private secretary was all that he could desire in efficiency. He wished him well, and the interview ended. He then thought that Wilde might be of service to him in the securing of employment, and wrote to the dramatist a very fulsome letter. Some days later Brookfield and I heard the young gentleman expatiating after lunch on Wilde's marvellous gifts, and we had something to say to him on the subject. He was a very good dispositioned young fellow, but remarkably weak in will. A single glass of port would start him on a monologue which, like the brook, unless it were 'dammed' would go on forever. Brookfield and I were constantly 'damming' it, and on one occasion we were aghast to learn that the young gentleman in a letter to Wilde had volunteered the statement that the famous statesman who had so kindly received him had expressed his admiration of *Dorian Grey*. I cannot imagine any public man – not excepting Mr. Gladstone himself – to whom the work in question would have been more repugnant. I bluntly put it, 'You must have known that was a lie,' and our young gentleman tearfully admitted that it was and he had put it in because he thought it would greatly please Wilde. Brookfield was still more forcible; but a certain amount of mischief had been done. More might have followed but for certain action taken at the time. When Mr. Littlechild, a former Chief Detective Inspector of Scotland Yard, got hold of some of Wilde's papers, the letter was among them. Brookfield and I knew Littlechild very well and had a great personal liking for him. He was very clever indeed at his calling, very human, and an excellent companion. He was placed in possession of the facts in the presence of the young Scot, who must have had the most unhappy time of his existence. At the outbreak of the trouble, Lord Queensberry sought out his solicitor, the Hon. Mr. Charles Russell. As already mentioned, Mr. Russell was both my solicitor and my friend. He called at my office one morning and at his request I introduced him to Brookfield. There had been considerable difficulty in getting hold of a key witness. 'Brooks' at once came to the rescue. The key witness, though I believe he was never called, was found in the person of a fine old Irish Commissionaire, who, with all an Irishman's gratitude, remembered the lavish tips bestowed upon him by Wilde. The sergeant was employed at the theatre where some of Wilde's pieces were produced. The old soldier would lend himself to nothing wrong, but he was able to furnish the addresses of Wilde's associates. The information was obtained with considerable difficulty, but it served its purpose. I was present during the action for libel and well remember the plaintiff's attitude towards Mr. Edward (now Lord) Carson. His insolence and his wit provoked the admiration of his admirers, who were present in unwholesome numbers. Some of them went so far as to indulge in applause, which was promptly suppressed in Court but boisterously expressed outside. They were a very unpleasant-looking lot, and Brookfield's comments were of a scarifying character. It was a very different Wilde who appeared in the dock at the Old Bailey, and a very deadly prosecuting counsel was Mr. Edward Carson. It is always a matter of grief when a man of genius disappears from the scene, and Wilde will always have his sympathisers; but not among those who for some years knew the misery that he was causing in many homes and the bad influence which survived his disappearance. I have no regret for any share that I took in connection with the case. On the contrary, I felt it my duty to act as I did.

## NOTES

In his recollections, John Boon records the impressions of a widely travelled journalist with more than forty years' experience as Parliamentary and Special Correspondent and Editor. From 1914 to 1921 he was in the service of *The Times*, acting as War Correspondent in the early days of the war.

1. Charles H. E. Brookfield (1860–1912) was one of Wilde's most vindictive enemies at the time of the troubles because he had once been rebuked by Wilde for wearing the wrong kind of suit off the stage. He wrote, with J. M. Glover, a parody of *Lady Windermere's Fan* called *The Poet and the Puppets*, which was produced at the Comedy Theatre on 19 May 1892. He was also largely responsible for collecting the evidence which brought about Wilde's downfall. After Wilde's conviction, Brookfield and some friends entertained the Marquis of Queensberry at a banquet in celebration of the event. In revenge for this, some of Wilde's admirers entered a protest at the Prince of Wales's Theatre on the night of Charles Hawtrey's revival of Brookfield's play, *Dear Old Charlie*, on 20 February 1912, shortly after the latter was made Examiner of Plays.

# Oscar Wilde: In Memoriam*

André Gide

## I

Those who came into contact with Wilde only toward the end of his life have a poor notion, from the weakened and broken being whom the prison returned to us, of the prodigious being he was at first. It was in '91 that I met him for the first time. Wilde had at the time what Thackeray calls 'the chief gift of great men': success. His gesture, his look triumphed. His success was so certain that it seemed that it preceded Wilde and that all he needed do was go forward to meet it. His books astonished, charmed. His plays were to be the talk of London. He was rich; he was tall; he was handsome; laden with good fortune and honors. Some compared him to an Asiatic Bacchus; others to some Roman emperor; others to Apollo himself – and the fact is that he was radiant.

At Paris, no sooner did he arrive, than his name ran from mouth to mouth; a few absurd anecdotes were related about him: Wilde was still only the man who smoked gold-tipped cigarettes and who walked about in the streets with a sunflower in his hand. For, Wilde, clever at duping the makers of worldly celebrity, knew how to project, beyond his real character, an amusing phantom which he played most spiritedly.

I heard him spoken of at the home of Mallarmé: he was portrayed as a brilliant talker, and I wished to know him, though I had no hope of managing to do so. A happy chance, or rather a friend, to whom I had told my desire, served me. Wilde was invited to dinner. It was at the restaurant. There were four of us, but Wilde was the only one who talked.

Wilde did not converse: he narrated. Throughout almost the whole of the meal, he did not stop narrating. He narrated gently, slowly; his very voice was wonderful. He knew French admirably, but he pretended to hunt about a bit for the words which he wanted to keep waiting. He had almost no accent, or at least only such as it pleased him to retain and which might give the words a sometimes new and strange aspect. He was fond of pronouncing *skepticisme* for 'scepticisme' . . . The tales which he kept telling us all through the evening were confused and not of his best; Wilde was uncertain of us and was testing us. Of his wisdom or indeed of his folly,

* *Oscar Wilde: In Memoriam (Reminiscences): De Profundis*, translated by Bernard Frechtman (New York: Philosophical Society, 1949) pp. 1–17.

he uttered only what he believed his hearer would relish; he served each, according to his appetite, his taste; those who expected nothing of him had nothing, or just a bit of light froth; and as his first concern was to amuse, many of those who thought they knew him knew only the jester in him.

When the meal was over, we left. As my two friends were walking together, Wilde took me aside:

'You listen with your eyes,' he said to me rather abruptly. 'That's why I'm going to tell you this story: When Narcissus died, the flowers of the field asked the river for some drops of water to weep for him. "Oh!" answered the river, "if all my drops of water were tears, I should not have enough to weep for Narcissus myself. I loved him!" "Oh!" replied the flowers of the field, "how could you not have loved Narcissus? He was beautiful." "Was he beautiful?" said the river. "And who could know better than you? Each day, leaning over your bank, he beheld his beauty in your water . . ." '

Wilde paused for a moment . . .

' "If I loved him," replied the river, "it was because, when he leaned over my water, I saw the reflection of my waters in his eyes." '

Then Wilde, swelling up with a strange burst of laughter, added, 'That's called *The Disciple.*'

We had arrived at his door and left him. He invited me to see him again. That year and the following year I saw him often and everywhere.

Before others, as I have said, Wilde wore a showy mask, designed to astonish, amuse, or, at times, exasperate. He never listened, and paid scant heed to ideas as soon as they were no longer his own. As soon as he ceased to shine all by himself, he effaced himself. After that, he was himself again only when one was once more alone with him.

But no sooner alone he would begin:

'What have you done since yesterday?'

And as my life at that time flowed along rather smoothly, the account that I might give of it offered no interest. I would docilely repeat trivial facts, noting, as I spoke, that Wilde's brow would darken.

'Is that really what you've done?'

'Yes,' I would answer.

'And what you say is true!'

'Yes, quite true.'

'But then why repeat it? You do see that it's not at all interesting. Understand that there are two worlds: the one that *is* without one's speaking about it; it's called the *real world* because there's no need to talk about it in order to see it. And the other is the world of art; that's the one which has to be talked about because it would not exist otherwise.

'There was once a man who was beloved in his village because he would tell stories. Every morning he left the village and in the evening when he returned, all the village workmen, after having drudged all day long, would gather about him and say, "Come! Tell us! What did you see today?" He would tell: "I saw a faun in the forest playing a flute, to whose music a troop of woodland creatures were dancing around." "Tell us more; what did you see?" said the men. "When I came to the seashore, I saw three mermaids, at the edge of the waves, combing their green hair with a golden comb." And the men loved him because he told them stories.

'One morning, as every morning, he left his village—but when he came to the seashore, lo! he beheld three mermaids combing their green hair with a golden comb. And as he continued his walk, he saw, as he came near the woods, a faun playing the flute to a troop of woodland creatures. That evening, when he came back to his village and was asked, as on other evenings, "Come! Tell us! What did you see?" he answered, "I saw nothing." '

Wilde paused for some moments, let the effect of the tale work its way in me, and then resumed, 'I don't like your lips; they're straight, like those of someone who has never lied. I want to teach you to lie, so that your lips may become beautiful and twisted like those of an antique mask.

'Do you know what makes the work of art and what makes the work of nature? Do you know what makes them different? For, after all, the flower of the narcissus is as beautiful as a work of art – and what distinguishes them can not be beauty. Do you know what distinguishes them? – The work of art is always *unique*. Nature, which makes nothing durable, always repeats itself so that nothing which it makes may be lost. There are many narcissus flowers; that's why each one can live only a day. And each time that nature invents a new form, she at once repeats it. A sea-monster in a sea knows that in another sea is another sea-monster, his like. When God creates a Nero, a Borgia or a Napoleon in history, he puts another one elsewhere; this one is not known, it little matters; the important thing is that *one* succeed; for God invents man, and man invents the work of art.

'Yes, I know . . . one day there was a great uneasiness on earth, as if nature were at last going to create something unique, something truly unique – and Christ was born on earth. Yes, I know . . . but listen:

'When, in the evening, Joseph of Arimathaea went down from Mount Calvary where Jesus had just died he saw a young man seated on a white stone and weeping. And Joseph approached him and said, "I understand that your grief is great, for certainly that Man was a just Man." But the young man answered, "Oh! that's not why I'm weeping. I'm weeping because I too have performed miracles! I too have restored sight to the blind, I have healed paralytics and I have raised up the dead. I too have withered the barren fig-tree and I have changed water into wine . . . And men have not crucified me." '

And it seemed to me more than once that Oscar Wilde was convinced of his representative mission.

The Gospel disturbed and tormented the pagan Wilde. He did not forgive it its miracles. The pagan miracle is the work of art: Christianity was encroaching. All robust artistic unrealism requires an earnest realism in life.

His most ingenious apologues, his most disturbing ironies were designed to bring the two ethics face to face with one another, I mean pagan naturalism and Christian idealism, and to put the latter out of countenance.

'When Jesus wished to return to Nazareth,' he related, 'Nazareth was so changed that He no longer recognized His city. The Nazareth in which He had lived had been full of lamentations and tears; this city was full of bursts of laughter and singing. And Christ, entering the city, saw slaves loaded with flowers hastening toward the marble stairway of a house of white marble. Christ entered the house, and at the rear of a room of jasper He saw lying on a regal couch a man whose disheveled hair was entwined with red roses and whose lips were red with wine. Christ approached him, touched him upon the shoulder and said, 'Why leadest thou this life?'' The man turned about, recognized Him and replied, "I was a leper; Thou hast healed me. Why should I lead another life?"

'Christ went out of that house. And lo! in the street he beheld a woman whose face and garments were painted, and whose feet were shod with pearls; and behind her walked a man whose coat was of two colors and whose eyes were laden with desire. And Christ approached the man, touched him upon the shoulder and said, 'Why dost thou follow that woman and regard her thus?'' The man, turning about, recognized Him and replied, "I was blind; Thou hast healed me. What should I do otherwise with my sight?"

'And Christ approached the woman. "The road which you follow," He said to her, "is that of sin; wherefore follow it?" The woman recognized Him and laughingly said to Him, "The road which I follow is a pleasing one and Thou hast pardoned me all my sins."

'Then Christ felt His heart full of sadness and wished to leave that city. But as He was leaving it, He saw at length beside the moats of the city a youth who was weeping. Christ approached him, and touching his locks, said to him, "My friend, wherefore weepest thou?"

'The youth lifted up his eyes, recognized Him, and replied, "I was dead and Thou hast raised me up; what should I do otherwise with my life?"'

'Would you like me to tell you a secret?' Wilde began another day – it was at the home of Heredia; he had taken me aside in the midst of a crowded drawing-room – 'a secret . . . but promise me not to tell it to anyone . . . Do you know why Christ did not love His mother?' This was spoken into my ear, in a low voice and as if ashamedly. He paused a moment, grasped my arm, drew back, and then bursting into laughter, said, 'It's because she was a virgin! . . .'

Let me again be permitted to quote this tale, a most strange one and a tough nut for the mind to crack – it is a rare spirit that will understand the contradiction, which Wilde hardly seems to be inventing.

'. . . Then there was a great silence in the Chamber of God's Justice. – And the soul of the sinner advanced stark naked before God.

And God opened the book of the sinner's life:

"Certainly your life has been very bad: You have . . . (followed a prodigious, marvelous enumeration of sins).[1] – Since you have done all that, I am certainly going to send you to Hell."

"You can not send me to Hell."

"And why can I not send you to Hell?"

"Because I have lived there all my life."

Then there was a great silence in the Chamber of God's Justice.

"Well, since I can not send you to Hell, I am going to send you to Heaven."

"You can not send me to Heaven."

"And why can I not send you to Heaven?"

"Because I have never been able to imagine it."

And there was a great silence in the Chamber of God's Justice.'[2]

One morning Wilde handed me an article to read in which a rather dull-witted critic congratulated him for 'knowing how to invent pleasant tales the better to clothe his thought.'

'They believe,' Wilde began, 'that all thoughts are born naked . . . They don't understand that I can not think otherwise than in stories. The sculptor doesn't try to translate his thought into marble; *he thinks in marble*, directly.

'There was a man who could think only in bronze. And one day this man had an idea, the idea of joy, of the joy which dwells in the moment. And he felt that he had to tell it. But in all the world, not a single piece of bronze was left; for men had used it all. And this man felt that he would go mad if he did not tell his idea.

'And he thought about a piece of bronze on the grave of his wife, about a statue he had made to adorn the grave of his wife, of the only woman he had loved; it was the statue of sadness, of the sadness which dwells in life. And the man felt that he would go mad if he did not tell his idea.

'So he took the statue of sadness, of the sadness which dwells in life; he smashed it and made of it the statue of joy, of the joy which dwells only in the moment.'

Wilde believed in some sort of fatality of the artist, and that the idea is stronger than the man.

'There are,' he would say, 'two kinds of artist: one brings answers, and the other, questions. We have to know whether one belongs to those who answer or to those who question; for the kind which questions is never that which answers. There are works which wait, and which one does not understand for a long time; the reason is that they bring answers to questions which have not yet been raised; for the question often arrives a terribly long time after the answer.'

And he would also say:

'The soul is born old in the body; it is to rejuvenate it that the latter grows old. Plato is the youth of Socrates . . . '

Then I remained for three years without seeing him again.

## II

Here begin the tragic memories.

A persistent rumor, growing with each of his successes (in London he was being played at the same time in three theatres),[3] ascribed strange practices to Wilde; some people were so kind as to rake umbrage at them with a smile, and others took no umbrage at all; it was claimed moreover that he took no pains to hide them, that, on the contrary, he flaunted them; some said, courageously; others, cynically; others, affectedly. I listened to this rumor with great astonishment. Nothing, since I had been associating with Wilde, could have ever made me suspect a thing. – But already, out of prudence, a number of former friends were deserting him. People were not yet repudiating him outright, but they no longer made much of having met him.

An extraordinary chance brought our two paths together again. It was in January 1895. I was travelling; I was driven to do so by a kind of anxiety, more in quest of solitude than in the novelty of places. The weather was frightful; I had fled from Algiers toward Blidah; I was going to leave Blidah for Biskra. At the moment of leaving the hotel, out of idle curiosity, I looked at the blackboard where the names of the travelers were written. What did I see there? – Beside my name, touching it, that of Wilde . . . I have said that I was longing for solitude: I took the sponge and rubbed out my name.

Before reaching the station, I was no longer quite sure whether a bit of cowardice might not have been hidden in this act; at once, retracing my steps, I had my valise brought up again and rewrote my name on the board.

In the three years that I had not seen him (for I can not count a brief meeting at Florence the year before), Wilde had certainly changed. One felt less softness in his look, something raucous in his laughter and something frenzied in his joy. He seemed both more sure of pleasing and less ambitious to succeed in doing so; he was bolder, stronger, bigger. What was strange was that he no longer spoke in apologues; during the few days that I lingered in his company, I was unable to draw the slightest tale from him.

I was at first astonished at finding him in Algeria.

'Oh!' he said to me, 'it's that now I'm fleeing from the work of art; I no longer want to adore anything but the sun . . . Have you noticed that the sun detests thought; it always makes it withdraw and take refuge in the shade. At first, thought lived in Egypt; the sun conquered Egypt. It lived in Greece for a long time, the sun conquered Greece; then Italy and then France. At the present time, all thought finds itself pushed back to Norway and Russia, places where the sun never comes. The sun is jealous of the work of art.'

To adore the sun, ah! was to adore life. Wilde's lyrical adoration was growing wild and terrible. A fatality was leading him on; he could not and would not elude it. He seemed to put all his concern, his virtue, into overexaggerating his destiny and losing patience with himself. He went to pleasure as one marches to duty. – 'My duty to myself,' he would say, 'is to amuse myself terrifically.'

Nietzsche astonished me less, later on, because I had heard Wilde say: 'Not happiness! Above all, not happiness. Pleasure! We must always want the most tragic . . .'

He would walk in the streets of Algiers, preceded, escorted, followed by an extraordinary band of ragamuffins; he chatted with each one; he regarded them all with joy and tossed his money to them haphazardly.

'I hope,' he said to me, 'to have quite demoralized this city.'

I thought of the word used by Flaubert who, when someone asked him what kind of glory he was most ambitious of, replied, 'That of demoralizer.'

In the face of all this, I remained full of astonishment, admiration, and fear. I was aware of his shaky situation, the hostilities, the attacks, and what a dark anxiety he did beneath his bold joy.[4] He spoke of returning to London; the Marquis of Q . . . was insulting him, summoning him, accusing him of fleeing.

'But if you go back there, what will happen?' I asked him. 'Do you know what you're risking?'

'One should never know that . . . They're extraordinary, my friends; they advise prudence. Prudence! But can I have any? That would be going backwards. I must go as far as possible . . . I can not go further . . . Something must happen . . . something else . . .'

Wilde embarked the following day.

The rest of the story is familiar. That 'something else' was *hard labor*.[5]

## NOTES

André Gide (1869–1951), French writer, whom Wilde met in Paris for the first time in 1891. Wilde's influence on him was so strong, so unsettling, that Gide destroyed several pages of his *Journal* for November and December of 1891 because 'he is always trying to instil into you a sanction for evil'. Gide fell under Wilde's charm again in Algeria when Wilde and Alfred Douglas arrived in 1895. Gide gave two versions of this meeting; one in *In Memoriam*, was fairly severe about Wilde's works, the other in *Si le Grain ne meurt* was more severe about the man. See Jean Delay, *La jeunesse d'André Gide, 1890–1895* (Paris: Gallimard, 1957) pp. 128–47, 447–64; 'Gide on Wilde', *Times Literary Supplement*, (9 Nov 1951) p. 706; François J. L. Mouret, 'La première rencontre d'André Gide et d'Oscar Wilde', *French Studies*, XXII (Jan 1968) 37–9; K. Hellwig, 'André Gide bei Oscar Wilde', *Der Kleine Bund*, X (1929) 279–80; and Jef Last, 'Gide en de invloed van Wilde', *Maatstaf*, XVII (1971) 386–93.

1. 'The written version which he later made of this tale is, for a wonder, excellent' – Gide.

2. 'Since Villiers de l'Isle-Adam betrayed it, everybody knows, alas! the "great secret of the Church": *There is no purgatory.*' – Gide.

3. Only two of Wilde's plays were produced at the same time in 1895: *An Ideal Husband* and *The Importance of Being Earnest.*

4. 'One of those last Algiers evenings, Wilde seemed to have promised himself to say nothing serious. . . . I grew somewhat irritated with his too witty paradoxes: "You've better things to say than witticisms," I began. "You're talking to me this evening as if I were the public. You ought rather talk to the public the way you know how to talk to your friends. Why aren't your plays better? You talk away the best of yourself; why don't you write it down?"

"Oh!" he exclaimed at once, "but my plays are not at all good; and I don't put any stock in them at all. . . . But if you only knew what amusement they give! . . . Almost every one is the result of a wager. *Dorian Gray* too; I wrote it in a few days because one of my friends claimed that I could never write a novel. It bores me so much, writing!" – Then, suddenly bending over toward me: "Would you like to know the great drama of my life? – It's that I've put my genius into my life; I've put only my talent into my works."

It was only too true. The best of his writing is only a pale reflection of his brilliant conversation. Those who have heard him speak find it disappointing to read him. *Dorian Gray*, at the very beginning, was a splendid story, how superior to the *Peau de Chagrin*! how much more *significant*! Alas! written down, what a masterpiece *manqué*. – In his most charming tales there is too great an intrusion of literature. Graceful as they may be, one feels too greatly the affectation; preciosity and euphuism conceal the beauty of the first invention; one feels in them, one can never stop feeling, the three moments of their genesis; the first idea is quite beautiful, simple, profound and certainly sensational; a kind of latent necessity holds its parts firmly together; but from here on, the gift stops; the development of the parts is carried out factitiously; they are not well organized; and when, afterwards, Wilde works on his phrases, and goes about pointing them up, he does so by a prodigious overloading of concetti, of trivial inventions, which are pleasing and curious, in which emotion stops, with the result that the glittering of the surface makes our mind lose sight of the deep central emotion.' – Gide.

5. 'I have invented nothing and arranged nothing in the last remarks I quote. Wilde's words are present to my mind, and I was going to say to my ear. I am not claiming that Wilde clearly saw prison rising up before him; but I do assert that the dramatic turn which surprised and astounded London, abruptly transforming Wilde from accuser to accused, did not, strictly speaking, cause him any surprise. The newspapers, which were unwilling to see anything more in him than a clown, did their best to misrepresent the attitude of his defense, to the point of depriving it of any meaning. Perhaps, in some far-off time it will be well to lift this frightful trial out of its abominable filth.' – Gide.

# Oscar Wilde*

## Coulson Kernahan

'To the memory of one who by some strange madness, beyond understand-ing, made shipwreck of his own life and of the life of others; one of whom the world speaks in whispers, but of whom I say openly that I never heard an objectionable word from his lips and saw in him at no time anything more vicious than vanity; to the memory of

### OSCAR WILDE,

actor (in a great life tragedy as in everything else), artist (in more crafts than one, including flattery), poet, critic, convict, genius, and, as I knew him, gentleman: I dedicate these pages in memory of many kindnesses.'

In these words I wished, soon after Wilde's death, to dedicate a book, but the publisher of the book in question was obdurate. He would not, he said, have Wilde's name on the dedication page of any work issued by him, and went so far as to urge me not to fulfil the intention I had even then formed of one day writing a chapter on Oscar Wilde as I knew him. Yet in Oscar Wilde as I knew him, as stated in the above dedication, except for his vanity there was no offence.

The preface, since my relations with the publisher of whom I speak were pleasant and friendly, I withdrew. If I have let sixteen years elapse before writing the chapter, it was for no other reason than that I felt the thing could wait – would perhaps be the better for waiting – and that the pressure of other work kept me employed.

But one day a man, who to my knowledge has eaten Wilde's salt and received many kindnesses from him in the season of Wilde's prosperity, called to see me concerning some literary project. On my shelves are books given and inscribed to me by Wilde and signed 'from his sincere friend,' and on my mantelshelf stands a portrait similarly inscribed and signed. Seeing this portrait, my caller observed:

'If I were you I should put that thing out of sight, and, if you happen at any time to hear his name mentioned, I should keep the fact that he had been a friend of yours to yourself.'

That decided me to write my long delayed chapter. I begin by a protest.

---

* *In Good Company; Some Personal Recollections* (London and New York: John Lane, 1917) pp. 189–235.

In his very interesting *Notes from a Painter's Life*, my friend Mr. C. E. Hallé speaks of Wilde's 'repulsive appearance.' At the time of Wilde's conviction some of the sketches of him, presumably made in court and published in certain prints, did so portray him, possibly because, as he was just then being held up to public execration, so to picture him fitted in with the popular conception. Mr. Hallé wrote 'after the event' of Wilde's downfall, when it is easy not only to be wise, but also to see in the outer man some signs of the evil within. But from the statement that Wilde's appearance was 'repulsive' I entirely dissent. It is true there was a flabby fleshiness of face and neck, a bulkiness of body, an animality about the large and pursy lips – which did not close naturally, but in a hard, indrawn and archless line – that suggested self-indulgence, but did not to me suggest vice. Otherwise, except for this fleshiness and for the animality of the mouth, I saw no evil in Wilde's face. The forehead, what was visible of it – for he disposed brown locks of his thick and carefully parted hair over either temple – was high and finely formed. The nose was well shaped, the nostrils close and narrow – not open and 'breathing' as generally seen in highly sensitive men. The eyes were peculiar, the almond-shaped lids being minutely out of alignment. I mean by this that the lids were so cut and the eyes so set in the head that the outer corners of the lids drooped downwards very slightly and towards the ears, as seen sometimes in Orientals. Liquid, soft, large and smiling, Wilde's eyes, if they seemed to see all things – life, death, other mortals and most of all himself – half banteringly, met one's own eyes frankly. His smile seemed to me to come from his eyes, not from his lips, which he tightened rather than relaxed in laughter. His general expression – always excepting the mouth, which, its animality notwithstanding, had none of the cruelty which goes so often with sensuality – was kindly.

The best portrait I have seen of Wilde is one in my possession which has never been published. It was taken when he was the guest of the late Lady Palmer (then Mrs. Walter Palmer), with whom I had at the time some acquaintance. She was a close friend of Wilde (who christened her 'Moonbeam') and of George Meredith (whom she sometimes half-seriously, half-playfully spoke of as 'The Master'). In the portrait, Lady Palmer is seated with Meredith, Mrs. Jopling Rowe being seated on her right and Mr. H. B. Irving on her left. Behind Meredith's chair stands Wilde with Miss Meredith (afterwards Mrs. Julian Sturgis), Sir J. Forbes-Robertson, and I think Mr. David Bisham on his right. The portrait of Wilde, if grave, is frank, untroubled, and attractive, for, when he chose to be serious, the large lines of his face and features sobered into a repose and into a massiveness which were not without dignity. Too often, however, Dignity suddenly let fall her cloak, and Vanity, naked and unashamed, was revealed in her place.

Yet there is this to be said of Wilde's vanity, that its very nakedness was its best excuse. A loin-cloth, a fig-leaf would have offended, but it was so artlessly naked that one merely smiled and passed on. Moreover, it was never a jealous or a malicious vanity. It was so occupied in admiring itself in the mirror that the smile on its face was never distorted into a scowl at sight of another's success. Wilde's vanity, I repeat, was as entirely free from venom as was his wit. No one's comments on society, on the men and women he met, the authors he read, were more incisive or more caustic, but I remember none in which the thought was slanderous or the intention spiteful.

*A propos* of Wilde's vanity, here is a story told me long ago by Lieutenant-Colonel Spencer, who then held a post of some sort in connection with the Masters in Lunacy. Visiting the Zoological Gardens one day – in his private capacity, I assume, not in connection with the Lunacy Commission – he entered the Monkey House. Within the big cement wire enclosure a certain liveliness – the war phrase seems to have come to stay – was evident. What it was all about Colonel Spencer did not know, but with one exception the occupants were very excited, leaping wildly from end to end of the cage, and from top to bottom, jabbering, groaning, snarling, emitting shrill shrieks of terror or hoarse howls of rage.

The one exception was an evil-looking and elderly monkey which sat humped and brooding in a corner, absolutely motionless except for the twitching of his nostrils and the angry way in which he switched his eyes first upon what he apparently thought to be the staring human idiots outside, and then at the capering and noisy monkey imbeciles within.

'What's the matter with that monkey?' Colonel Spencer inquired of a keeper. 'Is he ill? He seems too bored even to scratch.' The keeper shook his head. 'No, he isn't ill, sir,' he answered. 'Wot's the matter with 'im, sir? Why, wanity.' Then stirring up the sulking monkey with his cane, he added, ''Ere, get up – Hoscar Wilde!'

One day it was Wilde's caprice to amuse himself by talking the most blatantly insincere nonsense, directed against my own political views, and deliberately intended to 'draw' me. He was in his most exasperating mood, exuding, or affecting to exude, egotism at every pore, and fondling, or making pretence to fondle, his vanity as some spinsters fondle a favourite cat. At last I could stand it no longer, and wickedly told him the story of Colonel Spencer's visit to the Monkey House at the Zoo and the keeper's comment about the sulky monkey. 'Wot's the matter with 'im, sir? Why, wanity. 'Ere, get up – Hoscar Wilde.'

So far from being annoyed, Wilde simply rocked, or affected to rock with delight.

'I hoped once,' he said, 'to live to see a new shape in chrysanthemums or sunflowers, or possibly a new colour in roses, blue for choice, called after me. But that one's name should percolate even to the Zoological Gardens, that it should come naturally to the lips of a keeper in the Monkey House, is fame indeed. Do remind me to tell George Alexander the story. It will make him so dreadfully jealous.'

And I answered grimly:
'Your game, Wilde!'

## II

My friendship with Wilde was literary in its beginnings. Flattered vanity on my part possibly contributed not a little to it, for when I was a young and – if that be possible – a more obscure man even than I am now, Wilde, already famous, was one of the very first to speak an encouraging word. Here is the first letter I received from him:

> 16 Tite Street, Chelsea.
>
> Dear Mr. Kernahan,
> If you have nothing to do on Wednesday, will you come and dine at the Hotel de Florence, Rupert Street, at 7.45 – morning dress, and chianti yellow or red!
> I am charmed to see your book is having so great a success. It is strong and fine and true. Your next book will be a great book.
>
> Truly yours
> Oscar Wilde.

This letter, it will be observed, is undated. Apparently Wilde never dated his letters, for of all the letters of his which I have preserved not a solitary one bears a date, other perhaps than the name of the day of the week on which it was written, and that only rarely. He had the impudence once at a dinner-party, when taken to task by a great lady for not having answered a letter, to reply:
'But, my dear lady, I never answer or write letters. Ask my friend there, whose faithful correspondent I am.' Then turning to me, he said, 'Tell Lady —— when you heard from me last.'
As I had heard from him that morning, I dissembled by saying:
'How can I answer that, Wilde, for among my other discoveries of the eccentricities of genius I have discovered that genius, at least as represented by you, never dates its letters. I never had one from you that was dated.'
Not long after the receipt of this first letter, I proposed to write what I may call a 'grown-up fairy story,' and asked Wilde whether I might borrow as sub-title a phrase I had once heard him use of a fairy tale of his own making – 'A Story for Children from Eight to Eighty.' He replied as follows, then, as always, with a capital *D* for 'dear':

> 16 Tite Street,
> Chelsea, S.W.
>
> My Dear Kernahan,
> I am only too pleased that any little phrase of mine will find a place

in any title you may give to any story. Use it, of course. I am sure your story will be delightful. Hoping to see you soon.

> Your friend,
> OSCAR WILDE.

My story[1] written and published, I despatched it cap in hand to carry my acknowledgments to the teller of supremely lovely fairy stories – imagined, not invented – from whom my own drab and homespun-clad little tale had impudently 'lifted' a beautiful sub-title to wear, a borrowed plume, in its otherwise undecorated hat.

Here is Wilde's very characteristic reply. It needs no signature to indicate the writer. No other author of the day would have written thus graciously and thus generously:

> 16 TITE STREET,
> CHELSEA, S.W.

MY DEAR KERNAHAN,

I should have thanked you long ago for sending me your charming Fairy Tale, but the season with its red roses of pleasure has absorbed me quite and I have almost forgotten how to write a letter. However, I know you will forgive me, and I must tell you how graceful and artistic I think your story is – full of delicate imagination, and a symbolism suggestive of many meanings, not narrowed down to one moral, but many-sided, as I think symbolism should be.

But your strength lies not in such graceful winsome work. You must deal directly with Life – modern terrible Life – wrestle with it, and force it to yield you its secret. You have the power and the pen. You know what passion is, what passions are. You can give them their red raiment and make them move before us. You can fashion puppets with bodies of flesh and souls of turmoil, and so you must sit down and do a great thing.

It is all in you.

> Your sincere friend,
> OSCAR WILDE.

That Wilde was an artist in flattery as well as an egotist, is not to be denied, but when quite early in our friendship I was shown by a certain woman poet a presentation copy of Wilde's book of poems inscribed 'To a poet and a poem,' and within the next few weeks saw upon a table in the drawing-room of a very beautiful and singularly accomplished woman, the late Rosamund Marriott-Watson ('Graham Tomson'), who was a friend of Wilde's and mine, a fine portrait of himself also inscribed 'To a poet and a poem,' I was not so foolish as to take too seriously the flattering things he said.

Egotist as Wilde was, his was not the expansive egotism which, in spreading its wings to invite admiration, seeks to eclipse and to shut out its fellow egotists from their own little place in the sun. Most egotists are eager only for flattery and applause. Wilde was equally eager, but he was ready for the time being to forget himself and his eagerness in applauding and flattering others. Not many egotists of my acquaintance, especially literary egotists, write letters like that I have quoted, in which there is no word of himself, or of his own work, but only of his friend.

The last letter I ever received from Wilde is in the same vein. It is as usual undated, but as the play to which it refers was his first, *Lady Windermere's Fan*, I am, by the assistance of Mr. Stuart Mason's admirably compiled *Oscar Wilde Calendar*, enabled to fix the date as the middle of February, 1892.

HOTEL ALBEMARLE,
PICCADILLY LONDON.

MY DEAR KERNAHAN,

Will you come and see my play Thursday night. I want it to be liked by an artist like you.

Yours ever,
O.W.

Wilde came to see me, I think, the morning after the production of the play, or at all events within a morning or two after, and hugged himself with delight when, in reply to his question, 'Do tell me what you admired most in the play,' I said:

'Your impudence! To dare to come before the footlights in response to enthusiastic calls – smoking a cigarette too – and compliment a British audience on having the unexpected good taste – for your manner said as plainly as it could, "Really, my dear people, I didn't think you had it in you!" – to appreciate a work of art on its merits! You are a genius, Wilde, in impudence at least if in nothing else.'

'And you are a plagiarist as well as a flatterer,' he replied. 'You stole that last remark from a story you have heard me tell about Richard Le Gallienne.[2] I'm going to punish you by telling you the story, for, though you stole part of it, I am sure you have never heard it. No one ever has heard the story he steals and calls his own; no one ever has read – the odds are that he will swear he has never heard of – the book from which he has plagiarised. Our friend Richard is very beautiful, isn't he? Wasn't it you who told me that Swinburne described him to you as "Shelley with a chin"? I don't agree. Swinburne might just as well have described himself as "Shelley without a chin". No, it is the Angel Gabriel in Rossetti's National Gallery painting of the Annunciation of which Richard reminds me. The hair, worn long and fanning out into a wonderful halo around the head, always reminds me of Rossetti's angel. However, my story is that an American woman, in that terribly crude way that Americans have, asked Richard, "Why do you wear your hair so long, Mr. Le Gallienne?" Richard is sometimes brilliant as well as always beautiful, but on this occasion he could think of nothing less banal and foolish to say than "Perhaps, dear lady, for advertisement." "But you, Mr. Le Gallienne! You who have such genius!" Richard blushed and bowed and smiled until the lady added cruelly – "for advertisement!" '

Wilde was quite right in saying I had heard the story before. It had been told me as happening to himself in America in the days when wore his own hair very long, and I am of opinion that it was much more likely to have happened to Wilde, who was both a notoriety hunter and an advertiser, than to Le Gallienne, who is neither.

*A propos* of Wilde's love of advertising, I once heard the fact commented upon – perhaps rudely and crudely – to Wilde himself. Just as I was about to enter the Savage Club in company with a Brother Savage, who was well known as an admirer of Dickens, we encountered Wilde, and I invited him to join us at lunch.

'In the usual way,' he answered, 'I should say that I was charmed, but out of compliment to our friend here, I will for once condescend to quote that dreadful and tedious person Dickens and answer, "Barkis is willin'." Where are you lunching – Romano's?'

'No,' I said, 'the Savage Club.'

'Oh, the Savage Club,' said Wilde. 'I never enter the Savage Club. It tires me so. It used to be gentlemanly Bohemian, but ever since the Prince of Wales became a member and sometimes dines there, it is nothing but savagely snobbish. Besides, the members are all supposed to be professionally connected with Literature, Science, and Art, and I abhor professionalism of every sort.'

My Dickens friend, who shares every Savage's love for the old club (he told me afterwards, whether correctly or not I do not know, that Wilde's aversion was due to the fact that his brother Willie Wilde had unsuccessfully put up for membership), was annoyed by what Wilde had said both about the club and about Charles Dickens.

'I can understand your dislike of professionalism – in advertisement, Mr. Wilde,' he said bluntly. 'And, since you have condescended to stoop to quote Dickens, I may add that, in the matter of advertisement, Barkis as represented by Wilde is not only willing but more than Mr. Willing the advertising agent himself. Good morning.'

One other story of Wilde and Le Gallienne occurs to me. Wilde held Le Gallienne, as I do, in warm liking as a friend and in genuine admiration as a poet; but, meeting him one day at a theatre, bowed gravely and coldly and made as if to pass on. Le Gallienne stopped to say something, and, noticing the aloofness of Wilde's manner, inquired:

'What is the matter, Oscar? Have I offended you in anything?'

'Not offended so much as very greatly pained me, Richard,' was the stern reply.

'I pained you! In what way?'

'You have brought out a new book since I saw you last.'

'Yes, what of it?'

'You have treated me very badly in your book, Richard.'

'I treated you badly in my book!' protested Le Gallienne in amazement. 'You must be confusing my book with somebody else's. My last book was *The Religion of a Literary Man*. I'm sure you can't have read it, or you wouldn't say I had treated you badly.'

'That's the very book; I have read every word of it,' persisted Wilde, 'and your treatment of me in that book is infamous and brutal. I couldn't have believed it of you, Richard – such friends as we have been too!'

'I treated you badly in my *Religion of a Literary Man?*' said Le Gallienne impatiently. 'You must be dreaming, man. Why, I never so much as mentioned you in it.'

'That's just it, Richard,' said Wilde, smilingly.

Here is a recollection of another sort. About the time when Wilde's star was culminating, he boarded a Rhine steamer on the deck of which I was sitting. The passengers included a number of Americans, one of whom instantly recognised Wilde, and seating himself beside the new-comer, inquired:

'Guess, sir, you are the great Mr. Oscar Wilde about whom every one is talking?'

Smilingly, but not without an assumption of the bland boredom which he occasionally adopted toward strangers of whom he was uncertain, Wilde assented. The other, an elderly man wearing a white cravat, may or may not at some time have been connected with a church. Possibly he was then editing some publication, religious or otherwise, and in his time may have done some interviewing, for he plied Wilde with many curious and even over-curious questions concerning his movements, views, and projects. The latter, amused at first, soon tired. His eyes wandered from his interviewer to scan the faces of the passengers, and catching sight of me made as if to rise and join me.

The interviewer, who had not yet done with him, and was something of a strategist, cut off Wilde's retreat by a forward movement of himself and the deck-chair, in which he was sitting, so as to block the way. It was apparently merely the unconscious hitching of one's seat a little nearer to an interesting companion, the better to carry on the conversation, but it was adroitly followed by a very flattering remark in the form of a question, and Wilde relapsed lumpily into his seat to answer. For the next few minutes I could have imagined myself watching a game of 'living chess.' Wilde, evidently wearying, wished to move his king, as represented by himself, across the board and into the square adjacent to myself, but for every 'move' he made his adversary pushed forward another con- versational 'piece' to call a check. At last, shaking his head in laughing remonstrance, Wilde rose, and the other, seeing the game was up, did the same.

'It has been a real pleasure and honour to meet you, sir,' he said. 'Guess when I get home and tell my wife I've talked to the great Oscar Wilde she won't believe me. If you would just write your autograph there, I'd take it as a kindness.' He had been searching his pockets while speaking for a sheet of paper, but finding none opened his Baedeker where there was a blank sheet and thrust it into Wilde's hand.

The latter, with a suggestion in his manner of the condescension which is so becoming to greatness, scrawled his name – a big terminal Greek 'e' tailing off into space at the end – in the book, and bowing a polite, in response to the other's effusive, farewell, made straight for a deck-chair next to me, and plumping himself heavily in it began to talk animatedly.

Meanwhile, the interviewer was excitedly going the round of his party to exhibit his trophy.

'Oscar Wilde's on board, the great æsthete!' he said. 'I've had a long talk with him. See, here's his own autograph in my Baedeker. There he is, the big man talking to the one in a grey suit.'

The excitement spread, and soon we had the entire party standing in a ring, or perhaps I should say a halo, around the object of their worship, who though still talking animatedly missed nothing of it all, and by his beaming face seemed to enjoy his lionising. I suspect him, in fact, of amusing himself by playing up to it, for, seeing that some of his admirers were not only looking, but while doing their best to appear not to be doing so were also listening intently, his talk struck me as meant for them as much as for me. He worked off a witty saying or two which I had heard before, and just as I had seen him glance sideways at a big plate-glass Bond Street shop window to admire his figure or the cut of his coat, so he stole sideway glances at the faces around as if to see whether admiration of his wit was mirrored there.

Then he told stories of celebrities, literary or otherwise, of whom he spoke intimately, called some of them, as in the case of Besant and Whistler, by their Christian names, and so tensely was his audience holding its breath to listen, that when at Bingen he rose and said, 'I'm getting off here,' one could almost hear the held breath 'ough' out like a deflating tyre.

No sooner was he gone than the interviewer seated himself in the deck chair vacated by Wilde, and inquired politely:

'Are you a lit-er-ary man, sir?'

'Why, yes,' I said, 'I suppose so, in a way. That's how I earn my living.'

'May I ask your name?'

'Certainly,' I said (meaning thereby 'you may ask, but it does not follow that I shall tell you'). 'I am afraid "Brown" is not a very striking name, but don't tell me you have never heard it, for there is nothing so annoys an author as that.'

He was a kindly man, and made haste to reassure me.

'I know it well,' he protested. 'Yours is not an uncommon name, I

believe, in England. It is less common in the States. Your Christian name
is – is – is – ?'

'John,' I submitted modestly.

His brow cleared. 'Exactly,' he nodded. 'I know it well.'

Then he seemed uncertain again, and looked thoughtfully but absently
at a castle-crowned hill. I imagine he was running through and ticking off
as the names occurred to him the list of all the illustrious John Browns.
Possibly he thought of the author of *Rab and His Friends*, and decided that I
was too young. Possibly of Queen Victoria's favourite gillie, who was
generally pictured in kilts, whereas I wore knickerbockers.

'You have published books?' he asked.

I nodded.

'Only in England perhaps?'

'No, they have been issued in America too.'

'Sold?'

'The people who bought them were,' I said.

'Tell me the name of one of your books, please.'

I shook my head.

'Can't. Not allowed.'

'Not allowed? Why not?'

'Because,' I answered, rattling off the first nonsense which came to my
head, 'I'm a member of the famous "Silence Club," the members of which
are known as the W.N.T.S.'s. You have heard of the club of course, even if
you haven't heard of me?'

'Yes,' he said. 'I feel sure I have; but I was never quite sure what it
meant. What does W.N.T.S. stand for?'

'It means "We Never Talk Shop.' An author who so much as mentions
the title of his book except to his publisher, his bookseller, or an agent is
unconditionally expelled.'

Then I delivered my counter-attack. He had mentioned to Wilde that
he hailed from Boston. It so happens that at my friend Louise Chandler
Moulton's[3] receptions I had met nearly every eminent Boston or even
American author, so I put a few questions to my interviewer which showed
an inner knowledge of Boston and American literary life and celebrities
that seemed positively to startle him. He was now convinced that I was a
celebrity of world-wide fame, and that such a comet should come within
his own orbit, without his getting to know as much as the comet's name,
was not to be endured by a self-respecting journalist. He literally agonised,
as well as perspired, in his unavailing efforts to trick, wheedle or implore
my obscure name from me. For one moment I was minded to tell him my
name if only to enjoy the shock of its unknownness, but I resisted the
temptation and, tiring in my turn as Wilde had tired, I rose and said that as
I was getting off at the next stopping place I would wish him 'Good day.'

He did not even ask for John Brown's autograph. He even seemed suddenly
in a hurry to get rid of me, the reason for which I afterwards discovered. He

had, I suppose, heard me tell Wilde that my luggage was on board; and the last I saw of him was in the boat's hold, where he was stooping, pince-nez on nose, over the up-piled bags, boxes, dressing-cases and trunks, painfully raking them over, and every moment hoping to be rewarded by finding mine labelled 'Robert Louis Stevenson,' 'Rudyard Kipling,' 'Algernon C. Swinburne' or 'Thomas Hardy.' I trust he found it.

When we were back in town I told Wilde my own adventure with the interviewer after the former had left the boat. His comment was:

'It sounds like a terrible serial story that I once saw in a magazine, each chapter of which was written by a different hand. "The Adventures of Oscar Wilde, by himself, continued by Coulson Kernahan." How positively dreadful!'

I wonder what Wilde will have to say to me, if hereafter we should discuss together the brief and fragmentary continuation of his own story which in these Recollections I have endeavoured to carry on?

## III

Once when Wilde, a novelist and I were lunching together, and when Wilde, after declaring that the wine was so 'heavenly' that it should be drunk kneeling, was discoursing learnedly on the pleasures of the table – how the flesh of this or that bird, fish or beast should be cooked and eaten, with what wine and with what sauce, the novelist put in:

'If I were to adapt Bunyan, I should say that you ought to have been christened Os-carnalwise Wilde instead of plain Oscar.'

'How ridiculous of you to suppose that anyone, least of all my dear mother, would christen me "plain Oscar,"' was the reply. 'My name has two O's, two F's and two W's. A name which is destined to be in everybody's mouth must not be too long. It comes so expensive in the advertisements. When one is unknown, a number of Christian names are useful, perhaps needful. As one becomes famous, one sheds some of them, just as a balloonist, when rising higher, sheds unnecessary ballast, or as you will shed your Christian name when raised to the peerage. I started as Oscar Finghal O'Flahertie Wills Wilde. All but two of the five names have already been thrown overboard. Soon I shall discard another and be known simply as "The Wilde" or "The Oscar." Which it is to be depends upon one of my imitators – that horrid Hall Caine, who used to be known very properly as Thomas Henry;[4] quite appropriate names for a man who writes and dresses as he does. I can't say which he does worse as I have never read him, but I have often been made ill by the way he wears his clothes.

'And, by the by, never say you have "adapted" anything from anyone. Appropriate what is already yours – for to publish anything is to make it public property – but never adapt, or, if you do, suppress the fact. It is hardly fair to Bunyan, if you improve on him, to point out, some hundreds of years after, how much cleverer you are than he; and it is even more unfair, if you spoil what he has said, and then "hold him accountable."'

'That, I suppose,' said the novelist drily, 'is why when you said the other day that "Whenever a great man dies, William Sharp and the undertaker come in together," you suppressed the fact that the same thing had already been said in other words by W. S. Gilbert.'

'Precisely,' said Wilde. 'It is not for me publicly to point out Gilbert's inferiority. That would be ungenerous. But no one can blame me, if the fact is patent to all.'

Mention of Sir W. S. Gilbert prompted the other to say that a friend of his had occasion to take a cab at Harrow where the author of *The Bab Ballads* had built a house. Driving from the station to his destination, his friend noticed this house, and asked the cabman who lived there. 'I don't know 'is name, Sir,' said the cabman. 'But I do know (I have driven 'im once or twice) that 'e is sometimes haffable and sometimes harbitrary. They do say in the town, sir, that 'e's wot's called a retired 'umorist, whatever that may be.'

From Harrow the conversation shifted to the neighbouring city of St. Albans, where I was then living.

'That reminds me,' said Wilde, turning to me, 'that I want to run down to St. Albans once again to bathe my fingers in the mediaeval twilight of the grey old Abbey. We two will come to you tomorrow. You shall meet us at the station, give us lunch at your rooms – a cutlet, a flask of red chianti and a cigarette is all we ask – and then you shall take us over the Abbey.'

'I shall be delighted,' I said, 'but do you remember my meeting you the other day when you were coming away from the Royal Academy? I asked you how you were, and you replied, "Ill, my dear fellow, ill and wounded to the soul at the thought of the hideousness of what in this degenerate country, and these degenerate days, dares to call itself Art. Get me some wine quickly, or I'm sure I shall faint." Well, I'm living in bachelor diggings where it would be highly inconvenient to have dead or dying artists on hand or lying about. The pictures on show in my bachelor rooms, like the furniture, are not of my selection. If you were wounded by what you saw in the Academy, you would die at sight of one work of art on my walls. It is a hideous and vulgar representation of "Daniel in the Lions' Den," done in crude chromo, four colours.'

Wilde affected to shudder.

'How awful!' he said. 'But I can think of something more awful even than that.'

'What's that?' I asked.

'A poor lion in a den of Daniels,' was his reply.

## IV

A factor in Wilde's downfall was, I am sometimes told, evil association, but if so it was a factor on which I can throw no light, as if evil associates he had I saw nothing of them.

Louise Chandler Moulton sings of

> This brief delusion that we call our life,
> Where all we can accomplish is to die,

and of the many figures in the literary, artistic, and social world of the day whom I met in Wilde's company, some have achieved death, some, knighthood (Mr. Stephen Phillips once said in my hearing, he was not sure which was the better – or the worse), and some, distinction. Of the remainder, the worst that could be said against them is that they have since come a crash financially, as Wilde himself did. It was only in money matters that I ever had cause to think Wilde immoral.

In setting down these recollections and impressions I do not write as one of his intimates. We were friends, we corresponded, I dined with him and Mrs. Wilde at 16 Tite Street, and he with me, and we forgathered now and then at clubs, theatrical first nights, and literary at homes; but the occasions on which we met were not very many, all told; nor did I desire more closely to cultivate him, and for two reasons. One was that the expensive rate at which he lived made him impossible as other than a very occasional companion, and the other was that 'straightness' in money matters is to me one of the first essentials in the man of whom one makes a friend. On this point Wilde and I did not see alike. He laughed at me when I said that, while counting it no dishonour to be poor, I did count it something of a dishonour deliberately and self-indulgently to incur liabilities one might not be able to meet. In his vocabulary there were few more contemptuous words than that of 'tradesman,' as the following incident, which I may perhaps be pardoned for interpolating will show.

When *The Picture of Dorian Grey* was in the press, Wilde came in to see me one morning.

'My nerves are all to pieces,' he said, 'and I'm going to Paris for a change. Here are the proofs of my novel. I have read them very carefully, and I think all is correct with one exception. Like most Irishmen, I sometimes write "I will be there," when it should be "I shall be there," and so on. Would you, like a dear good fellow, mind going through the proofs, and if you see any "wills" or "shalls" used wrongly, put them right and then pass for press? Of course, if you should spot anything else that strikes you as wrong, I'd be infinitely obliged if you would make the correction.'

I agreed, went through proofs, made the necessary alterations, and passed for press. Two or three days after I had a telegram from Paris. 'Terrible blunder in book, coming back specially. Stop all proofs. Wilde.' I did so, and awaited events. Wilde arrived in a hansom.

'It is not too late? For heaven's sake tell me it is not too late?' he affected to gasp.

'Oh, make yourself easy. It was not too late. I stopped the proofs,' I answered.

'Thank God!' he exclaimed theatrically, throwing himself into a chair and making a great show of wiping away the perspiration from a perfectly dry brow. 'I should never have forgiven myself, or you, had my book gone out disfigured by such a blunder – by such a crime as I count it against art.'

Then in a faint undertone, as if the thing were too unholy to speak of above one's breath, he said:

'There's a picture framer – a mere tradesman – in my story, isn't there?'

'Yes,' I said.

'What have I called him?'

'Ashton, I think. Yes, Ashton,' I answered.

He simulated a shudder and seemed to wince at the words.

'Don't repeat it! Don't repeat it! It is more than my shattered nerves can stand. Ashton is a gentleman's name,' he spoke brokenly, and wrung his hands as if in anguish. 'And I've given it – God forgive me – to a tradesman! It must be changed to Hubbard. Hubbard positively smells of the tradesman!'

And having successfully worked off this wheeze on me, Oscar became himself again, and sat up with a happy smile to enjoy his own and my congratulations on the exquisiteness of his art.

Wilde's contempt for tradesmen, as instanced in this anecdote, I did not share. Once, when he had spoken thus contemptuously because a shopkeeper was suing a certain impecunious but extravagant artist acquaintance of his and mine for a debt incurred, I told Wilde that even if I despised 'tradesmen' as he and the artist did, I should despise myself much more were I to defraud a despised tradesman by ordering goods for which I had neither the means nor the intention to pay. He was not in the least offended, perhaps because the remark suggested an aphorism – the exact wording I forget, but it was to the effect that only mediocrity concerned itself with tradesmen's bills, that a writer of genius, whether a playwright or a novelist, ran into debt as surely as his play or his book ran into royalties. I remember the occasion well, though I do not remember the phrasing of his aphorism, for on that particular morning he had, for the first time within my experience, shown less than his usual nice consideration for others which – whether due merely to love of approbation or to finer feelings – made him so agreeable and delightful a companion.

When he came in I offered him my cigarette case. They were of a brand he had often himself smoked in the past – in fact it was he who had first recommended them to me – quite good tobacco and well made, but moderate in price, and with no pretence to be of the very best. He took one, lit it, drew a few puffs, and then tossing it practically unsmoked on the fire, drew out his own bejewelled case and lit up one of his own. That was very unlike Wilde as I had known him in his less prosperous days. Then he would have said, 'I have accustomed myself to smoke another brand lately and am something of a creature of habit. Do you mind if I smoke one of my own?'

Perhaps the omission was due only to preoccupation and forgetfulness. Perhaps the incident will be accounted too trivial, thus seriously to put on record. Possibly, but it is often by the cumulative effect of small and seemingly trivial details – not always by the bold broad strokes – that the truest portrait is drawn. Into the tragedy of human life we are not often permitted to look, but just as, since all fish swim against the stream, a minnow will serve to show the run of the current, no less than a pike, so trivial incidents serve sometimes to point the trend of life or of character as truly as great happenings.

Nor in Wilde's case were other signs of change in him wanting. His first play had just then been produced and with success. He struck me on that particular morning as unpleasantly flushed, as already coarsened, almost bloated by success. There was a suspicion of insolence in his manner that was new to me, and from that time onward he and I – perhaps the fault was mine – seemed to lose touch of each other, and to drift entirely apart. Wilde died in the late autumn of 1900. I never saw or heard from him again after the spring of 1892.

# V

Was it not Mr. Stead[5] who defined paradox as a truth standing on its head? Wilde's aim in paradox was so to manipulate truth and falsehood as to make the result startle one by appearing to reverse the existing standard. A paradox by him was sometimes a lie and a truth trotting side by side together in double harness like a pair of horses, but each so cleverly disguised that one was not quite sure which horse was which.

More often a paradox by Wilde was a lie (or a seeming lie) and a truth (or a seeming truth) driven the one in front of the other tandem-wise; but whichever Wilde had placed last was tolerably sure to take one by surprise by lashing out with its heels when one came to look at it. When Wilde had carefully arranged a paradox with a kick in it and wished to see one jump, he spoke the first half smilingly to put one off one's guard. Then he would pause, suddenly become grave and thoughtful as if searching his words. But the pause was not for loss of a word. It was no pause of momentary inaction. It was, on the contrary, if I may vary the simile, like the backward swing of a rifle, and was meant only to give fuller play and power to the forward thrust that bayonets an enemy. No sooner was one off one's guard by the smile and the momentary silence, than swift and sure came the sting of the stab.

Let me give an illustration. Wilde once asked me some question concerning my religious belief which I did my best to answer frankly and, as he was good enough afterwards to say, without the cant which he so loathed. When I had made an end of it, he said gravely:

'You are so evidently, so unmistakably sincere and most of all so truthful' (all this running smoothly and smilingly) 'that' (then came the grave look and the pause as if at a loss for a word, followed by the swift stab) 'I can't believe a single word you say.'

And so, having discharged his missile, Wilde, no longer lolling indolently forward in his seat, pulled himself backwards, and up like a gunner taking a pace to the rear, or to the side of his gun the better to see the crash of the shell upon the target, and then, if I may so word it, 'smiled all over.' He was so openly, so provokingly pleased with himself and with this particular paradox that not to be a party to the gratification of such sinful vanity, instead of complimenting him, as he had expected, on its neatness, I ignored the palpable hit, and inquired:

'Where are you dining to-night, Wilde?'

'At the Duchess of So-and-so's,' he answered.

'Precisely. Who is the guest you have marked down, upon whom – when everybody is listening – to work off that carefully prepared impromptu wheeze about "You are so truthful that I can't believe a single word you say," which you have just fired off on me?'

Wilde sighed deeply and threw out his hands with a gesture of despair, but the ghost of a glint of a smile in the corner of his eye signalled a bull's-eye to me.

'Compliments are thrown away on such coarse creatures as you,' he said. 'This very morning I called into being a new and wonderful aphorism – "A gentleman never goes east of Temple Bar" – notwithstanding which I have brought wit and fame and fashion to lighten your editorial room in the City. Why? To pay you the supremest compliment one artist can pay another one. To make you the only confidant of one of my most graceful and delicate fancies. I was about to tell you—'

'Yes, I know,' I interpolated rudely, 'you have coined a witty new aphorism, or thought out a lovely fancy. You do both and do them more than well. But you are going to the Duchess's dinner party tonight, and you will contrive so to turn what is said that your aphorism or fancy seems to rise as naturally and spontaneously to the surface of the conversation as the bubbles rise to the surface of the glass of champagne at your side. But you are not, as actors say, sure of your "words." You think it would be as well to have something of the nature of a dress rehearsal. So you have dropped in here, on your way to your florist's or to some one else, to try it upon me as somebody is said to try his jokes on his dog before publishing them. I don't mind playing "dog" in your rôle in the least, but I object to being made a stalking-horse for the Duchess's honoured guest.'

I have no intention in these Recollections to play the reporter to my own uninteresting share in the conversation, but one must do so sometimes for obvious reasons. In this case, I wish to illustrate the means by which I sometimes succeeded in inducing Wilde to drop attitudinising and to be his natural self.

There is a certain Professor of my acquaintance, a man of brilliant abilities and incomparable knowledge, whom I used to meet at a club – let us call him Clough. When Clough could be induced to talk upon the matters in which he was an expert, he was worth travelling many miles to hear. Unfortunately he had an aggressive, even offensive manner, and was troubled with self-complacent egotism. It was only after a systematic course of roughness and rudeness at the hands of his fellow clubmen that Clough was endurable, or could be got to talk of anything but himself.

One would sometimes hear a fellow clubman say, 'Clough is in the other room, just down from the 'Varsity; and more full of information than ever. Two or three capable members are administering the usual course of medicine – "Cloughing" we call it now – of flatly contradicting every word he says, "trailing" him, snubbing him, and otherwise reducing his abnormally swollen head to moderate dimensions. Then he will be better worth listening to on his own subjects than any other man in England. Don't miss it.'

Similarly, in my intercourse with Wilde, I found that a certain amount of 'Cloughing,' such as, 'Now then, Wilde! You know you are only showing off, as we used to say at home when I was one of a family of kids. Stow it, and talk sense,' had equally good result. He would protest at first when minded to let me off lightly, that such 'engaging ingenuousness' alarmed and silenced him. At other times he would vow that my coarseness made him shudder and wince – that it was like crushing a beautiful butterfly, to bludgeon a sensitive creature of moods and impulses with unseemly jibes and blatant speech. Having, however, thus delivered himself and made his protest, he would often stultify that protest and provide me with an excuse to myself for my Philistinism, by throwing aside his stilts (assumed possibly because he imagined they advertised him to advantage above the heads of those who walk afoot in the Vanity Fair of Literature and Art), and by showing himself infinitely more interesting when seen naturally and near at hand than when stilting it affectedly in mid-air above one's head.

At times, and when he had forgotten his grievance at being thus rudely pulled down, he would forget – egotist that he was – even himself, in speaking of his hopes, his ambitions and his dreams; and in his rare flashes of sincerity would show himself as greater and nobler of soul than many who met and talked to him only in the *salon* or in society perhaps realised.

There is a graceful fancy of Wilde's – I do not know whether he ever told it in print – the hero of which was a poet lad who had dreamed so often and written such lovely songs about the mermaid, that at last – since the dream-world was more real to him than the waking world – he was convinced that mermaids there really are in the seas around our shores, and that if one watched long and patiently they might by mortal eye be seen. So day and night the poet watched and waited, but saw nothing. And when his friends asked him, 'Have you seen the mermaids?' he answered, 'Yes,'by moonlight I saw them at play among the rollers,' telling thereafter what he had seen and with such vividness and beauty that almost he persuaded the listeners to believe the story. But one night by moonlight the poet did indeed have sight of the mermaids, and in silence he came away and thereafter told no one what he had seen.

So, of Wilde himself, I cannot but hope and believe that though he told many stories of exceeding beauty, none of which were true, yet hidden away in his heart was much that was gracious, true, noble and beautiful, the story of which will now never be known, for like the poet lad of his fantasy he told it to no one. Of what was evil and what was good in his life, only a merciful God can strike the balance, and only a merciful God shall judge.

## VI

As one who knew Wilde personally, I am sometimes asked whether I was not instinctively aware that the man was bad. Frankly I was not. Possibly because scandal does not interest me, and other things do, I had not heard the rumours which I now understand were even then prevalent, and so I took him as I found him, an agreeable companion, a brilliant conversationalist, a versatile and accomplished man of letters. On the crime of which he has since been committed, I make no comment, if only for the reason that I did not follow the evidence at his trial, just as I abstained from reading Mr. W. T. Stead's *Maiden Tribute to Modern Babylon* – not because of any innate niceness on my part, but for the same reason which causes me to turn aside if, in my morning's walk, I come across offal which it is not my business to remove. The Wilde of the days of which I am writing was foppish in dress and affected in manner. He talked and wrote much nonsense, as I held it to be, about there being no such thing as a moral or an immoral book or picture; that the book or picture was either a work of art, or was not a work of art, and there the matter ended; but much of this talk I attributed to pose, and I had even then learned that some of the men who are most anxious to have us believe them moralists – and stern moralists at that – are often less moral in their life than some of those who make no pretence of any morals at all.

To the folk who objected that Wilde has boasted of being a 'pagan' I replied that he probably used the word – just then very much in vogue – in the same sense in which Mr. Kenneth Grahame[6] used it when he entitled a volume, bubbling over with the joy of life, with animal spirits, keen observation, and exquisite humour, *Pagan Papers*. Wilde's 'paganism' I took as meaning no more than that he claimed for himself freedom from formula, most of all freedom from cant in his attitude towards the accepted conventions, whether literary, artistic, social, or even religious.

That he was not an irreligious man, I had reason to know. One day when we were chatting together, Wilde mentioned a little book of mine of which I will say no more here than that it made no uncertain confession of the writer's faith in Christianity. This led Wilde – uninvited by me, for I make it a rule never to obtrude my religious views upon others – to express himself upon the subject of religion, especially of Christianity, and with such intense reverence, such manifest earnestness, that I perhaps looked something of the surprise I felt.

'You are surprised,' he said, 'to hear Oscar Wilde, the *poseur*, as people call him, the man who is supposed to hold nothing too sacred, talking seriously and on serious things. *No*, I am *not* making believe to be earnest, as I do make believe about so much else. I am speaking as I feel, and you will perhaps hardly realise what an intense relief it is to meet some one to whom one can talk about such matters without cant. It is cant and officialdom' (he spoke bitterly) 'which is keeping the men and women who think out of the churches to-day. It is cant which more than anything else stands between them and Christ. Shall I tell you what is my greatest ambition – more even than an ambition – the dream of my life? Not to be remembered hereafter as an artist, poet, thinker, or playwright, but as the man who reclothed the sublimest conception which the world has ever known – the Salvation of Humanity, the Sacrifice of Himself upon the Cross by Christ – with new and burning words, with new and illuminating symbols, with new and divine vision, free from the accretions of cant which the centuries have gathered around it. I should thereby be giving the world back again the greatest gift ever given to mankind since Christ Himself gave it, peerless and pure two thousand years ago – the pure gift of Christianity as taught by Christ.

'Yes,' he went on, 'I hope before I die to write the Epic of the Cross, the Iliad of Christianity, which shall live for all time.'

On another occasion Wilde unfolded to me the opening scene in a sort of religious drama which he intended one day to write – the finding to-day of the body of the Christ in the very rock-sepulchre where Joseph of Arimathea had laid it, and a great and consequent eclipse of faith in Him and in His resurrection. Thereafter, by a new revelation of the Christ, Wilde was, in his drama, newly to recreate Christianity and faith in Christianity, but of this Second Act of his World-Drama I heard no more, as our talk was at this point interrupted, and he never renewed it.

I speak of this proposed religious drama here for the singular reason that I, too, had long been turning over in my mind some such work and some such opening scene as in Wilde's drama – I mean the finding of the body of Christ.

Wilde went no further with his project, but in a book of mine, written some years after, I carried my own project into effect. To this day I am uncertain how much of my opening scene was Wilde's, and how much mine. The idea appears to have occurred to both, but whereas, in Wilde's mind, it was clear and defined, in mine it was then no more than an idea. I sometimes wonder whether his words did not make vivid to me what before was vague. Of one thing at least I am sure, that he was the first to speak of such an opening scene, which fact in itself constitutes some sort of previous claim. The rest of the book was entirely mine, and probably the whole, but the facts seem to me not uninteresting, and having made confession of the possibility at least of some debt incurred, I must leave it to the reader to say whether I ought or ought not to be condemned in 'conscience money.'

I have already said that I have reason to know that Wilde was not irreligious, and I propose now to give my reasons for refusing to believe him to be irreclaimably bad. One has some hesitation in quoting oneself, but, in a dream-parable booklet of mine, there is a passage which I may perhaps be forgiven for printing here, when I say that I had Wilde in my mind when I wrote it. In my dream-parable, Satan, even as once of old he had presented himself to speak with God concerning Job, appears to-day before the Most High, urging that men and women have become godless and faithless. He craves permission to prove this by putting them to certain tests. The permission is accorded on condition that Satan himself becomes mortal, even as they. In the following passage Satan is supposed to be speaking, after the failure and defeat of his projects.

Master and Maker, hear me ere I die. For until Thou didst in Thy wisdom decree that ere I might work my will on mortals, myself must become mortal even as they – until then, the thoughts of these mortals were as foreign to my understanding as are the thoughts in the brain of a bird, to the fowler who spreads his net to catch the little creature. Like the fowler, I knew that I must change my bait, according to the creature that I set out to snare, that this one could be taken by avarice, that one by vanity, a third by spiritual pride, a fourth by bodily lust. When they came to my lure, and I caught them; when I saw the poor fools struggling in my net, I laughed and hugged myself to think of their misery and of the impotent anguish of God. And so I grew wise in the ways and the weaknesses of men and women, while knowing nothing of the hearts which beat in their breasts.

But now that I have become mortal, even as they, – now at last, to the wonder and the mystery of mortal life, are my eyes opened. Now perceive I that, in the least and most shameful of these lives is to be seen, even in uttermost wreckage, something so sacred, so august, so beautiful, so divine, that the very angels of light might stand amazed in envious wonder and awe.

For if men and women have failed greatly, at least they have striven greatly – how greatly, how valiantly, how desperately, only the God Who sees all may know.

It may be that by Him, that very striving itself, even the unsuccessful striving, shall mercifully be taken into account. The sin and the shame are human: the wish and the effort to overcome them are divine. For that which in a man's truer, nobler moments, he has longed unutterably to be, *that in some sense he is, and shall be accounted*, in the eyes of the God, Who taketh not pleasure in remembering sin, but in rewarding righteousness.

That even in sin, a man should think such thoughts, should carry unsullied in his heart some white flower of his childhood, and, in spite of what is ugly and impure in himself, should project so pure and perfect a vision of hoped-for, longed-for Loveliness and Purity, sets that man, even in his sins, a world removed above the angels. When I who was once an angel fell, I fell from uttermost light to uttermost dark. Ceasing to be an angel, I became a devil. Man falls, but even in his fall retains something that is divine.

Yonder man into whose great brain I entered, working strange madness within! Him first I thought to love Beauty, because it is of Thee. Him I haunted of beauty, haunted with visions of forms more fair than earthly eyes may know, luring him at last to look upon Beauty as of greater worth than all else, and as a law unto itself.

And because the love of beauty is not far removed from the love of pleasure, it was not difficult for me to lead on such as he to love pleasure for itself. With innocent pleasures at first I plied him, and when they staled, I enticed him with grosser joys, till the pleasure-seeker became the voluptuary, and, in the veins of the voluptuary, desire soon quickened into lust.

Next, because wine, like water to drooping flowers, lent fictitious strength to his flagging pulse, made the live thoughts to quicken in his tired brain, and set the tongue of his wit a-wagging; because he loved to stand well with his comrades, among whom to chink glasses together was the sign of fellowship – because of all these I enticed him to drink and yet again to drink, until Alcohol, the Arch Destroyer, had stolen away his will power, silenced his conscience, perverted his moral sense, inflamed with foul passion his degenerate brain, and made the wreck and the ruin of him that he now is.

Yet even now, as I steal gloatingly through the dark chambers of that House of Shame which was once the fair temple of the living God, even now there still smoulders under the ashes of a fouled hearthstone some spark of the fire which was kindled of God, a fire which I strive in vain to trample out, since, because it is of God, it is inextinguishable and eternal.

If therefore when I seem most to have conquered, there never yet was God wholly defeated – of what use is it further to wage the unequal conflict? For God never entirely lets go His hold on a human soul; and that to which God holds fast, Satan shall never finally wrest from Him. Say the world, think the world, what it will, in the warfare for souls God wins, and has won all along the line.

It was, as I say, Wilde who was in my mind when I penned that passage commencing 'Yonder man into whose great brain I entered, working strange madness within.' To me he seems to have been less hopelessly bad than partly mad.

We are told that it is possible, by locating and destorying certain cells or nerve-centres in the brain, so to affect the mind of the subject as to destroy his sense of colour, his sense of touch, or even, it is believed, to destroy his sense of right and wrong.

Wilde died of meningitis, which is a brain affection, and I think that the fact should be considered retrospectively. A post-mortem examination would possibly have revealed some disease or degeneration of certain brain-cells which may account for much that is painful in his career and character. This degeneration of brain-cells may have been inherited and congenital, in which case, condemnation on our part is silenced; or it may have been due to excesses of his own choosing and committing. Even if this be so, the price he paid was surely so terrible, and so tragic, as in a sense to be accounted an atonement, and even to entitle him to our pity. In the passage quoted from my dream-parable, I have hinted at some form of demoniacal possession which may or may not be a positive, as opposed to a negative form of madness. There is a brain derangement by which the power to reason aright and to co-ordinate ideas is lost; a brain derangement which results mainly in vacancy of mind. But there is yet another and more terrible form of derangement in which, so it seems to me, that unseen evil powers, outside himself, seize upon and possess the brain chambers, thus vacated, and direct and rule the unhappy victim, not according to his own will, which indeed has passed out of his control, but according to the wish or will of the power by which he is possessed.

On such a question we dare not dogmatise; but I am humbly of opinion that in the great re-awakening to the realities (not to the outward forms) of religion, which some of us think will follow the war, there will be a return to simplicity of belief, and that the too often disregarded New Testament explanation of certain mysterious happenings will be proved to be more in accordance with the later discoveries of Science than some advocates of the Higher Criticism now think. For my own part I have never doubted the accuracy of the Gospel records in regard to demoniacal possession. We have Christ's own words: 'For this saying go thy way; the devil is gone out of thy daughter,' 'Howbeit this kind goeth not out but by prayer and fasting,' and 'I charge thee come out of him and enter no more into him.'

That some men and women whose wills are weakened – possibly by habitual disregard of conscience or by continued wrongdoing for which they cannot be held irresponsible – *do* commit, under the urging and direction of evil spirits by which they are possessed, crimes and cruelties for which they are not in the fullest sense responsible, I think more than possible. My friend, the late Benjamin Waugh, Founder of the Society for the Prevention of Cruelty to Children, on more than one occasion placed before me the full facts and the indisputable proofs of acts so fiendish as to be difficult to ascribe to human motive or passions.

In the most terrible sonnet ever penned, Shakespeare says:

> The expense of spirit in a waste of shame
> Is lust in action, and till action, lust
> Is perjured, murderous, bloody, full of blame,
> Savage, extreme, rude, cruel, not to trust,

and, to lust, some particularly bestial outrages which came before the Society were clearly attributable. Others were as clearly the outcome of avarice, greed, hatred, jealousy and blind fury of anger. But some crimes there were, such as the torturing of her own children by a mother, and, in another case, the deliberate jabbing out of the eyes of an unoffending pony by a woman, not under the influence of drink, and in whom the medical experts declared they otherwise found no symptoms of insanity, which, if only for the sake of our common humanity, one would be relieved to think were due to demoniacal possession, for which the victim was, in this last stage at least, irresponsible.

In the near future it is possible that Science will by closer inquiry and by completer records be found once more in harmony with Scripture. Hypnotism, a science which as yet is not a science, but merely a haphazard accumulation of unorganised data, pointing to the possession of un-explained powers and possibilities by the individual, has established the fact that the living can thus be influenced and obsessed by the living. If so, why not by the dead, who, when emancipated from the body, may possibly be able to concentrate even greater spiritual force upon the living than when they were themselves alive?

I am not likely to live to see it, but my belief is that all these so-called occult matters, Hypnotism, Thought-reading, Obsession, Clairvoyance, Spiritualism, and the like will one day fall into line with Science, and be proved to be not supernatural, but merely the manifestation of natural laws – of certain psychical powers and forces which may be easily explainable and demonstrable with further and exacter knowledge, but concerning the working of which we are at present very much in the dark.

I have written at greater length than I intended, in hinting and in hoping that Wilde was at times under the subjection of powers and forces of darkness outside himself. I say 'at times' intentionally, and for the following reason. It would be gratifying to one's *amour propre* (I use a French term for once, as it expresses my meaning more nearly than any English equivalent) could I take high ground, and aver that I was vaguely conscious – warned, as it were, by some fine instinct – of evil in the presence of Wilde, but so to aver would be untrue. I have not lived to nearly threescore years without meeting men from whom one does thus instinctively shrink, and concerning whom one found it impossible to breathe the same air. I experienced nothing of the sort in Wilde's company, and, since his guilt seems uncontrovertible, I ask myself whether it is not possible that Wilde lived a sort of Jekyll and Hyde life, of the latter of which I saw nothing, inasmuch as just as some wounded or plague-stricken creature withdraws itself from the herd, so, during the Hyde period of madness or of obsession, some instinct moved him to withdraw from his home, his haunts and the companions of his everyday life, only to return when the obsession or madness had passed, and once again he was his sane and normal self.

This 'periodicity' is not infrequent in madness, whether the madness be due to a brain derangement, explainable by pathology, or to some such demoniacal possession as that of which I have spoken. A memorable instance is that of Mary Lamb, who was herself aware of the return of homicidal mania, and at such times of her own accord placed herself under restraint. Recalling the fact that I saw in Wilde no sign either of the presence of evil or of insanity, I ask myself whether in picturing Dorian Grey as at one season living normally and reputably, and at another disappearing into some oblivion of iniquity, he was not consciously or unconsciously picturing for us his own tortured self. I write 'tortured' advisedly, for whether he were wholly, or only partly, or not at all, responsible, I refuse to believe that the man, as in his saner moments I knew him, *could* sink thus low, without fighting desperately, if vainly – how desperately only the God who made him knows – before allowing himself in the hopelessness of despair to forget his failures in filth, as other unhappy geniuses have before now drowned their souls in drink.

One talk with him I particularly remember. I had been reading the proofs of *Dorian Grey*, and, on our next meeting, I said that he had put damnable words into the mouth of one of his characters.

'Such poisonous stuff is not likely to affect grown men and women,' I said, 'but for a writer of your power and persuasiveness to set up a puppet like Lord Henry to provide ready-made excuses for indulgence, and to make evil seem necessary, unavoidable, and easy, by whispering into the ears of readers, of impressionable age and inflammable passion, that "the only way to get rid of a temptation is to yield to it" – when you do that, you are helping to circulate devils' doctrines in God's world.'

Wilde was visibly perturbed.

'You are quite right,' he said. 'It *is* damnable; it *is* devils' doctrine. I will take it out.'

But, alas, other influences, whether within himself in the shape of the whisperings of some evil spirit, but which he was, as I believe, at times possessed, or in the form of so-called friends, whose influence over him was of the worst, I cannot say, but some days after the conversation recorded above I received the following letter:

GRAND HÔTEL DE L'ATHENÉE,
15 RUE SCRIBE, PARIS.

My DEAR KERNAHAN,
Thank you for your charming letter. I have been very ill and unable

to correct my proofs, but have sent them off now. *I have changed my mind about the passage about temptation.* One can't pull a work of art about without spoiling it, and after all it is merely Luther's 'Pecca Fortiter' put dramatically into the lips of a character.

Do you think I should add to preface the definition of 'morbid' and 'unhealthy' art I gave in the *Fortnightly* for February? The one on morbidity is really good.

Will you also look after my 'wills' and 'shalls' in proof! I am Celtic in my use of these words, not English.

You are excellent on Rossetti. I read you with delight.

Your sincere friend,<br>OSCAR WILDE.

When next I met Wilde I recurred to the matter, but it was then too late, for the book, he said, was in great part printed. Moreover, he had now another excuse to put forward.

'After I had left you,' he said, 'I remembered that a friend of mine, a well-known critic, had read the book in manuscript when it was first written. He said something to the same effect as you did, but less strongly. Honestly it was that, more than anything else, which finally decided me to leave the passage in. Had I taken it out, he would have claimed that I did so in deference to his strictures, and haul down my flag to a professional critic I never have and never will.'

This incident (though Wilde has been dead sixteen years I have neither written of it nor spoken of it before) shows Wilde as weak, it shows him as yielding – as we all, alas, too often yield – to evil influences, and to inclination as opposed to conscience, and as a man who was determined to shine at all costs. His vanity would not allow him to withhold the word that he was pleased to think daring, original, and above all brilliant, though he knew that word to be only brilliantly bad. Even in his sinning, it seems to me, he fed and flattered his insatiable vanity, by electing, even in sin, to be unlike others; and how far vanity, even more than viciousness, was accountable for Wilde's downfall, only the God who made him and the devil who fostered and fed that vanity, till it less resembled a pardonable human weakness than a hideous excrescence and disease, can ever truly say.

The setting of Wilde's sun (which had risen on so fair a prospect, and with such promise of splendour) in foul quagmires of sin and shame, was the greatest tragedy I have known. I met his friend and mine, Mr. Hall Caine, immediately after the verdict and sentence. I have seen Caine ill, and I have seen him deeply moved, even distressed, but I remember always to his honour (for Wilde not seldom made Caine's writing the butt of his wit) the anguish in his face as he said:

'God pity him in this hour when human pity there seems none! To think of it! that man, that genius as he is, whom you and I have seen fêted and flattered! whose hand we have grasped in friendship! a felon, and come to infamy unspeakable! It haunts me, it is like some foul and horrible stain on our craft and on us all, which nothing can wash out. It is the most awful tragedy in the whole history of literature.'

## NOTES

Coulson Kernahan (1858–1943), English author and journalist. He was for many years literary adviser to Messrs Ward, Lock, the publishers of Wilde's *The Picture of Dorian Gray* (1891).
 1. The story, entitled 'The Garden of God', was included in Kernahan's *A Book of Strange Sins* (1893).
 2. For a note on Richard Le Gallienne see p. 398.
 3. Louise Chandler Moulton (1835–1908), American poet.
 4. Sir Thomas Henry Hall Caine (1853–1931), English novelist.
 5. William Thomas Stead (1849–1912), English journalist.
 6. Kenneth Grahame (1859–1932), British writer.

# Oscar Wilde in Prison*

## Richard Burdon Haldane

I had also, towards the end of the 'nineties,' served on the Committee appointed by the Home Office to investigate the organization of our prisons. As an aid to the discharge of my duties on this Committee I had a warrant which enabled me to go to any prison, at any hour, and call on the Governor to produce any prisoner. During the time of our work Oscar Wilde had been sentenced to a term of imprisonment under circumstances which are well remembered. I used to meet him in the days of his social success, and, although I had not known him well, was haunted by the idea of what this highly sensitive man was probably suffering under ordinary prison treatment.[1] I went to Holloway Gaol,[2] where I knew he was, and asked the Governor to let me see him. The Chaplain was called in, and he said that he was glad I had come, for with Wilde he had wholly failed to make any way. I then saw Wilde himself, alone in a cell. At first he refused to speak. I put my hand on his prison-dress-clad shoulder and said that I used to know him and that I had come to say something about himself. He had not fully used his great literary gift, and the reason was that he had lived a life of pleasure and had not made any great subject his own. Now

---

 * *An Autobiography* (London: Hodder & Stoughton; Garden City, New York: Doubleday, 1929) pp. 177–9. Editor's title.

misfortune might prove a blessing for his career, for he had got a great subject. I would try to get for him books and pen and ink, and in eighteen months he would be free to produce. He burst into tears, and promised to make the attempt. For the books he asked eagerly, saying that they would only give him the *Pilgrim's Progress*, and that this did not satisfy him. He asked for Flaubert's works. But I said that the dedication by that author to his advocate, who had successfully defended Flaubert from a charge of indecent publication, made such a book as *Madame Bovary* unlikely to be sanctioned. He laughed and became cheerful. We hit on St. Augustine's Works and on Mommsen's *History of Rome*. These I got for him, and they accompanied him from prison to prison. I afterwards visited him at Wandsworth Prison, and persuaded the Home Secretary to transfer him to Reading. I saw Lady Cowper, and with her aid his wife and children were looked after. On his release there came to me anonymously a volume, *The Ballad of Reading Gaol*.[3] It was the redemption of his promise to me.

## NOTES

Richard Burdon Haldane (1856–1928), British lawyer, philosopher, and statesman whose greatest importance lay in the military reforms he instituted while serving as Secretary of State for War (1905–12).

1. On Wilde's life in prison from 1895–97 see Shane Leslie. 'Oscar Wilde', *Sir Evelyn-Ruggles-Brise; A Memoir of the Founder of Borstal* (London: John Murray, 1938) pp. 128–36; C. J. Björklund, 'I Oscar Wildes fängelse', *Studiekamraten*, XLVII (1965) 27–8; Carlo Bronne, 'Parallèlement: Wilde et Verlaine en Prison', *Synthèses*, (Apr 1955) 297–314; Albert Camus, 'The Artist in Prison', *Encounter*, II, no. 3 (Mar 1954) 26–9; Hentry-D. Davray, 'Oscar Wilde et la vie de prison en Angleterre', *Mercure de France*, CXCI (15 Oct 1926) 313–35; 'Entre Nous', *Truth* (London), XXXVII (13 June 1895) 1443; Robert Merle, 'Oscar Wilde en prison', *Les Temps modernes*, X (1954–55), 613–36; and William White, 'A Bribe for Oscar Wilde', *American Notes and Queries*, II (Nov 1963) 38–9.

2. When Wilde was charged at Bow Street Police Court on 6 April 1895 and refused bail, he was imprisoned at Holloway Gaol until his first trial began at the Old Bailey on 26 April. On 25 May he was found guilty and sentenced to two years' imprisonment with hard labour. The first six months of his sentence were served in Pentonville and Wandsworth prisons, the rest at Reading.

3. Oscar Wilde, *The Ballad of Reading Gaol* (London: Leonard Smithers, 1898). Wilde began working on this long poem in Berneval, near Dieppe, in the summer of 1897 after his release from prison. He took the hanging of his fellow convict C. T. Wooldridge as the central theme; it was as simple as that, and as great: the expiration of a soul in pain for the sin which society judged without understanding.

# Prison Chaplain's Memories of Oscar Wilde*

Rev. M. T. Friend

With a record of over forty years as chaplain of Reading Gaol, the Rev. M. T. Friend has just retired from prison service.

Of the thousands of prisoners who have passed through his hands in that period one, of course, the author of the most poignant poem of prison life ever written, stands out above all others in the interest of his personality and his career.

The picture given in Wilde's 'Ballad of Reading Gaol' Mr. Friend accepts as a substantially fair representation of prison life, though with a great many imaginative touches added.

'DE PROFUNDIS.'[1]

'How far,' he was asked yesterday by a 'Daily News' representative, 'did Wilde's bearing and conversation in prison throw light on the sincerity or otherwise of his religious professions in "De Profundis"?'[2]

'That of course touches the great question about Wilde's whole life,' he replied. 'There is no doubt that he wrote for effect, but at the same time I should say, from my acquaintance with him, that the spiritual side of his nature was thoroughly real. He was certainly not an atheist, though he never when I knew him came within measurable distance of anything that could be described as orthodox religion. Yet, strangely enough, he ended his life a member of the Roman Church.'[3]

Of Wilde's personal fascination Mr. Friend retains a vivid impression. 'The prison routine was naturally peculiarly trying to such a temperament,' he said, 'but sometimes in conversation in his cell his eye would light up, his body would straighten, and he would pull himself together and seem, as it were, almost to endeavour to project himself physically back into his old intellectual life.'

* *The Daily News and Leader* (London), (11 December 1913) p. 2, where the complete title is 'Forty Years in Gaol: Prison Chaplain's Memories of Oscar Wilde.'

THE DEATH SENTENCE.

Reference to the verses on the execution described in Wilde's poem led to some interesting remarks on one or two practical points in connection with the carrying out of the death sentence.

'The establishment of the Court of Criminal Appeal and the regularity with which a reprieve is applied for,' Mr. Friend explained, 'makes the chaplain's position very difficult. Three weeks are supposed to elapse between sentence and execution in order that the prisoner may have time to prepare himself for the punishment he must face. As it is, often the man is hanging between fear and hope till within a day or two of his death, and it is impossible for the Chaplain to influence him while such uncertainty has possession of his mind. The three weeks should date from the day when the final and irrevocable judgment has been given.'

Mr. Friend can recall no instance in his experience of a condemned man protesting his innocence.

## NOTES

1. *De Profundis* (London: Methuen, 1905). Reprinted in its fullest form in *The Letters of Oscar Wilde*, ed. Rupert Hart-Davis (London: Rupert Hart-Davis, 1962) pp. 423–511. It is a long letter addressed to Alfred Douglas written by Wilde in jail. In it Wilde spoke from the depths of his anguished spirit. The title was suggested by E. V. Lucas.

2. For Wilde's references to religion in this long letter see particularly pp. 468, 476–89 in the *Letters*.

3. When Robert Ross, Wilde's friend, heard that Wilde's state was 'almost hopeless', he went to Paris. Remembering an old promise, he brought a native of Dublin, attached to the Passionist Church of St. Joseph in the Avenue Hoche, Father Cuthbert Dunne, who asked Wilde whether he wished to be received and put the usual questions. Wilde consented. See Cecily Lambert. 'Oscar Wilde – A Death-Bed Convert', *Eirigh*, (Nov 1973) 28–30.

# In the Depths*

I never saw a man who looked
With such a wistful eye
Upon that little patch of blue
Which prisoners call the sky;
And at every wandering cloud
That trailed
Its revealed fleeces by.

Thus in 'The Ballad of Reading Gaol,' under his prisoner pseudonym of 'C.3.3,' wrote the late Oscar Wilde, whose book, 'De Profundis,' has just been published, and revealed the secret sorrows and humiliations of one who rightly claimed to have been 'a lord of language.'

An ex-prison warder who was at Reading Gaol during the entire period of Wilde's incarceration, has further drawn aside the veil that hid the ill-fated man of genius during his degradation and despair 'in the depths.'

The publication of the posthumous book by the great literary genius, who 'sinned and suffered,' has induced this warder, who had charge of Oscar Wilde during his imprisonment, to tell 'Evening News' readers how that unhappy man of letters 'circled the centre of pain,' as he in poignant phrase described the daily prison ordeal.

The warders strutted up and down,
And watched their herd of brutes.

wrote Wilde on his release, and in this fragment of verse can be read his own bitter self-contempt. Of the warders themselves, he made no complaint – he regarded them as simply instruments of an iron, soul-killing system that might be right – or wrong.

## SYMPATHETIC WARDERS

The warders, on their side, knew how terrible was the punishment the former pampered pet of society must be undergoing, for they could see he was suffering a thousandfold because of his strangely sensitive temperament and previous ignorance of all hardships and iron discipline.

\* *The Evening News and Evening Mail* (London), (1 March 1905) p. 4; and (2 March 1905), p. 2, where the complete title is 'In the Depths: Account of Oscar Wilde's Life at Reading. Told by his Gaoler.'

'Poor Wilde,' writes his former prison custodian, who is by no means the iron-hearted creature warders are generally supposed to be.

'I remember, before he was transferred from Wandsworth Prison, the governor of Reading Gaol said to us. 'A certain prisoner is about to be transferred here, and you should be proud to think the Prison Commissioners have chosen Reading Gaol as the one most suitable for this man to serve the remainder of his sentence in.'

'The governor never told us the name, but directly the prisoner arrived, we saw that "C.3.3" which was his prison letter and number, afterwards made famous by him thus signing the "Ballad of Reading Gaol," was none other than Oscar Wilde.

### CAUSE OF HIS TRANSFER

'The probable cause of his transfer from Wandsworth Prison was his inability to comply with the regulation tasks allotted to his class of prisoner. On one or two occasions he had been brought up before the governor there for idleness at oakum-picking or talking.

'I remember my first sight of the fallen literary idol of whom all the world was then talking in terms of infamy.

'A tall figure with a large head and fat, pendulous cheeks with hair that curled artistically, and a hopeless look in his eyes – that was Oscar Wilde as I first met him.

'Not even the hideous prison garb, or "C.3.3," the badge of ignominy he bore could altogether hide the air of distinction and ever-present intellectual force that lifted him always far above "the herd of brutes," as he so bitterly afterwards styled his fellow convicts and himself.

'From the first it was apparent to us that he was totally unfitted for manual work or hardships of any kind, and he was treated accordingly.

'He was no good for anything – except writing, and that, as a rule, has small place inside a prison. But on account of his former greatness a small concession was made him, and he was allowed to read and write as much as he liked.

### 'A BUNDLE OF BRAINS'

'Had this boon not been granted him he would, I am confident, have pined away and died. He was so unlike other men. Just a bundle of brains – and that is all.

'When he arrived his hair was long and curly, and it was ordered to be cut at once.

'It fell to my lot as warder in charge to carry out this order and cut his hair, and never shall I forget it.

'To Oscar Wilde it seemed as though the clipping of his locks, and thus placing him on the same level as the closely shorn, bullet-headed prisoners round him was the last drop in the cup of sorrow and degradation which he had to drain to the bitter dregs.

' "Must it be cut," he cried piteously to me. "You don't know what it means to me," and the tears rolled down his cheeks.

'It may seem somewhat ludicrous to some who do not know, as I do, what a curiously constituted character was that of Oscar Wilde, but I know it cut me to the heart to have to be the person to cause him his crowning shame. Warders have feelings, although their duty will not always allow them to show it.

'The only task Wilde was put to was to act as "schoolmaster's orderly," which was in the nature of a great privilege, for it meant that he could take charge of the books and go round with them to other prisoners, besides having the pick of the literature for himself. Strange as it may seem considering his literary bent, he failed to accomplish even this task satisfactorily.

WITH HIS BOOKS

'Chiefly he remained in his cell occupied with his books, of which in his cell he had a large supply, consisting of poetic works and foreign authors. On his table was always a manuscript book – full of writing in some foreign language – French or Italian I believe, and Wilde often seemed busily engaged writing in this.

I think this must have been "De Profundis" – the work of self-analysis that has just been published.

'His hair was always kept closely cut until about five months before his discharge, and I remember when he was told that it need not be prison-cropped any more owing to his impending release, how pleased he seemed. And he was a man who so seldom lifted his bowed head of shame to smile.

'Wilde was superstitious to a degree, and I recall one striking incident that proved his superstitious fears to be well grounded.

'I was sweeping the walls of his cell, for he seldom followed the prison regulations with regard to scrupulously cleansing his cell daily, and I disturbed a spider which darted across the floor.

'As it made off I raised my foot and killed it, when I saw Wilde looking at me with eyes of horror.

'BRINGING BAD LUCK'

' "It brings bad luck to kill a spider," he said. "I shall hear worse news than any I have yet heard."

'At the time I paid little attention to it, but the following morning he received the news that his mother, whom he had deeply loved and honoured, had died, and that his shame had hastened her end.[1]

'The saddest story I know of Wilde was one day when his solicitor called to see him to get his signature, I think, to some papers in the divorce proceedings then being instituted by his wife – a suit which, of course, Wilde did not defend.

'Unknown to Wilde his wife had accompanied the solicitor, but she did not wish her husband to see her.

'The interview with the solicitor took place in the consultation room, and Wilde sat at a table with his head on his hands opposite the lawyer.

'Outside, in the passage with me, waited a sad figure in the deepest mourning. It was Mrs. Wilde – in tears.

'Whilst the consultation was proceeding in the "solicitor's room," Mrs. Wilde turned to me and begged a favour. "Let me have one glimpse of my husband," she said; and I could not refuse her.

HER LAST LOOK

'So silently I stepped on one side, and Mrs. Wilde cast one long lingering glance inside, and saw the convict-poet, who, in deep mental distress himself, was totally unconscious that any eyes save those of the stern lawyer and myself witnessed his degradation.

'A second later, Mrs. Wilde, apparently labouring under deep emotion, drew back, and left the prison with the solicitor.

'I fancy Wilde, when she saw him, was putting the final signature to the divorce papers, and I do not know if she ever saw her unhappy husband again. I do not think she ever did.

'At exercise, when he tramped what he called "The Fools' Parade" with his companions of "The Devil's Own Brigade," he would pace along with bended head as though deep in thought, and usually muttering snatches of prose or verse from his favourite authors.

'The monotony of the life seemed appalling to Wilde, and when he was released he wrote, you remember:

> I know not whether laws be right
> Or whether laws be wrong;
> All that we know who be in gaol
> Is that the walls are strong.
> And that each day is like a year,
> A year whose days are long.

'I have good reason to know that Oscar Wilde was satisfied with the way two of the warders treated him.

'After his release he sent us through the Governor copies of his soul-stirring poem, "The Ballad of Reading Gaol."

'My copy is inscribed "From his friend, the author, Naples, February 1898."

'You remember the masterly way in which Wilde worked out the theme of that wonderful poem which told of the last days in prison of Trooper C. T. Woolridge, of the Royal Horse Guards, who was hanged for the murder of his wife at Clewer, near Windsor.

### A TERRIBLE MOMENT

'Wilde, of course, never saw the murderer after his condemnation, but he heard the bell tolling for the execution, and it made a terrible impression on his mind.

'He wrote: –

> The memory of Dreadful Things
> Rushed like a dreadful wind,
> And Horror stalked before each man,
> And Terror crept behind.
> The warders with their shoes of felt
> Crept by each padlocked door,
> And peeped and saw with eyes of awe
> Grey figures on the floor,
> And wondered why men knelt to pray
> Who never prayed before.

'Wilde told me that those moments when the bell rang out, and his imagination conjured up the execution scene, were the most awful of a time rich in horrors.

'I always found Wilde extremely good-natured, and he wrote several little things out for me.

'I had recently been married, and a certain weekly paper offered a silver tea service to the young couple who could give the best reason why this service should be given to them.

'I told Wilde of this, and he wrote out several witty "reasons," which I have kept.

'Here are some, very apt, that should have secured the tea service: –

(1) Because evidently spoons are required, and my girl and I are two.
(2) Because it would suit us to a T (tea).
(3) Because we have good "grounds" for wanting a coffee pot.
(4) Because marriage is a game that should begin with a love set.
(5) Because one cannot get legally married without a proper wedding service.'

## NOTE

1. Wilde's mother died at her residence, 146 Oakley Street, London, on 3 February 1896.

# The Poet in Prison*

## [Thomas Martin]

For the first eighteen months of his imprisonment all the rigours of the system were applied to him relentlessly. He had to pick his quantity of oakum, or bear the punishment that was sure to follow; turn the monotonous crank, along with his fellows, by which the prison was supplied with water; read the silly books from the library, or pace his cell, a prey to his own sad thoughts, until his health broke down under the unnatural strain, and, to prevent his being sent to a madhouse, he was allowed the privilege of having a limited number of books, which were sent by friends, and which afterwards found a place amongst others less abstruse on the shelves of the prison library.

Later he was allowed a more important privilege – the privilege of writing – and to this concession the world owes 'De Profundis.' He wrote mostly in the evenings, when he knew he would be undisturbed. In his cell were two wooden trestles, across which he placed his plank bed. This was his table, and, as he himself observed: 'It was a very good table, too.'

His tins he kept scrupulously clean; and in the mornings, after he had arranged them in their regulated order, he would step back, and view them with an air of child-like complacency.

He was dreadfully distressed because he could not polish his shoes or brush his hair. 'If I could but feel clean,' he said, 'I should not feel so utterly miserable. These awful bristles' – touching his chin – 'are horrid.' Before leaving his cell to see a visitor he was always careful to conceal, as far as possible, his unshaven chin by means of his red handkerchief. He showed great agitation when a visitor was announced. 'For I never know,' he said, 'what fresh sorrow may not have entered my life, and is, in this manner, borne to me, so that I may carry it to my cell, and place it in my already overstocked storehouse, which is my heart. My heart is my storehouse of sorrow!'

It was during the latter part of the Poet's imprisonment that the order was issued for 'first offenders' to be kept apart from the other prisoners. They were distinguished by two red stars, one of which was on the jacket

    * Extracted from Robert Harborough Sherard, 'The Poet in Prison (Written by one of the warders in Reading Gaol)', *The Life of Oscar Wilde* (London: T. Werner Laurie; New York: Dodd, Mead, 1906) pp. 386–97.

and the other worn on the cap, and in consequence were known as 'Star-class men.' The order, not being retrospective, did not apply to the Poet, and in consequence he, like the remainder, had to stand with his face to the wall when any of the 'star-class' were passing in his vicinity. The framers of the order were, no doubt, actuated by the best of motives, but its too literal interpretation caused it to look rather ludicrous. I have seen the Poet having to stand with his face to the wall while a villainous-looking ruffian, who had been convicted for half killing his poor wife, passed him. In fact, nearly every day he was forced to assume this undignified position, which might have been obviated but for the crass stupidity of officialdom.

In Church the Poet seemed to suffer from *ennui*. He sat in a listless attitude with his elbow resting on the back of his chair, his legs crossed, and gazed dreamily around him and above him.

There were times when he was so oblivious of his surroundings, so lost in reverie, that it required a friendly 'nudge' from one of the 'lost sheep' beside him to remind him that a hymn had been given out, and that he must rise and sing, or at least appear to sing, his praises unto God.

When the Chaplain was addressing his shorn and grey-garbed flock, telling them how wicked they all were, and how thankful they should all be that they lived in a Christian country where a paternal Government was as anxious for the welfare of their souls as for the safe-keeping of their miserable bodies; that society did not wish to punish them, although they had erred and sinned against society; that they were undergoing a process of purification; that their prison was their purgatory, from which they could emerge as pure and spotless as though they had never sinned at all; that if they did so society would meet and welcome them with open arms; that they were the prodigal sons of the community, and that the community, against which they had previously sinned, was fattening calves to feast them, if they would but undertake to return to the fold and become good citizens, – the Poet would smile. But not his usual smile: this was a cynical smile, a disbelieving smile, and often it shadowed despair. 'I long to rise in my place, and cry out,' said he, 'and tell the poor, disinherited wretches around me that it is not so; to tell them that they are society's victims, and that society has nothing to offer them but starvation in the streets, or starvation and cruelty in prison!'

I have often wondered why he never did cry out, why he was able to continue, day after day, the dull, slow round of a wearisome existence – an existence of sorrow: sorrow benumbed by its awful monotony; an existence of pain, an existence of death.

But he faithfully obeyed the laws, and conscientiously observed the rules, prescribed by Society for those whom it consigns to the abodes of sorrow. I understand he was punished once for talking. I have no personal knowledge of the circumstance, but I know that it would be almost a miracle for one to serve two years' imprisonment without once being reported. Some of the rules are made with no other object than to be broken, so that an excuse may be found for inflicting additional punishment. However, he could not have been punished by solitary confinement for fifteen days, as has been stated. A governor is not empowered to give more than three days. But twenty-four hours' bread and water is the usual punishment for talking, and, if it be the first offence, the delinquent is generally let off with a caution.

During the period of his incarceration the Poet suffered in health, but he seldom complained to the doctor. He was afraid of doing so lest he should be sent to the sick-ward. He preferred the seclusion of his cell. There he could think aloud without attracting the glances or the undertone comments of the less mobile-minded. There he could be alone – alone with the spectre of his past, alone with his books, alone with his God!

When I entered his cell on a certain bleak, raw morning in early March I found him still in bed. This was unusual, and so I expressed surprise. 'I have had a bad night,' he explained. 'Pains in my inside, which I think must be cramp, and my head seems splitting.' I asked whether he had better not report sick. 'No,' he said; 'not for anything; I shall be better, perhaps, as the day advances. Come back in a few minutes, when I will be up.'

I returned to his cell a few minutes afterwards, and found he was up, but looking so dreadfully ill that I again advised him to see the doctor. He declined, however, saying he would be all right when he had had something warm to drink.

I knew that in the ordinary course of events he would have nothing for at least another hour, so I resolved to find something to give him in the meanwhile myself. I hastened off, and warmed up some beef-tea, poured it into a bottle, placed the bottle inside my jacket, and returned towards his cell. While ascending the staircase the bottle slipped between my shirt and skin. It was very hot. I knew that there was an unoccupied cell on the next landing, and I determined to go there and withdraw the bottle from its painful position. But at that moment a voice called me from the central hall below. I looked down, and saw the Chief Warder. He beckoned me towards him. I went back. He wished to speak concerning a discrepancy in the previous night's muster report. I attempted to elucidate the mystery of two prisoners being in the prison who had no claim on its hopitality. I am afraid I threw but little light on the mystery. I was in frightful agony. The hot bottle burned against my breast like molten lead. I have said 'there are supreme moments in the lives of men.' Those were supreme moments to me. I could have cried out in my agony, but dared not. The cold, damp beads of perspiration gathered on my brow; I writhed and twisted in all manners of ways to ease myself of the dreadful thing, but in vain. I could not shift that infernal bottle – try as I might. It lay there against my breast like a hot poultice, but hotter than any poultice that was ever made by a cantankerous mother or by a cantankerous nurse. And the strange thing about it was that the longer it lay the hotter it became. The Chief eyed me curiously. I believe he thought I had been drinking. I know I was incoherent enough for anything. At last he walked off, and left me, for which I felt truly thankful. I bounded up the iron stairs, and entered the Poet's cell, and, pulling out the burning bottle, I related, amid gasps and imprecations, my awful experience. The Poet smiled while the tale was being told, then laughed – actually laughed. I had never seen him laugh *naturally* before, and, with the same qualification, I may add that I never saw him laugh again.

I felt angry because he laughed. I told him so. I said it was poor reward for all I had undergone to be laughed at, and, so saying, I came out, and closed the door – I closed it with a bang.

When I took him his breakfast he looked the picture of contrition. He said he wouldn't touch it unless I promised to forgive him.

'Not even the cocoa?' I asked.

'Not even the cocoa,' he replied; and he looked at it longingly.

'Well, rather than starve you, I'll forgive you.'

'And supposing I laugh again?' said he, with a smile.

'I sha'n't forgive you again,' I said.

The following morning he handed me a sheet of foolscap blue official paper. 'Here is something,' said he, 'which is not of much value now, but probably may be if you keep it long enough.'

I had no opportunity of reading then, but when I had read it I was struck by the power and beauty of its expression. It was headed: 'An Apology,' and written in his old, original, and racy style. The flow of subtle humour, the wit and charm of the many epigrams, the naïvete contained in some of the personal allusions, were captivating. As a lover of style, I was captivated, and told him so.

'Ah!' said he, 'I never thought to resume that style again. I had left it behind me as a thing of the past, but yesterday morning I laughed, which showed my perversity, for I really felt sorry for you. I did not mean to laugh: I had vowed never to laugh again. Then I thought it fitting when I had broken one vow to break the other also. I had made two, and I broke both, but now I have made them again. I never intend to laugh, nor do I intend ever again to write anything calculated to produce laughter in others. I am no longer the Sirius of Comedy. I have sworn solemnly to dedicate my life to Tragedy. If I write any more books, it will be to form a library of lamentations. They will be written in a style begotten of sorrow, and in sentences composed in solitude, and punctuated by tears. They will be written exclusively for those who have suffered or are suffering. I understand them, and they will understand me. I shall be an enigma to the world of Pleasure, but a mouth-piece for the world of Pain.'

## NOTE

Thomas Martin, a native of Belfast, came to Reading Gaol as a warder some seven weeks before Wilde's release. He was always kind to Wilde and constantly broke the regulations to bring him extra food, as well as *The Daily Chronicle* and other papers. See Wilde's letter to him in *The Letters of Oscar Wilde*, p. 528. This reminiscence is an extract from the chapter Martin contributed to Robert Harborough Sherard's *The Life of Oscar Wilde*. In a footnote Sherard said:

> This chapter has been contributed to this biography by a man who was a warder in Reading Gaol at the time of Oscar Wilde's imprisonment there. The express condition under which it was contributed was that it should be printed exactly as it stood in the manuscript, with no alteration of a single phrase or word or expression. This condition has been faithfully observed, and the chapter has been printed as it was written.

# Wilde's God*

### Robert Harborough Sherard

In spite of the stringent prison regulations he appears to have had many opportunities for conversation, and records of such conversations have been jealously preserved. At the time when he was writing 'De Profundis' he had one afternoon a long talk with a man in Reading Gaol, who, writing from memory, supplies for the purpose of this biography the following account of it:—

'We had been talking of Robert Emmet,[1] when I incidentally remarked that it was curious that he an atheist should have made so many allusions to the Supreme Being and a future state in the course of his speech from the dock.

'"That was no doubt due to his Celtic temperament," said Oscar Wilde. "Those who are governed by their emotions are more given to hero-worship and the worship of the gods than practical people who believe in logic and are governed by what they choose to term their reason. Imaginative people will invariably be religious people for the simple reason that religion has sprung from the imagination."

'I pointed out that Shelley and Voltaire were highly imaginative people and were sceptics.

'"Of course," he replied, "we must allow for exceptions. I am one myself, but it is an open question whether the two poets you mention were unbelievers or simply agnostics. Besides, one's religious opinions are often greatly influenced by private and local events or national contingencies. I

---

* *The Life of Oscar Wilde* (London: T. Werner Laurie; New York: Dodd, Mead, 1906) pp. 377–83. Editor's title.

daresay the oppression of Church and State on the poor in France was the direct cause of Voltaire's apostasy."

' "And may have led to yours," I ventured to say.

'He remained silent for some time, then stepped aside to allow a fly, which was floating round the door, to enter his cell. "You see," he observed, watching its movements, "it will be company for me when you have gone." I laughed, and repeated my question.

' "What," he said, "was the cause of my becoming a man? Remember I once was a child."

' "Well," I said hesitatingly, "I suppose it was natural development."

' "Just so," he answered, "and the cause of my apostasy is spiritual development, or the natural evolution of the mind. You will observe that the various races of the world have various forms of supernatural belief, and if you examine closely into those forms you will find they accord more or less with the racial characteristics of the people who hold them. And what is true in regard to races is equally true when applied to individuals, I mean individuals who can claim individuality – each one makes his own God, and I have made mine. My God might not suit you, nor your God suit me, but as my God suits myself I wish to keep him, and when I feel so inclined to worship him."

' "What is your God, then?" I asked. "Art?"

' "No," he said, "Art is but the disciple, or, perhaps, I should say the Apostle. It was through Art I discovered him, and it is through Art I worship him. Christ, to me, is the one supreme Artist, and not one of the brush, or the pen, but, what is more rare, he was an Artist in words. It was by the voice he found expression – that's what the voice is for, but few can find it by that medium, and none in the manner born of Christ."

' "If we acknowledge the divinity of Christ," said I, "neither his words nor his books, his fastings nor his final sufferings should excite our admiration any more than the strength of the elephant or the fleetness of the deer. If we allow he was a supernatural being, gifted with miraculous power, his sufferings became a farce; they resemble a millionaire choosing to suffer the pangs of hunger in the midst of plenty, or the fanatic who deliberately inflicts pain on his body for the purification of his soul."

' "The divinity of Christ," said he, "in its generally accepted sense, I, of course, do not believe, but I see no difficulty whatever in believing that he was as far above the people around him as though he had been an angel sitting on the clouds." (Here followed a panegyric of Christ something similar to that drawn in "De Profundis.")

'On another occasion when speaking on the same subject I wished to know which label I would present him with, supposing I had a bundle containing the names of the world's religions and non-religions, and to say "Take this it fits you."

'He smiled and said he would not accept any one of them. "This," he said, touching the round piece of cardboard on his coat, "indicates my address, or rather the number of my room, and does so correctly, I daresay. But you couldn't find a card in your supposititious bundle that would correspond with my religion."

' "Yours is a unique creed, then," I responded, "why not explain its tenets and you may make a convert?"

' "I do not want any converts," he replied, "the moment I discovered that anyone else shared my belief I would flee from it, I must either have it all to myself or not at all."

' "Selfish man!" I cried.

' "To be a supreme Artist," said he, "one must first be a supreme Individualist."

' "You talk of Art," said I, "as though there were nothing else in the world worth living for."

' "For me," said he sadly, "there is nothing else."

' "Do you know," he said suddenly, "the Bible is a wonderful book. How beautifully artistic the little stories are! Adam and his wife alone in the beautiful garden, where they could have enjoyed all the pleasures of life by simply obeying the laws. But he refuses to become a machine, and so eats the apple – I, also, would have eaten that apple – and in consequence is expelled."

' "Then, young Joseph sold into Egypt as a slave, when he blossoms out as the ruler of a kingdom, and his subterfuge to obtain his brother. In nearly every chapter you can find something so intensely interesting that one pauses to wonder how it all came to be written. The Psalms of David; the Song of Solomon – how grand it is! – And the story of Daniel; all appeal to me as a lover of language, and as a lover of Art. And if I am delighted with the Old Testament imagery I am charmed with the New. Christ, Paul, and most of the other characters in the book have for me a singular fascination. Then take the last book of all. How powerful must have been the imagination of the writer! Why, I know of nothing in the whole world of Art to compare with it, especially those tenth, eleventh and twelfth chapters. Really, I have no sympathy with stupid people who cannot admire a book unless they believe in its literal truth."

'I reminded him that the leading agnostics of the century had paid tribute to the beauty of the scriptures, and mentioned Renan, Huxley and Ingersoll.

' "I very much admire," he said, "Renan's[2] 'Life of Jesus'; and Huxley had a captivating style which is seldom to be met with in men of science, for instance, I remember reading where he said 'that one could not be a true soldier of science and a soldier of the Cross,' and I thought it a very fine sentence, although I did not believe it, for between matter of fact and matter of faith there is a wide gulf which science cannot bridge."

' "When I go out from here I should like to find a quiet, nice little Church, I shouldn't in the least mind what its denomination was so long as it had a nice, simple-minded and good-hearted clergyman, one who had religion within himself and did not preach somebody else's opinions and practise somebody else's formulas, a man who thought of the sinner more than the stipend. I can never belong to any of the conventional forms of religion, but I should like to be able to extract the good there may be in all."'

## NOTES

Robert Harborough Sherard (1861–1943), author and journalist.

  1. Robert Emmet (1778–1803), Irish patriot.

  2. Joseph Ernest Renan (1823–92), French philologist and historian; a leader of the school of critical philosophy in France. On Renan's influence on Wilde's thought see Joan N. Harding, 'Oscar Wilde and Ernest Renan', *Contemporary Review* (London), CLXXXIII (May 1958) 283–9.

# His Wit Never Failed*

### Sir Chartres Biron

I only met that unhappy man once. It was at a quiet family dinner given by a county court judge at Dinard; a party respectable even to the verge of dullness. There were then unpleasant rumours about Wilde, and I was strongly prejudiced against him. His appearance was not in his favour, heavy and sensual; but directly he spoke his whole face lit up, the aspect of the man changed and he seemed a different personality. I have never heard such talk in my life. The whole company was held spellbound. It was no monopoly, for his wit and wisdom all arose out of the general conversation, and much of the talk was as wise as it was witty. Discussing Browning's poems someone regretted his obscurity. 'You must remember', was the comment, 'every great truth is unintelligible. Then the master wants an audience and waters it down to the level of a disciple; then it becomes popular and is lost.' In a moment he would turn to simple fun. In life it was suggested one had to begin at the bottom of the ladder. 'No,' was the comment, 'begin at the top and sit upon it.'

A boy who was just going to Sandhurst, he urged to go to Oxford. 'But I am going to be a soldier,' was the answer. 'But if you took a degree at Oxford they would make you a colonel at once.' And then, pausing: 'At any rate in a West Indian regiment.'

I never met him again, but such was the effect of the meeting that until the crash came I would never believe anything against him.

* *Without Prejudice; Impressions of Life and Law* (London: Faber & Faber, 1936) pp. 211–12. Editor's title.

Even in his downfall the wit never failed. The Governor of the prison sent for him to tell him that a relation had died, and added: 'It may interest you to know that Mr. Poynter[1] has been made President of the Academy.'

'I am grateful to you for your kindness in telling me about my poor aunt, but perhaps you might have broken Poynter to me more gently,' was the answer.

## NOTE

Sir Chartres Biron (1863–1940), English magistrate and author.
 1. Sir Edward John Poynter (1836–1919), English historical painter.

# Oscar Regains His Freedom[*]

## Hesketh Pearson

All Wilde's friends who could afford it subscribed to a fund which would give him several months of leisure after his imprisonment: amongst others, Adela Schuster,[1] the Leversons,[2] Ross,[3] Adey[4] and Charles Ricketts.[5] The last-named contributed £100, though he could ill afford it, and three days before Oscar regained his freedom went to see him in the company of Ross and Adey. He had to wait while the others discussed with their friend certain details about clothes, where he wanted or did not want to go on leaving prison, etc., and Ricketts heard afterwards that Oscar had been refractory, unreasonable and impatient on these points, though everything had been talked over and agreed upon some time before; but of this there was no sign when Ricketts entered the room, where an inspector and two warders stood against the wall, and where Oscar sat at a green baize table looking wonderfully well and in excellent spirits. After a cordial greeting, Oscar said laughingly:

'Both my dear friends would wish me to retire to a monastery . . . Why not La Trappe? . . . or worse still, to some dim country place in England: I believe it was Twyford . . . They speak of Venice later with its silence and dead waterways. No, I have had enough of silence!'

'But, Oscar, is not Venice, with its beauty and stillness, the very place for work and privacy? There you could see your friends if . . .'

'No! . . . Privacy! work! my dear Ricketts. I wish to look at life, not to become a monument for tourists . . .'

* *The Life of Oscar Wilde* (London: Methuen, 1946) pp. 332–4. Editor's title.

They talked of the French production of *Salomé*, and Ricketts asked whether he had thought of a new play.

'A play! the Theatre!' exclaimed Wilde. 'My dear boy, what folly was mine! I held the future of the English stage in the hollow of my hand, to make or mar. To-day, in London, who would produce a work of mine?'

Ricketts reported that *Lady Windermere's Fan* had recently been done at Richmond, that Ellen Terry had praised him, and that Henry Irving had expressed his sympathy.

'I must return to literature, and you must print *the Portrait of Mr. W. H.*', said Wilde. 'I know it needs retouching, though one of my early masterpieces. Your picture, Ross tells me, has vanished; it was not in the sale;[6] but you must design me another wonderful frontispiece.'

'My dear Oscar, of course I will publish a book of yours, but for the moment let it be some other work, your *Sainte Courtisane*, for instance.'

'Alas! she no longer says marvellous things; the robbers have buried her white body and carried away her jewels . . . Yes, perhaps you are right . . . *Mr. W. H.* might be imprudent . . . the English public would have to read Shakespeare's Sonnets.'

'Why not the play about Pharaoh?' suggested Ross.

'Yes, of course, the King is tremendous when he cries to Moses "Praise be to thy God, O prophet, for he has slain my only enemy, my son!" . . . But I must have books about Egypt, full of the names of beautiful things, rare and curious meat for the feast, not the mere flesh-pots the Jews regretted. At night, in the cold . . . when I felt hungry . . . I have often thought of fantastic feasts . . . Yes, I have sometimes been cold and hungry . . . cold is worse than hunger . . . in time one gets used to this . . . but many of my warders have been friends . . . Don't mention this; it might lead to trouble. . . . Knowing that I had not enough food, they have brought me curious things to eat, Scotch scones, meat pies and sausage rolls, believing that a hungry man can eat anything, just as the British throw Bibles to bears.' He laughed; and their interview was at an end.

## NOTES

1. Adela Schuster was the daughter of Leo Schuster, a wealthy Frankfurt banker who had settled in a large villa called Cannizaro at Wimbledon. Wilde nicknamed her Miss Tiny on account of her size. She was a woman of great perception and generosity. While Wilde was out on bail she gave him £1000 for his personal use.

2. For a note on Leverson see p. 270.

3. Robert Baldwin Ross (1869–1918), Canadian literary journalist and art-critic who was brought up in England. He first met Wilde in 1886 and later became his literary Executor and editor of *The Collected Works of Oscar Wilde* (London: Methuen, 1908). See Ross, Margery (ed.), *Robert Ross; Friend of Friends* (London: Jonathan Cape, 1952).

4. William More Adey (1858–1942) was a close friend of Robert Ross, with whom he later ran the Carfax picture gallery. In 1891 he published, under the pseudonym William Wilson, the first English translation of Ibsen's *Brand*. He became joint editor of the *Burlington Magazine* 1911–19.

5. Charles Ricketts (1866–1931), British painter, sculptor, art critic, and stage-set designer. He first met Wilde in 1889 and visited him in Reading Gaol. See his *Oscar Wilde: Recollections* (London: Nonesuch Press, 1932).

6. When Wilde was arrested, his creditors obtained judgment against him, an execution was put into his house, and his library and possessions were sold by auction on 24th April 1895. Nearly everything went for a song, though some of his personal belongings were bought by friends and eventually restored to him.

# 'I Want a Change of Scene'*

## Ada Leverson

Very early one very cold May morning my husband, I, and several other friends drove from our house in Deanery Street to meet Oscar at the house in Bloomsbury of the Rev. Stuart Headlam. The drawing-room was full of Burne-Jones and Rossetti pictures, Morris wallpaper and curtains, in fact an example of the decoration of the early 'eighties, very beautiful in its way, and very like the aesthetic rooms Oscar had once loved.

We all felt intensely nervous and embarrassed. We had the English fear of showing our feelings, and at the same time the human fear of not showing our feelings.

He came in, and at once he put us at our ease. He came in with the dignity of a king returning from exile. He came in talking, laughing, smoking a cigarette, with waved hair and a flower in his button-hole, and he looked markedly better, slighter, and younger than he had two years previously. His first words were, 'Sphinx, how marvellous of you to know exactly the right hat to wear at seven o'clock in the morning to meet a friend who has been away! You can't have got up, you must have sat up.' He talked on lightly for some time, then wrote a letter, and sent it in a cab to a Roman Catholic Retreat, asking if he might retire there for six months. While waiting, he walked up and down, and said: 'The dear Governor, such a delightful man, and his wife is charming. I spent happy hours in their garden, and they asked me to spend the summer with them. They

---

* 'Reminiscences', *Letters to the Sphinx from Oscar Wilde* (London: Duckworth, 1930) pp. 44–7. Editor's title.

thought I was the gardener.' He began to laugh. 'Unusual, I think? but I don't feel I can. I feel I want a change of scene.'

'Do you know one of the punishments that happen to people who have been "away?" They are not allowed to read *The Daily Chronicle*! Coming along I begged to be allowed to read it in the train. "No!" Then I suggested I might be allowed to read it upside down. This they consented to allow, and I read all the way *The Daily Chronicle* upside down, and never enjoyed it so much.It's really the only way to read newspapers.'

The man returned with the letter. We all looked away while Oscar read it. They replied that they could not accept him in the Retreat at his impulse of the moment. It must be thought over for at least a year. In fact they refused him.

Then he broke down and sobbed bitterly. I left, and heard later that he went to Berneval with friends. Oscar had a wonderful power of recuperation, and soon recovered his spirits.

Later I went to Paris to see him, and found him at that time leading the life of a student in a tiny room at the Hotel d'Alsace. He was unique in his power of making people fond of him. It is known that his landlord lent him hundreds of pounds.

## NOTE

Wilde left Reading Gaol on the evening of 18 May 1897. Accompanied by two prison officers, he was driven in a cab to Twyford station, where they took the London train. They left it at Westbourne Park and travelled by cab to Pentonville prison, where Wilde spent the night. At 6.15 next morning he was fetched in a cab by his friend More Adey and the Rev. Stewart Headlam. They managed to avoid the press, and drove straight to Headlam's house, where Wilde changed and breakfasted. Soon afterwards he was visited by Earnest and Ada Leverson, who records the scene in this memoir. For a note on Ada Leverson see p. 270.

# An Evil Influence*

Gertrude Atherton

I had been at work for about three weeks when I suddenly found myself with a companion nearer my own age. Madame d'Oliviera came to me in a state of manifest perturbation one morning shortly after the arrival of the postman.

* *Adventures of a Novelist* (New York: Liveright, 1932) pp. 276–9; (London: Jonathan Cape, 1932) pp. 181–4. Editor's title.

'Oh, Madame! Madame!' she exclaimed. 'How shall I say it? Something so unexpected has happened. I must ask you to leave . . .'

'What!' I interrupted her. 'Leave? I won't leave! I shan't stir until I've finished my book.'

She wrung her hands in despair, and it was evident she was very much upset; not only had she grown quite fond of me but was persuaded the Virgin or one of the saints was writing that book. 'You know what I told you, dear Madame. If my young men came . . .'

'But it is too soon for them . . .'

'I hoped so, but one has just written that he is not very well and is coming tomorrow. If he finds you here, he'll leave at once and never come again. I'm afraid the others wouldn't either!'

It was impossible not to pity her; she looked so distracted, and I knew she could not afford to lose those Englishmen who had been faithful to her for a number of years. She was too far out of town for the unattached men of Rouen, unless they were humble clerks, and these she scorned. Her Englishmen were all gentlemen, although some of them were forced to economize in their yearly outings; the others came to be with them.

'I'll tell you what to do,' I said. 'He won't mind if he thinks I'm only here for a day or two. Tell him I'm looking round for another place. Leave the rest to me. I've never met the man yet I couldn't get along with – if I chose.'

And at that it was left, but she went away shaking her head.

I met him next night at the dinner table. He greeted me with a scowl on his gnome-like face, but thawed somewhat before the meal was over. His was a gregarious soul and he liked to talk. We had acquaintances and literary ideals in common, and exchanged opinions in the parlor until ten o'clock. Needless to say he also talked about himself and that I encouraged him. He had a small income which relieved him of the necessity of work, and he loved art, literature, and travel. Many of his friends were blinding lights in the literary world, and although he had no talent of his own, he had much to give in the way of wit, intelligence, and critical appreciation. Before two days had passed we were the best of friends and he informed me graciously that I could remain; glad to have me.

For that matter he was in the house for dinner and the night only. Some time during the morning he emerged from his room, very sprucely dressed, and sauntered off, cane under his arm, to sit in one of the cafés on the quay, lunch in a fashionable restaurant, sit in the cafés again. It was his idea of an interesting continental vacation.

We spent every evening together, and he had a great deal to say of Oscar Wilde. He had sat at his feet, worshipping him, listening to such talk as never before since the Fifth Century B.C. had flowed from any man's lips, enchanted at being one of his circle, clay in his hands.

'But I now regret bitterly that I ever knew him,' he said to me in a burst of confidence one day. 'He was an evil influence for any young man, and distorted one's outlook upon life. I'll never see him again. Never! He's coming out of prison in a day or two, and several of his friends will meet him and bring him over to Dieppe. But not I! I'm trying to live now as if I had never known him. He and the others may think I'm heartless. I don't care.'

And then, less than a week later, he was very glum at dinner, and when we were alone in the parlor told me he had received a letter from Wilde. 'He's coming to Rouen tomorrow!' he exclaimed, looking as if about to cry. 'He wants me to meet him at a certain restaurant. He says he must talk to me, and as I won't go to him . . .'

'Well, you won't meet him, I hope,' I said as his voice trailed off. 'You'd be an idiot if you did.'

'I must!' he wailed. 'If I don't he'll come out here. And his letter is full of reproaches, and very pitiful. It's a horrible fix to be in. How I wish I had never met him!'

'If you must go, then get rid of him once for all. If you have any character now is the time to show it. Tell him you are leading a different life and he must let you alone in the future.'

'Character!' He sighed deeply. 'You don't know Oscar.'

He went off next morning, dragging his feet, all the jauntiness gone out of him.

I was in the parlor when he returned. His face looked three inches longer. He fell into a chair, leaned his elbows on the table, and clutched his hair with both hands.

'I'm done for,' he moaned. 'Oscar wouldn't listen to me. He says it is my duty to stand by him, that he must have companionship or go mad. The others are too busy . . . I have the leisure to devote myself to him . . . He has been through hell. He reminded me of all he had done for me in the past –'

'But I thought the man had a large nature despite the rest of him,' I interrupted. 'Didn't you tell him you wanted to break with the past? That it would be your social ruin to associate yourself with him again?'

'He has suffered too much to think of anything else. Oh, yes, I told him everything I could think of. I even told him I didn't want to leave you –'

'Confound you!' I cried in wrath. 'A nice thing to tell him! What will he think?' And then I looked at that gnome-like little face and laughed. 'Well, what did he say to that?'

'He said: "Oh, Mrs. Atherton! She is young and has all life before her. While I – I am a soul in purgatory"!'

'Very touching. But you are even younger, and I see no reason why you should wreck your life for the sake of an old sinner like that.' I looked at him sharply. 'Answer this question honestly, do you really want to go back to Oscar Wilde?'

'No!' he exclaimed violently. 'A thousand times no! I wish to God I could get out of it. But I don't see . . . He says he'll stay here in Rouen until I promise to go back to Dieppe with him.'

'Then there's but one thing for you to do. Pack your bags and leave for England by the first boat tomorrow. Write him a note which he will receive when you are out of his reach, telling him that you had a telegram recalling you to London at once. Leave the rest to time.'

He looked up hopefully. 'I might do that . . . he certainly couldn't follow me to England! But – but – it does seem like an act of desertion. He made me feel . . .'

I argued with him for an hour longer. He veered back and forth. But the upshot was that he ran away, and, as far as I know, did not see Wilde again until that dethroned Lord of Language had fallen into such depths of poverty and illness that all his old friends rallied about him once more and eased him into another world.

## NOTE

Gertrude Atherton (1857–1948), American novelist.

# Fritz Thaulow and Oscar Wilde at Dieppe, 1897[*]

### Christian Krogh

From early morning till seven at night Fritz Thaulow[1] sat painting, painting. Even when talking with him in his studio one never saw his face, but only his back. The conversation turned mainly on his new method of painting, of which I had seen some examples in the last Salon. This method was called in Paris the Thaulow process. However, he had no intention of giving the secret away, and though I observed him closely behind a mask of assumed indifference, I could not by merely watching him paint discover the secret myself. At last I gave it up, and was leaving the room when he called me back and told me all about his method.

But, he said, that's not what I'm doing now. Far from it. I'm doing something much finer, much more delicate. What do you say to tubes of glass? – But that secret I'll never give away.

[*] *The New Age* (London), (10 December 1908) 132–3.

After some time I heard him calling all over the house for me. After all, he might tell me, he said, because the method was far too complicated for me to follow. It proved, in fact, difficult – far too difficult for me . . . For several days he had been talking of inviting two young French painters who were working in the neighbourhood. I had seen these young fellows. They looked bright and pleasant enough, and also penniless. I particularly noticed that one of them never wore stockings.

Great arrangements were made for the dinner. The menu was carefully studied, and the wine-list well conned. There was no need to do this, I thought. Those brigands would be just as delighted with Chianti or cider.

I was still more surprised on finding that Thaulow, a little before dinner, had changed his grey velvet knee-breeches that bore the marks of painting and cycling for a pair of dove-grey striped trousers, white vest, long dress coat, and smart tie. So I went in and rubbed off one of my paint-spots.

But I understood it all when I came back. For to my amazement, Thaulow, who was evidently enjoying his little joke, introduced me, not to the young French painters, but to a tall, elegant gentleman of striking physiognomy – Mr. Oscar Wilde!

At dinner the conversation turned upon the Queen of England's Jubilee.

'I suppose it's really because she represents the greatness of England that the enthusiasm is so enormous,' said Thaulow.

'Not at all; it's because of her personality. She is really a personality. She's a woman, a thorough woman, and superlatively aristocratic.'

'Have you ever met her?'

'Yes, in a big garden party given by the Prince of Wales. I shall never forget her. She walked through the garden on the Prince's arm. She has the most exquisite bearing: thus –(he made waving motions in the air with his hands to indicate what he meant. He very often used his hands in this way to express his ideas.) She looked like a ruby mounted in jet. She is very small, and she moved thus – (here he imitated her walk with his hand on the table cloth.) Everybody moved aside as she approached. By the rules of Court etiquette no one is allowed to look at her face in front, but only in profile. This makes it rather difficult, for you have to take care when her eye rests on you. Then you must bow and move towards her. She gives her hand like this. (Here he lifted his delicate, aristocratic hand; and it struck me that he himself bore a resemblance to Queen Victoria.) She has the most beautiful hands and the most beautiful wrists. I stood there with Bastien Lepage. He was simply wild with enthusiasm. "I must paint this woman," he said. "If I may paint her, I'll swear never to paint another woman in my life.' I promised to ask the Prince of Wales. The Prince replied that it was impossible. Bastien Lepage was inconsolable.

'She has the most delicate feeling and the rarest tact. Once she was going to open Parliament. There's a very ancient rule that on State occasions the Queen must not venture out unless accompanied by her chief lady-in-waiting. The chief lady must also be the first duchess in the land. At that time it was the Duchess of Sutherland.

'All the Court functionaries stood in the hall whispering to each other that the Duchess had not yet arrived. They were horrified. It was only a very few minutes to the time fixed for starting; and that, you know, is always to the second. Still the Duchess did not arrive. Another minute passed. Then they got a shock; the Queen herself appeared at the top of the stairs. What was to be done? Who dared tell her the incredible thing that the Duchess had not arrived? The Queen came to the very bottom of the stairs. She looked calmly round and asked, "Where is the Duchess?" For a moment or two no one dared answer. At last one of the ladies advanced, "Your Majesty, the Duchess has not arrived." What would happen? The Queen did not move. She only folded her hands, those beautiful hands. She remained standing and waiting. Profound silence reigned. All eyes were rivetted on the entrance. Five minutes passed. No Duchess. Ten minutes. A carriage was heard. It is the Duchess, a young and very beautiful lady. She sees the Queen standing in waiting. She approaches with bowed head, stammering broken words. What would happen? Disgrace? Dismissal? "It appears to me," said the Queen, "that your watch does not go well. Allow me." She lifted with both hands, those beautiful hands, a priceless chain over her head, and hung it round the neck of the kneeling Duchess. On the chain was suspended the Queen's watch, set with diamonds forming her name.'

'It must be intolerable to live under such etiquette,' said Thaulow.

'Oh, they all become slaves, all of them. They don't live their own lives; they live other people's lives. The first and only question for them every morning is: How is Her Majesty to-day, happy or sad? The question begins right down below, and climbs the stairs until it reaches the attendants surrounding Her Majesty's bed-chamber. The lady-in-waiting who can give any information acquires an enormous prestige. And as the answer returns, sounding through all the rooms downstairs, the expression on all faces becomes either happy or sad. Before the answer arrives the faces have no expression at all. A courtier's face has absolutely no expression in the morning till the bulletin appears. They are slaves.'

'How revolting!'

'Oh, but they get to like it. It becomes second nature to them. If an old courtier is dismissed from Her Majesty's service, he grows wretched. He often dies of it. You see he cannot breathe in any other air. Courtiers and actors all live other people's lives. And most people really do so more or less. Everybody has someone concerning whom he asks: Is Her Majesty happy to-day or peradventure sad?'

'The Royal Family, I suppose, is very popular in England; even the foreign section of it?'

'Not the Emperor of Germany. He doesn't care much for England or English ways. He was extremely annoyed because he wasn't allowed to wear a uniform at the garden-party. He has, you know, marvellous uniforms. When he turns out in one he creates a sensation. Well, he was informed that it was not the custom to attend a garden-party in uniform. He addressed himself to his uncle, the Prince of Wales. But he was told it was quite impossible. Then he appealed to his grandmother, the Queen. She replied, "I have never heard of a uniform at a garden-party." So he had to come in an ordinary black coat like everybody else. And nobody looked at him; and nobody asked who he was. But he made up for it in the evening at the Opera. There in his box he looked magnificent in his gold and white, and everybody's eyes were fixed on him the whole evening.'

'Well, he's quite an interesting man, quite amusing; not like the others.'

'I don't know if he's anything in himself. But there have been two Royal personages really interesting—Rudolph of Austria and Ludwig of Bavaria. The one was murdered by his lover's brother. The other killed his doctor and then himself. They didn't live other people's lives.'

'Don't you find that all actors are slaves? Sarah Bernhardt, for instance?'

'Oh, no, not Sarah. Sarah is a splendid exception in that, as in everything else. She is a great woman as well as a great genius.'

Strange that she can keep young so long.'

'Oh, that's due to her caprices. She says herself, "You never grow old so long as you indulge your caprices. When you cease, you grow old immediately." '

'You have a famous actress in England now – Ellen Terry. Is she as great as Sarah Bernhardt?'

'No, she is only great as a woman. She is more of a woman than anyone I have even seen, except Queen Victoria.'

'Don't you think Watts the greatest English painter?'

'No, Whistler, far and away. Have you seen his portrait of Sarasate, and have you seen Sarasate? The portrait is much better than Sarasate. Sarasate was immensely flattered by the furore his portrait produced. He stayed the whole time in the room where it hung. But he looked shockingly ordinary by the side of it. I met him there one day, and I said to him, "For God's sake, don't stay in this room. You must never come into this room." And I led him out.'

'What do you think of our friend the young poet, with whom I met you the other day?'

'Oh, he is very talented. I'm a great admirer of his.'

'It's a pity he drinks too much absinthe.'

Oscar Wilde shrugged his shoulders.

'If he didn't drink, he would be somebody else. Il faut accepter la personalité comme elle est. Il ne faut jamais regretter qu'un poete est soûl, il faut regretter que les soûls ne soient pas toujours poetes.'[2]

'Well, anyhow, the worst thing, he can drink is absinthe – it's absolutely destructive.'

'Absinthe,' answered Wilde, 'has a wonderful colour, la coleur verte. Il faut maintenant boire des choses vertes. A glass of absinthe is as poetical as anything in the world. Quelle différence y a-t-il entre un verre d'absinthe et un coucher de soleil?'[3]

'By the way, have you got into your villa?' asked Thaulow.

'Yes, I gave a banquet there yesterday in honour of the Queen's jubilee. I had the place lit up with myriads of coloured lamps and decorated with English flags. I also hired a band to play "God Save the Queen." '

'Have you got a good valet?'

'I had one. He was very clever. But he became impossible. It was my own fault: I'm very unhappy about it. I gave him a blue uniform; a thing I ought not to have done. Of course he got conceited about it at once. He went to a ball, and made quite a hit with his blue uniform. Naturally he wanted to go to dances every evening. Then, of course, he wanted to sleep in the mornings. And I had to wait and wait for my hot water. One morning I got up myself and took him hot water. That helped for one day, but no more. Now he is dismissed and I have found another one. He is to have a black uniform, and that has given me an idea. The next book I write shall be about the effect on men of the colour blue. For instance, take Mr. Thaulow. He's all blue – blue character, blue temperament. And to-day he's bluer than ever.'

Thaulow looked incredulous.

'Good gracious! are you all mad with this nonsense? May I ask if, like my wife, you think Friday is yellow?'

'Think,' he cried, with a look of astonishment. 'Can anybody doubt for an instant that Friday is yellow?'

No one ventured to deny it. Even Thaulow only muttered something to himself.

Later on, a well-known young American painter, a mutual friend of Thaulow and Wilde, paid a visit. He made a hard, dry impression, and seemed to take no interest in anything, not even in his art. When he had gone, one of the ladies remarked that he was not a human being, but merely an American patent, 'une invention americaine de fer.'[4]

'No,' answered Oscar Wilde, 'no, he's not that. He's quite dead. And the dead ought to be good enough to keep to their graves. If they do come out, it should be by moonlight, and on the sea-shore with lanterns in their hands. But the dead ought never to go visiting or go to the cafés.'

Thaulow asked Wilde if he was beginning any new book.

'Yes,' he said, 'I'm writing an essay to be called, "A Defence of Drunkenness." '

Thaulow looked disapprovingly.

'Good gracious, my dear Wilde, why always such provoking titles?'

'Why? London must be shocked at least twice a year.'

'Then you don't always mean what you write?'

'Oh, yes; the soul is never liberated except by drunkenness in one form or another. Here in a small place like Dieppe your soul can listen to the words and harmonies and behold the colours of the Great Silence. And that intoxicates. But one is not always at Dieppe. And it is difficult to find the Great Silence. But a waiter with a tray will always find it for you. Knock; and the door will always open, the door of le paradis artificiel.'[5]

'What do you think of the horrid weather Felix Faure had going into Paris?' interrupted Thaulow.

'Oh, it always does that under a frock-coated Republic. During the Empire it never rained when the Empress drove through the Champs Elysées.'

## NOTES

Translated from the Norwegian of Christian Krogh. Wilde refers to this dinner in a letter to William Rothenstein written from Berneval, near Dieppe, on 21 June 1897.

1. Fritz Thaulow (1847–1906), Norwegian landscape-artist and designer.
2. One must accept a personality as it is. One must never regret that a poet is drunk, but that drunkards are not always poets.'
3. 'What difference is there between a glass of absinthe and a sunset?'
4. An American invention made of iron.
5. The artificial paradise.

# Oscar Wilde in Dieppe*

Jacques-Émile Blanche

Conder[1] and Sickert[2] received without enthusiasm the news of Oscar Wilde's coming arrival at Dieppe on his release from prison. What attitude was to be taken with regard to the outlaw? In discussing the matter with me Conder said:

'You have only been married recently, and it's hardly fair to inflict a man who has just served a sentence of hard labour on your family'.

'I quite agree that it is unusual, but my people are broad-minded and accustomed to strange characters'.

'I'm sure that at the Villa Olga he'll be put on the index'.

'After all, I've known Oscar Wilde for a long time and I consider him a man of undisputed talent. Now that he's a wreck I should never forgive myself if I didn't do what I could for him'.

* *Portraits of a Lifetime*. Translated and edited by Walter Clement (London: J.M. Dent, 1937) pp. 97–100. Editor's title.

'I am told that he is to go by another name, although he may not like it.
He's sure to make trouble here; he'll harangue the ignorant under the
Arcades. He'll use the Café Suisse as his platform and he'll make an
exhibition of himself. . . .'

One day while Sickert and I were going for a walk, Oscar, who was
sitting in the Café Suisse, beckoned to me. I pretended not to see. I know
for a fact that he was wounded to the quick by my action, and the
recollection of that episode still fills me with remorse.

I had known Oscar Wilde since the early 'eighties, and in 1883 I had
exhibited the portrait of a young woman reading a book of Wilde's verse.
He acknowledged the compliment by writing to me in the following terms:

'Hôtel Voltaire,
'*avril* 5.

'CHER MONSIEUR BLANCHE, – Je vous remercie beaucoup pour ces trois
charmants souvenirs de votre art: quant à la petite fille qui lit mes poèmes
je l'adore déjà, mais hélas! elle ne veut pas lever ses yeux de mon livre,
même pour un instant:

'Traître, vous l'avez faite préférer le poète à mant, et les vers à les baisers!

'Cependant c'est intéressant de trouver une femme comme ça, car elle
n'existe pas.

'A dimanche prochain,
'votre bien devoué
'OSCAR WILDE'.[3]

I have also another letter from him, written at the same period, in which he
accepts an invitation to tea at my studio: 'J'aime tant voir votre atelier,
avec sa porte bleu de paon, et la petite chambre verte et or; car c'est pour
moi une fraiche oasis de beauté dans le désert de Louis seize que je trouve à
Paris'.[4]

When Wilde came back from his lecturing tour in the United States,
about 1889,[5] and walked about Paris with a sunflower in his buttonhole
and with his famous sphinx ring on his finger, his reputation was already
tainted with scandal. Barrès[6] was struck with admiration for the Englishman who spoke such brilliant French. At the Restaurant Voisin,
which was so famous in those days, Barrès arranged a resplendent banquet
in Wilde's honour, with Anatole France[7] in the chair. Artists and writers
representing new movements were there; Edouard Dujardin[8] on behalf of
the symbolists made a speech in genuine symbolist jargon. George Moore
was furious with Dujardin and refused to take any part in the proceedings;
Whistler and Sickert poured scorn and ridicule on Wilde. As far as I was
concerned, my relations with Wilde were a little strained because I had a
foot in both camps, and, although I was not in any sense Whistler's pupil,[9]
and was never very much influenced by him, Wilde knew that Whistler
and Sickert were friends of mine.

But, to return to Dieppe, the Thaulows were less cowardly in their attitude towards Wilde. Fritz,[10] the Norwegian landscape painter, was living in a house in the Faubourg de la Barre which over looked the citadel, the town, the roadstead, and the valley of Arques, an extensive panorama which offered him countless subjects for pictures that dealers took off his hands by dozens. Packing cases addressed to all parts of the world encumbered the stations. The Fritz Thaulows, with their brood of fair-haired children, had descended upon Holland, gone on to Belgium, and reached Boulogne and Montreuil-sur-Mer like a tribe of bohemians. As soon as the subjects of a picturesque place were exhausted, the caravan proceeded on its way. These good people, obeying the orders of Fritz, had settled amongst us on the hill to the south of the Faubourg de la Barre, the stronghold of the English colony. Soon the house belonging to Delamare, the grocer, became a kind of Wahnfried, a miniature artists' Bayreuth. Oscar Wilde was there received with kindness and hospitality during the first days he spent on the Continent. After a few weeks he was forced to leave Dieppe, for he felt that he was being followed, and then he took a room at an inn at Berneval-sur-Mer.[11] The experiences which made him seek shelter in Paris are well known.

## NOTES

Jacques-Émile Blanche (1861–1942), French portrait painter. Wilde met him in Paril and often went to see him at his studio in Auteuil. It was Blanche who introduced Wilde to Marcel Proust. Blanche's writings on Wilde include 'Oscar Wilde', *La Pêche aux Souvenirs* (Paris: Flammarion, 1949) pp. 187–9.

1. Charles Conder (1868–1909), English artist. Wilde much admired his work. See references to him in *The Letters of Oscar Wilde*; A. E. John, 'Wilde and Conder', *Golden Horizon*, ed. Cyril Connolly (New York: British Book Centre, 1953) pp. 321–5; and John Rothenstein, *The Life and Death of Conder* (London: Dent, 1938) *passim*.

2. For a note on Walter Sickert see p. 272.

3. 'Dear Mr. Blanche – Thank you very much for these three charming momentos of your art: as for the little girl that reads my poems I adore her already, but alas! she does not want to lift her eyes from my book, even for one moment.

'Traitor, you made her prefer the poet to the lover, and the poetry to the kisses!

'In the meantime, it is interesting to find a woman like this, because she does not exist.

'Until next Sunday,
'Yours sincerely,
'Oscar Wilde'

4. 'I would like very much to see your studio, with its peacock-blue door, and the small green room, etc.; because to me it is a fresh oasis of beauty in the desert of Louis the Sixteenth which I find in Paris.'

5. Wilde sailed from New York on S.S. *Bothnia* on 27 December 1882 and arrived in Liverpool on 6 January 1883, not 1889.

6. Auguste Maurice Barrès (1862–1923), French writer and politician.

7. Anatole France (1844–1924), French novelist, critic, poet, and playwright.

8. Edouard Dujardin (1861–1949), French journalist and writer.

9. 'Sickert – at the time when I was on the committee of the New English Art Club, and there were quarrels and bickerings among the members, and he was undecided whether to send his pictures to Suffolk Street – wrote to me: "Vous allez me trouver très indécis. J'ai vu qu'on tirerait de mon exposition à Suffolk Street des conclusions exagérées et que j'aurais tort de vouloir publiquement offenser Whistler ce dont j'aurais horreur. J'ai été toujours affiché comme son élève. Pendant que ce n'était que question de se disputer en *private* cela ne faisait rien, mais cette fois j'ai aperçu que c'eût été trop fort. Aussi à la fin je n'avais rien de prêt. Je vous ai télégraphié au moment de ma décision pour ne pas vous tromper, mais il me parait que vous avez complètement le droit d'y exposer, vous, et que vous auriez tort de ne pas le faire. *Vous n'êtes pas élève de Whistler*"' – Jacques-Émile Blanche.

10. For a note on Fritz Thaulow see p. 351.

11. On Wilde's life in Berneval see André Germain, 'Wilde à Berneval', *La Revue Européenne*, I (December 1923) 37–40; Léon Lemonnier, 'Oscar Wilde en exil, d'après des documents nouveaux', *La Grande Revue*, (January 1931) 373–98; and Gerald Hamilton, 'Wilde at Berneval', *The London Magazine*, VII (June 1967) 73–7.

# An Interview with Oscar Wilde*

## Gedeon Spilett

The following scene takes place at Dieppe where the English novelist spent the last fine days of autumn before embarking for the resort of Naples where, I believe, he has decided to spend the winter.

A group of young poets and men of letters surrounds Oscar Wilde. He answers my somewhat prying questions good-naturedly, but with a trace of irony or bitterness in his voice.

Oscar Wilde expresses himself with ease in a modern, highly-coloured French to which his slight British accent adds a certain charm of its own.

Although he denies that he is English, and flouts his Catholicism and his Irish origin, you would have to be blind not to recognise him at first sight as a true representative of the Anglo-Saxon race. His height, his heavy build, his grey-blue eyes, his fair hair, and his long, powerful jaw-line leave no doubt at all about his origins.

When he laughs – and he laughs often, rather like a contented ogre – you

* *Gil Blas* (Paris), (22 November 1897) p. 3. This is the first appearance in English.

can see his long, broad, splayed teeth and the gold that fills the gaps between them.

Wilde is very much the fatalist, and wears a ring set with an emerald on the little finger of each hand. These precious stones are engraved with cabbalistic symbols, and come from an Egyptian pyramid. He claims that the emerald on his left hand is the real cause of all his happiness, and that the one on his right hand is the cause of all his unhappiness. To my observation – which was logical enough, I think – that he should have taken off the evil ring, he replied with a changed voice: 'To live in happiness, you must know some unhappiness in life.'

Besides, green is Oscar Wilde's favourite colour. For him it is all important, and the symbol of Hell. He has his own very personal interpretation of what Hell is. He says that Heaven is made for decent people, for the upright members of the middle class, and, generally speaking, for all the ordinary people who are unaware of their new freedom of Will. God is good. He is merciful, far too merciful. It is easy enough to ring the bell at St Peter's door, but Satan demands far more of his followers. With him a certain ceremony is required. 'To enter Paradise you only have to knock once at the door, but you must knock three times to get into Hell. Believe me, love the green, love Hell. The colour green and Hell are both made for thieves and artists.'

Oscar Wilde loves France because she alone stands up for freedom of speech, because she alone offers help to the weak, and because she alone satisfies man's longing for justice. I ask Wilde whether one could put on any mediocre French vaudeville whatsoever before an English audience. I pass on his answer for the benefit of those authors who write for the export market: 'You can put anything on for the English, anything . . . except *Tartuffe!*'[1]

However, he doesn't bear even the slightest grudge against the English. He has experienced such a Redemption through his sentence and his two years of hard labour that he admits that he speaks of his Exile in poetic terms. 'It is the sin of pride which has always destroyed men. I had risen too high, and I fell sprawling in the mire.' He is very grateful to the French Press which so warmly championed his cause. He is especially grateful to those who took up his defence without even knowing him. Judging from what he says, what he regrets most is to have been unable to see the production of his *Salomé* which the Théâtre de l'Oeuvre put on during his imprisonment. He speaks readily enough of those two lost years, and of the remarks made about his fellow-prisoners whose mood he tried very hard to define. He doesn't seem to have suffered much physically, but he must have suffered great tortures of mind and soul. He had to pass through all the phases and anguish of the 'nuit de fâmes' Huysmans talks about concerning St John of the Cross. When I asked him to describe all the hardships he suffered in prison, he replied with a sudden tremor in his voice, 'Excuse me, I never speak of that.'

Seeing him so gay, so lucid, so quick to deliver a retort, one forgets in the end the terrible ordeal he has undergone.

He is amazingly familiar with modern literary movements and their representatives. It's even a bit disconcerting, for he cited me the names of budding young writers whom I had barely heard of.

As everyone knows, Wilde was very intimately acquainted with Verlaine. He considers him one of the Nineteenth century's greatest writers, as much for his poetry as for the changes he was able to effect upon the writing of his time. Wilde enjoys recounting the conversations about aesthetics which he has with Verlaine at the Café François I under the benevolent eye of the indescribable Bibi-la-Purée. He would like the statue of the poor Lelian to be erected not in the Luxembourg, nor in the street, but in one of the cafés where Verlaine spent his life. In this way his image will be sheltered from inclement weather, especially from the rain the poet feared so much:

Il pleure dans mon coeur comme il pleut sur la ville.

'The hero's statue must be placed on his life's battle-field', Wilde told me with reference to this matter.

As for Stéphane Mallarmé,[2] Oscar Wilde prefers this poet when he writes in French, – everyone knows Mallarmé writes in English as well – 'because, at least in French Mallarmé is incomprehensible, whereas in English, unfortunately, one can understand him.' Perhaps to soften the biting nature of his criticism Wilde adds, 'That's a gift (not to be understood), that not everybody enjoys. See here, for example, poor Moréas[3] lacks it, but does Moréas really exist?'

– And to my assurance that the poet Moréas exists in flesh and blood, Wilde adds with a smile: 'I always believed it was a myth.' And he quoted me the names of two or three other French writers whose existence has always seemed a legend to him, perhaps even a hoax.

The author of the *Portrait of Dorian Gray* praises *Aphrodite*[4] without reservation. As I was drawing a parallel between Pierre Louÿs' novels and *Salammbô*,[5] he interrupted me, his gaze filled with a kind of ecstasy: 'Nothing is as beautiful as that book! . . . And the Goncourt brothers,[6] what artists! And proud, and arrogant, and jealous of their fame, and rightly so . . . !'

Little by little the critic grows silent, and Oscar Wilde speaks to me of his plans, his books. He is going to write one in French right away. Then he will follow Mallarmé's example and translate it into English. He describes the theatre he dreams of, the plays he wants to write, and the unsurpassed worship he pays 'the princess of beautiful gestures and postures', Sarah Bernhardt, on whom he is counting to bring to life one of his heroines.

Next he relates to me in a lively fashion the scenario of a satiric play in three scenes which he planned to write but has given up, at least for the present.

Let him speak for himself:

'The Gospel often speaks of the sick whom Christ cured; but nowhere in the holy books is there mention of what became of them. It's a missing piece in the story which a short story writer's or playwright's imagination ought to try to fill.

'Here's my idea.

'In the first scene we see a young man with a garland of roses on his head. He is getting drunk on wine. Christ happens to be passing by and He upbraids him for his drunkenness. The young man recognises Him, and after doing homage to Him says, "Master, I am the cripple whom you cured."

'Christ comes in the second scene to a place where another man is indulging in debauchery with three courtesans. He upbraids him for his vice. The man recognises Him, and prostrating himself says, "Master, I am the leper whom you cured."

'Then Christ, very sad, goes to the desert (scene 3). Seeing a young man crying, Christ says to him softly, "Why do you weep?" And the young man, recognising Him, answers "Master, I was dead and you brought me back to life!"

– 'But', adds Oscar Wilde as he ends his tale, 'I don't think I'll carry out the idea, for one must respect Christ in His majesty.'

M. Jules Lemaître[7] does not share the same scruples, for if my memory serves me correctly he has already written a *Christmas Tale* based on a similar idea which appeared last year in a political and literary magazine.

## NOTES

1. By the French dramatist Molière (1622–73).

2. Stéphane Mallarmé (1842–98), French poet and prose-writer.

3. Jean Moréas (1856–1910), French poet, of Greek birth.

4. By the French prose-writer Pierre Louÿs (1870–1925).

5. By the French novelist Gustave Flaubert (1821–80).

6. Edmond Louis Antoine Huot de Goncourt (1822–98) and Jules Alfred Huot de Goncourt (1830–70), French novelists, historians and art critics.

7. François Élie Jules Lemaître (1853–1914), French playwright, short-story writer and critic.

# A Trip to Naples*

## Vincent O'Sullivan

By accident, I presided at that first journey of his to Italy a few months after his release, which was not approved of by some of his close friends at the time, and has since been variously commented on.[1]

\*     \*     \*

Those who have read his biographers know that upon coming out of prison he passed some months at a place on the French coast called Berneval, near Dieppe. One day at the end of that summer, after he had come to Paris, I received a letter from him. He asked if I was in Paris, and if I were would I come to see him.

The next day I went about twelve o'clock to the address given – an hotel in the rue du Helder, just off the Boulevard. He was expecting a friend of his named Rowland Strong.[2] After waiting about a quarter of an hour, seeing that Strong did not turn up, he left a letter for him and we went out to lunch.

In the cab, I asked him who was Rowland Strong? He said he was an English journalist – the Paris correspondent, I think he said, of some London paper, and, what he seemed to think more important, a descendant on his mother's side of Chateaubriand. He seemed in very good spirits and launched out into a description of Strong's valet, an elderly man, who, he said, was the extreme type of the English well-trained servant. When Strong heard that Verlaine was dying, as he did not care to go himself to the mean street and the squalid abode, he sent this man to get news. The valet returned imperturbable.

'Well?' asked Strong.

'I saw the gentleman, sir, and he died immediately'.

As Wilde finished this story we arrived at the restaurant, a restaurant chosen by himself, which still exists at the moment of writing, up a flight of stairs over a passage giving on the Boulevard Montmartre, having somehow survived the drastic overhauling of Paris since the war. It was a kind of restaurant where nobody would recognize Wilde, and he did not want to be recognized.

---

* *Aspects of Wilde* (London: Constable; New York: Henry Holt, 1936) pp. 194–7, Editor's title.

Towards the end of the meal he said that he was rather troubled – as well as I remember, he said he was 'passing through a crisis'. It seemed that some friends of his family in England wanted him to go into a mountain village and write plays. This, it may be said in passing, was a most stupid suggestion which took no account of the havoc wrought in his brain and nerves by his trial and imprisonment. What he required was to forget, to be stimulated, distracted from his black thoughts. How could he find that in a mountain village? It would have continued the penal cell. He himself was inclined to go to Italy.

He talked of all this for some time, giving details, some of which it was hard for me to follow from lack of knowledge of the elements of the matter. So far as I remember, the main difficulty was that his wife's friends and relations wanted to keep him from rejoining Lord Alfred Douglas, who was at Naples. Then he added: 'I am not telling all this to you because I want advice. I have thought it all out and I would not take advice from anyone.' I assured him that nothing was farther from my thoughts than to offer him advice. That indeed was so, both because I should have thought it presumptuous to offer advice to a man so much beyond me both in years and achievement, and also because it was utterly indifferent to me what he did or where he went.

Finally he declared: 'I shall go to Italy tonight. Or rather, I would go, but I am in an absurd position. I have no money.'

Upon leaving the restaurant we drove to the Banque de Paris et des Pays-Bas in the rue d'Antin where I had an account. He stayed in the cab and I brought him out the sum he wanted. It is one of the few things I look back on with satisfaction. It is not every day that one has the chance of relieving the anxiety of a genius and a hero. I think he left Paris the same evening; certainly very soon. When I saw him next it was a good while after, and in Italy.

## NOTES

Vincent O'Sullivan (1868–1940), Irish-American poet and novelist who spent most of his life in France.

1. This is the only record of Wilde's journey from Berneval to Naples.

2. Rowland Strong (1865–1924), Paris correspondent of the *New York Times*, *Observer* and *Morning Post*.

# Confusion in Naples*

Norman Douglas

There was a curious little episode here. Oscar Wilde had arrived in Naples and was staying with his young friend[1] on the Posilipo [sic][2] (? Villa Giudice).[3] This came to the ears of Matilda Serao, a literary woman who, with Scarfoglio, edited the *Mattino* newspaper. Somehow or other she also heard of my building the Villa Maya, and of Campo Alegre's arrival there in a shattered state of health. The first indication we had of this was when Rolfe, the Consul-General, sent me a cutting from the *Mattino* and said he had already written to rectify the blunder. From the cutting it appeared that Matilda had confused Campo Alegre with Wilde, and me – owing to a similarity of name – with his friend. She spoke of the arrival of Wilde at the Villa Maya, which she described as having been built by this friend, and added that Wilde must have been disgracefully treated in his English prison, as he could hardly stand on his legs. Even Rolfe's letter did not quite convince Matilda, for she came out with a second communication entitled *C'è o non c' è* – is it (Wilde) or is it not? I forget how the affair ended.

* *Looking Back; An Autobiographical Excursion* (London: Chatto & Windus, 1934) pp. 461–2. Editor's title.

## NOTES

Norman Douglas (1868–1952), English writer.

1. Lord Alfred Douglas.
2. Posilippo. In a letter to Dalhouse Young written from Naples on 21 September 1897 Wilde said: 'I am living here without any money, and want to move into apartments at Posilippo as soon as possible.'
3. Wilde wrote a letter to Robert Ross on 1 October 1897 from 'Villa Giudice, Posilippo, Naples'.

# 'Oh, My Poor Dear Boys!'*

'It so happened that I saw your father nearly every day for several months on end. I was ten or eleven years old at the time, a rather small, shy, quiet little boy. My own father did not like his work interrupted by a mid-day meal, and he used to send my mother and me out to lunch "Chez Béchet", a small restaurant run by Monsieur Béchet and his wife at No. 42, Rue Jacob. Madame Béchet claimed to have been cook in "a big house" and, indeed, she cooked efficiently, simply and cleanly. A few days ago I looked through the curtain over the door, to see if the place retained anything of its former character. It seemed to me to be lighter and brighter, but it was still recognisable. The spiral staircase, for instance, in the far right hand corner, which went up to the first floor, was still there.

'In those days, the ground floor was frequented by casual visitors, but the first floor was kept for regular clients. All the tables there were reserved and you had to be a friend of Madame Béchet, a charming woman, to be allowed into it. My mother and I went there every day, and the table reserved for us was the one next to "Monsieur Sébastien"[1] whose personality attracted my mother very much, as she noticed that there was a certain style about him which was lacking in the other clients, who were mostly minor commercial travellers and clerks. It was a most respectable clientèle; the noisier, more conversational patrons were put by the window, and from there they descended, in order of quietness, to the table occupied by "Monsieur Sébastien", who ate with his back to the far wall, silent and alone.

'As we occupied neighbouring tables, we used to bow to him on arriving and on leaving, or he would bow to us if we were the first to come or to go. My mother held him up to me as a model of deportment, elegance and good breeding, and often used to talk to me about him on our way to the restaurant. What was the sorrow that weighed him down and made him so sad? He must be very unhappy; what had happened to him? My mother, who was as tender-hearted as she was pretty, worried about him. She would have liked to have talked to him, but he himself never talked. Once or twice a thin, rather dark man came to luncheon with him: I discovered afterwards that he was Ernest Lajeunesse.[2]

'I must describe Monsieur Sébastien as he appeared to me. The first

* Vyvyan Holland, *Time Remembered after Père Lachaise* (London: Gollancz, 1966) pp. 10–12. Editor's title.

thing that struck me was the width of his shoulders, and his height; he was like a man who had been very big but was wasted by illness. His face must have been handsome, indeed it retained traces of this; but his features were extremely tired. He made gentle movements with his hands. I think that his eyes, which he seldom raised, must have been a rather dark blue, but I have not a very good eye for colour. An expression of great kindness, but of infinite weariness.

'He ate what Madame Béchet put before him, and she looked after him like a child. She would prepare special dishes for him and kept coming to see whether he was eating them. If things were not going to her liking she would say: "Come, Monsieur Sébastien, you must not give up!"

'One autumn evening, while putting on my overcoat after finishing my meal, I clumsily upset something, perhaps a salt-cellar, on Monsieur Sébastien's table. He said nothing, but my mother scolded me and told me to apologise, which I did, distressed by my clumsiness. But Monsieur Sébastien turned to my mother and said: "Be patient with your little boy, one must always be patient with them. If, one day, you should find yourself separated from him . . ." I did not give him time to finish his sentence, but asked him: "Have you got a little boy?" "I've got two," he said. "Why don't you bring them here with you?" My mother interrupted, saying: "You mustn't ask questions, Lucien!" "It doesn't matter: it doesn't matter at all," he said, with a sad smile. "They don't come here with me because they are too far away . . ." Then he took my hand, drew me to him and kissed me on both cheeks. I bade him farewell, and then I saw that he was crying. And we left.

'While kissing me, he had said a few words which I did not understand. But on the following day we arrived before him and a Bank employé who used to sit at the table on the other side of us asked us: "Did you understand what Monsieur Sébestien said last evening?" "No," we replied. "He said, in English: 'Oh, my poor dear boys!'"

'The Bank employé went on to say: "I am almost certain that he is a great English writer who became mixed up in a scandal which rocked England." My mother retorted that she could not imagine such a sympathetic man being mixed up in a scandal, and he replied:

'"When a man is too successful, people are envious of him."

'A few weeks later, "Monsieur Sébastien" ceased to go there. Thanks to the other client who was the only one to witness what had happened, I realised that I had been given those two kisses vicariously – I was just at the age at which you had last seen him. I ask myself whether my clumsiness was not, perhaps, well-timed, since it was an opportunity for him to send you an indirect message.'

## NOTES

Vyvyan Holland (1886–1967), Oscar Wilde's son, told of his childhood and of his early youth in his book *Son of Oscar Wilde* (1954). This biography created a great deal of interest, and the author received letters from friends, from chance acquaintances, and from total strangers. Of all the letters he received he was most affected by this one, which came from France after the appearance of the translation of his book there. It was written from Issyles-Moulineaux and this is a translation of it.

  1. Monsieur Sebastien was, of course, Sebastian Melmoth, the name assumed by Oscar Wilde when he went into exile; from the 'Wandering Jew', hero of *Melmoth the Wanderer* (1820) by the Irish writer Charles Robert Maturin (1782–1824), who was Wilde's great-uncle. Robert Ross and More Adey had collaborated in an anonymous biographical introduction to a new edition of the novel in 1892, and Ross suggested this alias to Wilde.

  2. Ernest Harry La Jeunesse (1874–1917), French littérateur. For a note on him see p. 481.

# I Disliked Oscar Wilde*

### Ford Madox Ford

Wilde I can never forgive. You may maintain that he had a right to live his own life and, for the sake of sheer vanity, get himself into Reading Gaol. For there was no reason for his going to prison and the last thing that the British authorities wanted to do was to put him there. On the day of his arrest his solicitor received warning that the warrant would not be issued until after seven P.M., the night train for Paris leaving at 6:50 from Charing Cross. I remember still the feeling of anxiety and excitement of that day. Practically everybody in London knew what was agate.

Wilde went to his solicitor – Mr. Robert Humphreys; I once had him for my lawyer – about eleven in the morning. Humphreys at once began to beg him to go to Paris. Wilde declared that the authorities dared not touch him. He was too eminent and there were too many others implicated. To that he stuck. He was immovable and would listen to no arguments. There came a dramatic moment in the lawyer's office. Wilde began to lament his wasted life. He uttered a tremendous diatribe about his great talents thrown away, his brilliant genius dragged in the mud, his early and

---

\* *Return to Yesterday* (London: Victor Gollancz, 1931) pp. 40–5; (New York: Horace Liveright, 1932) pp. 46–50. Editor's title.

glorious aspirations come to nothing. He became almost epic. Then he covered his face and wept. His whole body was shaken by his sobs. Humphreys was extremely moved. He tried to find consolations.

Wilde took his hands down from his face. He winked at Humphreys and exclaimed triumphantly:

'Got you then, old fellow.' He added: 'Certainly I shall not go to Paris.' He was arrested that evening.

I always intensely disliked Wilde, faintly as a writer and intensely as a human being. No doubt, as a youth he was beautiful, frail and illuminated. But when I knew him he was heavy and dull. I only once heard him utter an epigram. He used to come to my grandfather's with some regularity at one time – every Saturday, I should say. My grandfather was then known as the Grandfather of the pre-Raphaelites and Wilde passed as a pre-Raphaelite poet.

He would sit beside the high fireplace and talk very quietly – mostly about public matters: Home Rule for Ireland and the like. My grandfather was a rather down-to-the-ground sort of person, so that Wilde to him talked very much like anyone else and seemed glad to be in a quiet room beside a high fireplace.

Once, at a garden party at the Bishop of London's, I heard a lady ask him if he were going to the dinner of the O. P. Club that evening. The O. P. Club had some grievance against Wilde. It was a dramatic society or something of the sort. Dramatic organisations are excitable and minatory when they disliked anybody. It was a dramatic society that booed and hissed at Henry James when he took his curtain call after *Guy Domville*. But really they were venting their wrath against Sir George Alexander, the actor manager who had that evening for the first time made a charge for programmes. So Wilde would have had a rough-house at the dinner of the O. P. Club. He therefore replied to the lady at the Bishop's party:

'I go to the dinner of the O. P. Club! I should be like a poor lion in a den of savage Daniels.'

I saw Wilde several times in Paris and he was a truly miserable spectacle, the butt usually of a posse of merciless students. He possessed and it was almost his only possession – a walking stick of ebony with ivory insertions, the handle representing an elephant. This he loved very much because it had been the gift of some one – Lady Mount Temple, I think. He would be of an evening in one or another disagreeable *bouge*[1] in Montmartre. The students would get about him. It was the days of the apaches. There would be a fellow there called Bibi La Touche or something of the sort. The students would point him out to Wilde and declare that Bibi had taken a fancy to his stick and would murder him on his homeward way if he did not surrender it. Wilde would cry, the tears pouring down his great cheeks. But always he surrendered his stick. The students would return it to his hotel next morning, when he would have forgotten all about it. I, once or perhaps twice, rescued his stick for him and saw him home. It would not be agreeable. He did not have a penny and I had very little more. I would walk him down the miserably lit Montmartrois streets, he completely silent or muttering things that I did not understand. He walked always as if his feet hurt him, leaning forward on his precious cane. When I thought we were near enough to the Quartier for my resources to let me pay a cab—usually in the neighbourhood of the Boulevard de la Madeleine – we would get into one and would at last reach the rue Jacob. This happened I think twice, but the memory is one as if of long-continued discomfort. It was humiliating to dislike so much one so unfortunate. But the feeling of dislike for that shabby and incoherent immensity was unavoidable. It had proved so strong that, the locality taking on an aspect of nightmare, I have only once since visited Montmartre at night in, say, thirty-five years and then found it very disagreeable. Of course, the sight of the young people, like starlings, tormenting that immense owl had a great deal to do with my revulsions.

On one occasion – I should think in the *Chat Noir* – I was with Robert de la Sizéranne and, looking at Wilde who was across the room, he said: '*Vous voyez cet homme là. Il péchait par pur snobisme.*'[2]

He meant that, even in his offences against constituted society, Wilde was out to *épater les bourgeois* – to scandalise the middle classes. Sizéranne added: '*Cela le faisait chaque fois vomir!*'[3]

That was pretty generally the French view and, on the face of it, I should say it was just. Sizéranne who was then accounted a very sagacious critic of art, mostly pre-Raphaelite, moved in French circles where Wilde had once throned it almost as an Emperor.[4]

## NOTES

Ford Madox Ford (1873–1939), English writer.

1. Haunt.

2. Do you see that man over there? He sinned through pure snobbishness.

3. That would make him throw up every time.

4. On Wilde's life in Paris and his later days see Ernest Raynaud 'Oscar Wilde à Paris', *La Mêlée Symboliste*, 2ᵉ partie: 1890–1900 (Paris: Renaissance du Livre, 1920) pp. 125–45; Paul Wiegler, 'Hotel d'Alsace', *Genius in Love and Death* (New York: Albert & Charles Boni, 1929) pp. 116–25; Cecil Georges-Bazile, 'Les Derniers Jours d'Oscar Wilde', *La Revue Hebdomadaire*, xi (28 November 1925) 387–99; André Gide, 'The Last Days of Oscar Wilde', *Saturday Review* (New York), xlii (13 June 1959) 10–12, 56–7; and Arthur Ransome, 'Oscar Wilde in Paris', *T. P.'s Magazine* (London), (June 1911) 427–35.

# 'I Used You in *Dorian Gray*'*

## Sir Peter Chalmers Mitchell

One afternoon I was taking coffee with two London friends in front of a café near the palace gates.[1] They were quite nice people, one a stockbroker, the other a partner in a publishing house, and both what may be called 'men of the world'. A heavy-jowled, large grey-faced man, looking as if his suit were too big for him, shuffled past us and sat down at a table near by. 'Why,' I said, 'that is Oscar Wilde! He must have come here from Paris.'

My friends got up to go.

'You can stay if you like,' they said; 'he is probably here under a false name; the hotel should be warned.' And they went off.

The trial and the two years in prison were over. *The Ballad of Reading Gaol* had been published and Wilde had left England. But still some of the almost gleeful ferocity with which his fall had been received was there. I could not understand it. The sin, at that time at least, had a lure for very few, and to most merely was an unpleasant mania requiring treatment rather than punishment. But probably there was something else. Wilde's character and personality were against the Victorian taste. He had the manners of an advertising charlatan and yet he was a poet, a scholar and a successful playwright. And he was not a 'mixer', but flaunted a kind of insolence. I suppose that if there had been anything abnormal about Whistler, although he was a very fine gentleman by birth and instincts, he would have been hunted with the same glee.

I went across to Wilde's table, raised my hat and said: 'Mr. Wilde, I don't suppose you remember me, but a long time ago Ion Thynne introduced me to you at the Café Royal.'

He raised his grey face and the thick lips mumbled:

'Ion Thynne. Yes! Isn't he dead?'

'I think so. It is years since I've heard anything of him. Robbie Ross is a friend of mine.'

'Ah! Robbie, with the face of Puck and the heart of an angel. Would you care to sit with me?'

I sat down.

'Of course I remember you. We talked and talked and I asked you how

* *My Fill of Days* (London: Faber & Faber, 1937) pp. 183–4. Editor's title.

to get rid of the body. I used you in *Dorian Gray*, but I don't think you would be easy to blackmail. Ion! In the days when I made phrases I called Ion "exquisitely corrupt".'

We talked for more than two hours, on crimes and punishments, on the management of gaols in England, on poems and poets, and on science. I wish to record the impression for which I was least prepared. Oscar Wilde was a man of very wide information and interests, and of commanding intelligence. When I got up to go I asked him to dine with us at night.

'No!' he said, 'Your friends would not stand it. I am going back to my little inn where they don't know me. Good-bye; thank you.' I never saw him again.

### NOTE

Sir Peter Chalmers Mitchell (1864–1945), British zoologist.

1. In Fontainebleau, a town in northern France about 35 miles south-east of Paris. It is famous for the magnificent palace which stands just outside the town in a park-like clearing of the Forest of Fontainebleau. The palace was a summer residence for many kings, and the scene of Napoleon's abdication in 1814.

# Oscar Wilde Loved My Mother*

Jack Smithers

And Oscar Wilde; what shall I say, when so many have spoken? Frank Harris's picture of him[1] is, in my opinion, perfectly true, but there are gaps in the story, and those gaps could be filled up by Bedford Square.[2] I wonder if Harris knew that Wilde was in love with my mother, and that he had been fool enough to tell her so, and that she first laughed at him, afterwards ordering him from the house, and that all that night he lay on the doorstep to sleep. Even I, as a child, knew that Wilde was what he was, and that his main source of income was by cadging and scrounging from his friends, who hoped to recoup their donations by securing some of his possible future work, which work only materialized in small, insufficient quantities. Any work that did materialize was sold many times to different people, and many times Wilde should have been in prison for offences in addition to

* *The Early Life & Vicissitudes of Jack Smithers* (London: Martin Secker, 1939) pp. 18–23. Editor's title.

those he committed and for which he suffered. He worked when he came out of Reading Gaol, but gradually fell off work, due solely to being unable to obtain any further advances from my father, who at last insisted on work being delivered before payment.

My father never liked Wilde very much, for there was that about Wilde which did not harmonize with a practical business man. Robbie Ross first introduced Wilde after he had been released from gaol, and broached the question of publishing his works, and incidentally Ross had a finger in the pie of all these works. Ross was a friend of my father's and not until years later did my father realize what a fraud Ross was. Wilde had plenty of money from his own resources, but this was not enough, or rather would not last long enough for the extravagant life of sheer idleness in which he lived. My father advanced him hundreds of pounds, fully expecting that he would work and earn them. *The Ballad of Reading Gaol* certainly brought in some remuneration to both, but where Wilde scored was in the continual sale of the same thing to many friends. For instance, the copyright of the *Ballad* was bought by my father just before Wilde's death. I was well informed at the time of my father's death that the *Ballad* copyright had been sold many times, to different people, all of whom had paid Wilde, so that if this was so, then the owner would apparently be hard to find; yet surely the first buyer was the owner. The account by Frank Harris of the sale of *Mr. and Mrs. Daventry*[3] is true in every detail, in fact, all the details of this fraud are not recorded. This play was not the only fraud that Wilde perpetrated on gullible friends. He had sold for cash *all* his copyrights to his publisher, my father, and later sold them again to others. Anything and everything to get money, no matter who suffered in the process.

I have said that Wilde was not a friend of my father's; this will be understood in the sense of the relativity of friendship and its meaning. My father helped him as no other man had done. The beginning of this unhappy friendship was Ross's begging and pleading to my father that Wilde was a genius whose literary works should be published despite the notoriety of the author; in fact, it was put by Ross that the notoriety would enhance sales enormously, quite apart from the merit of the *Ballad* itself. My father demurred, yet in generosity was persuaded to publish the *Ballad*. As it was, from a publisher's point of view, the market value of the *Ballad* was nil, in fact it was, if one takes into account the then state of society with reference to Wilde's imprisonment and offence, positively dangerous for any publisher to touch anything of Wilde's, and in certain sections of society even to mention his name. However, my father was persuaded and *The Ballad of Reading Gaol* was published. He had not reckoned on the morbidness of humanity, the morbid side of those who will stand outside a house where a murder has been committed although nothing is to be seen, and so the sales streamed in from two sources of interest. One from the morbid and sensational aspects of Queensbury [*sic.*] Trial, Wilde's downfall, his release, and the immediate publication of the poem, the other from literary people, those who recognized, despite the moral offence of the author, the merit of the *Ballad*. Many of these bought openly; many did not, they sneaked in to buy when no one was looking. Some even came to our house to buy at night. There was yet another little stream, those who bought the *Ballad*, and this was very amusing to the family, because they thought it was a trifle *outré*, a trifle obscene; their disappointment was rather amusing.

I will not weary readers with regard to the further publications of Wilde, which my father undertook, all the plays with the exception of *Lady Windermere's Fan*, for the facts are public property. He was cultivated for his work and was never really intimate with us. He visited Bedford Square frequently and never left without asking for money, and usually getting it. His works were saleable, and so my father tried to get him to work in a business-like manner, allowing for the possible inspiration period of the artistic temperament in Wilde. Unlike Beardsley, who could produce work to order, and did so, Wilde could not, he had to intermingle work with play and more play than work. In fact, if Wilde was in funds he would not do a stroke until almost, if not quite 'broke.' And even then, he would beg and cadge; this begging did not fail him at any time, for he was of the type hard to refuse despite his faults, but sometimes the begging, or rather its results would be insufficient to supply his expensive tastes and then work had to be done to augment matters.

On reading through Harris's life of Wilde, one is struck by Wilde's complex nature. It is recorded that all men of genius have faults, personal faults and weaknesses. This one for women, that one for drink and so on. This is as it should be, for a genius is but a specialist, and made of clay like all men. His speciality may be music, painting, writing and so on, yet society subconsciously places the genius on a pedestal, and cannot realize or wilfully close their minds to the faults of their genius. Not many have passed through the depths of humiliation as did Wilde, yet, and this is the surprising part of it, he did not realize that the humiliation lay in his offence and offences; he accepted the humiliation as being objective, in that it brought him to the lack of applause, of comforts, and the general good-for-nothing life which he led. It has been said that Dowson was dirty, and neglected himself. Be it so, at least he worked for his bread, and his dissolute life was his own. With Wilde, his dissolute life was not his own, for he threw the burden on other people. Utterly selfish, idle, a thief and cadger to boot. Perhaps I shall be chided for calling him such names, yet what would you have in one who, professing friendship, would sell you something for much money which you had laboured for, which he had already sold to others. Is this not thieving? Although I have suffered in this world, I am not in the least bitter. I do not chide Wilde because he robbed my father and others, but because there are those who would gloss over these things that Wilde may attain to a false position. Let it be said that Wilde was woefully weak, for Ross egged him on to many things. Wilde was weak, in that he had no masculinity, he was not wholly man; he was mostly feminine, his homosexual instincts being gratified quite unashamedly, and as he thought quite rightly, from a moral point of view.

When Wilde found that it was easier to beg from his friends and live an easy life, he ceased to work; the stories of his being unable to work through the thoughts of his imprisonment tormenting him, are just so much bunk. Nothing tormented Wilde, all he worried about was to scheme whom he should 'touch' next, and for how much, until at the last he even ceased to reckon in terms of 'how much,' but went all out for what he could get. When my father realized that no more work was forthcoming he saw Wilde and bought his copyrights, every one of them, and paid Wilde cash for them. He found that some of these had been sold already.

I would say but one word more, and that is, Frank Harris was a friend of my father's, though he was not liked very much by my mother, for he had this one fault which at times was very disconcerting; in mixed company, and generally important company outside the pale of Bedford Square, he would come out with some dirty remark apt to embarrass some people; also he had a habit of telling you just what he thought of you. Otherwise he was sound; rough, yes, but thoroughly sound, and from my own knowledge of the state of affairs at that time, and from what I have heard between my father and mother in conversation, and also from others, I believe that Frank Harris's picture of Wilde is true in detail. This is not a matter of 'insulting the dead' but of putting things in the place where they belong.

## NOTES

Jack Smithers, son of Wilde's publisher Leonard Smithers.

1. Frank Harris, *Oscar Wilde: His life and Confessions*, 2 vols (London, 1916). For a note on Harris see p. 426.

2. 6A Bedford Square, where the Smitherses lived.

3. *Mr. and Mrs. Daventry* by Frank Harris, based on a scenario by Oscar Wilde, was first produced at the Royalty Theatre, London, in the winter of 1900. Wilde outlined the plot of this play in a letter to George Alexander sent from Worthing in August 1894. The final play, however, was written by Harris. See H. Montgomery Hyde, 'Introduction', *Mr. and Mrs. Daventry; A Play in Four Acts by Frank Harris. Based on the Scenario by Oscar Wilde* (London: The Richards Press, 1956) pp. 7–43; and T. H. Bell, 'Oscar Wilde's Unwritten Play', *The Bookman* (New York, LXXI, no. 2 (Apr-May 1930) 139–50.

# After the *Débâcle**

Nellie Melba

It was at Gladys de Grey's[1] house in Paris that I first met Oscar Wilde. I had never seen anything in the least like Wilde before (we did not seem to breed that type in Australia) – and my memory of him is firstly the inimitable wit and brilliance of his conversation, and secondly a strange, almost *macabre* element in his character which made me feel always a little uneasy when he was in the room.

When I entered the room where I was first to meet him, I had a momentary impression either that I had interrupted a reading of poetry or that some dreadful scene had just occurred, for nobody was talking except a large heavy-jowled man, of a sallow and unhealthy appearance, clad in a frock coat, with a large bunch of violets in his buttonhole. I soon learnt that this was Wilde, and that while he was talking, the rest of us were expected to be silent. However, nobody minded, for as long as that brilliant fiery-coloured chain of words fell from his coarse lips, one felt it would be almost an impertinence to interrupt. If only he had had a Boswell, what a treasure we might have inherited.

Most of his wit I have forgotten, but one of the first things he ever said to me was: 'Ah, Madame Melba! I am the Lord of Language, and you are the Queen of Song, and so I suppose I shall have to write you a sonnet.' He never wrote the sonnet, although he wrote me some charming letters – lost long ago – and often came to see me. If I happened to be out, I could always tell when he had been, by the quantity of cigarettes which were afterwards discovered in the fire-place. In fact, so insatiable was his appetite for cigarettes that he used to have his pockets stuffed with cigarette-cases. I counted no less than six once – gold, silver and leather – and soon saw the reason for them, for he would light a cigarette, take two puffs and then throw it away, and light another five minutes later.

I think Wilde used to reserve his best stories for the public, but a thing he said once to me lingers in my memory, because, as one knew later, it was terribly true. He had been talking to me about his little sons. 'I was telling them stories last night,' he said, 'of little boys who were naughty and who made their mothers cry, and what dreadful things would happen to them

* *Melodies and Memories* (London: Thornton Butterworth, 1925) pp.74–5. Editor's title.

unless they became better, and do you know what one of them answered? He asked me what punishment could be reserved for naughty papas who did not come home till the early morning, and made mother cry far more?'

My last meeting with Wilde was terrible in its contrast to those happy times. I was walking one morning along the streets of Paris, three years after his *débâcle*, when there lurched round the corner a tall shabby man, his collar turned up to his neck, a hunted look in his eyes. I was about to pass on, when he stopped.

'Madame Melba – you don't know who I am? I'm Oscar Wilde,' he said,'and I'm going to do a terrible thing. I'm going to ask you for money.'

I could hardly bear to look at him, not from hatred but from shame and pity. I took all I had from my purse – about ten louis – and he quickly took it – almost snatched it – muttered a word of thanks and was gone. I never saw him again.

## NOTE

Dame Nellie Melba, stage name of Helen Porter Mitchell (1861–1931), Australian operatic soprano.
  1. Constance Gladys (1859–1917) married the fourth Earl of Lonsdale in 1878. After his death in 1882 she married Lord de Grey. Wilde dedicated *A Woman of No Importance* to her.

# Oscar Wilde*

### Augustus John

Rothenstein, who was not without a decided streak of romanticism himself, once suggested that he would like to play the part of Vautrin to my Lucien de Rubempré! Neither of us would have been suitably cast in these rôles. He used to talk of his friend Oscar Wilde, and quoted this wit's *mot*, 'The death of Lucien was the greatest tragedy of my life.' Wilde was now at large, and Rothenstein proposed a visit to Paris where he was to be found. Accordingly, the Vattetot expedition concluded, Will and Alice Rothenstein, Charles Conder and myself proceeded thither to pass a week or two, largely in the company of the distinguished reprobate. I had heard a lot about Oscar, of course, and on meeting him was not in the least disappointed, except in one respect: prison discipline had left one, and apparently only one, mark on him, and that not irremediable: his hair was

* *Chiaroscuro; Fragments of Autobiography* (London: Jonathan Cape, 1952) pp. 53–5.

cut short . . . We assembled first at the Café de la Régence. Warmed up with a succession of Maraschinos, the Master began to coruscate genially. I could only listen in respectful silence, for did I not know that 'little boys should be obscene and not heard'? In any case I could think of nothing whatever to say. Even my laughter sounded hollow. The rest of the company, better trained, were able to respond to the Master's sallies with the proper admixture of humorous deprecation and astonishment: 'My *dear* Oscar . . . !' Conder alone behaved improperly, pouring his wine into his soup and so forth, and drawing upon himself a reproof: 'Vine leaves in the hair should be *beautiful*, but such childish behaviour is merely *tiresome*.' When Alice Rothenstein, concerned quite unnecessarily for my reputation, persuaded me to visit a barber, Oscar, on seeing me the next day, looked very grave: laying his hand on my shoulder, 'You should have consulted me,' he said, 'before taking this important step.' Although I found Oscar thoroughly amiable, I got bored with these séances and especially with the master's entourage, and was always glad to retire from the rather oppressive company of the uncaged and now manless lion, to seek with Conder easier if less distinguished company.

The Monarch of the Dinner-table seemed none the worse for his recent misadventures and showed no sign of bitterness, resentment or remorse. Surrounded by devout adherents, he repaid their hospitality by an easy flow of practised wit and wisdom, by which he seemed to amuse himself as much as anybody. The obligation of continual applause I, for one, found irksome. Never, I thought, had the face of praise looked more foolish.

Wilde seemed to be an easy-going sort of genius, with an enormous sense of fun, infallible bad taste, gleams of profundity and a romantic apprehension of the Devil. A great man of inaction, he showed, I think, sound judgment when in his greatest dilemma he chose to sit tight (in every sense) and await the police, rather than face freedom in the company of Frank Harris, who had a yacht with steam up waiting for him down the Thames. I enjoyed his elaborate jokes, had found his *De Profundis* sentimental and false, the *Ballad* charming and ingenious, and *The Importance of Being Earnest* about perfect. When I read *The Picture of Dorian Gray* as a boy, it made a powerful and curiously unpleasant impression on me, but on re-reading it since, I found it highly entertaining. By that time it had become delightfully dated.

One evening Conder, Wilde, Bibi la Purée and I foregathered in the old seventeenth-century Café Procope. Bibi had been the devoted friend and factotum of Verlaine. He was indeed a strange bird. A member of the underworld, he traded in other people's umbrellas. When Verlaine died, Bibi followed the funeral cortége to the cemetery, weeping copiously all the way, but, combining business with burial, he returned, it was said, with a sheaf of his favourite stock-in-trade under his arm. No umbrella-user myself, I liked Bibi and enjoyed his company. He looked like an undernourished and fugitive Voltaire: bat-like, he was only seen to flit at night; a figure from Toulouse de Lautrec's sketch-book.

Now enters a superb specimen of blond manhood. It is Robert Sherard. As he approaches Oscar rises, and without a word, leaves the building. Sherard had been staunch champion of Wilde, one of the few who stood by him in his trouble. He only got snubbed for his pains. Oscar had said: '*Dear* Robert is *wonderful, quite* the *worst* writer in the *world*, but alas! he defends me at the *risk of my life!*' Sherard, addressing himself to me, denounced his former hero whose complete works, autographed and inscribed, he offered to present me with; but 'Not one of them is worth a damn,' he assured me. Taking him at his word, I declined the gift. Moving from one *boite de nuit* to another, with a young woman of my fancy in attendance, it was not till the first gleams of dawn appeared that we dispersed.

## NOTE

Augustus John (1878–1961), English painter, muralist, and print-maker, known primarily for his portraits, which vigorously characterised many of the political and artistic luminaries of his time.

# A Reminiscence of 1898*

### Wilfred Hugh Chesson

In 1894 I saw a manuscript by a very well-known woman author lying – a new and purchased commodity – upon the table of a famous publisher. The publisher was a liberal in politics and religion; his catalogue, impressively comprehensive, almost declared him to be the patron of Thought, pure, unspecified, unadjectived. The publisher turned over the preliminary pages of the manuscript and read these words:

To Oscar Wilde, with admiration.

'I'm not going to print that,' he said, and a faithful pencil chained to his person pounced upon the offending dedication and slew it.

That incident was the first which disturbed my view of Wilde as a young man's ideal, happy and secure in his free thought and originality. Hitherto he had been almost a humorous nursery figure, over whom Paterfamilias uttered a tolerant 'Pooh,' deeming his hedonism to be as rootless as most men's Christianity. Wilde had worn his hair long and curly, and his

* *The Bookman* (New York), xxxiv (December 1911), 389–94.

somewhat sudden sacrifice of its Postlethwaitian excess was audibly noticed, in his presence, by a girl to whom Wilde said, 'It was a pity, wasn't it?' This anecdote, a trifle insipid, is typical of those anecdotes from which the British public obtained an idea of Wilde, unjust to his power, but favourable to his liberty. Indeed, just after his death, a journalist employed the sieve, which I will designate his memory, to remember that the best of Wilde's wit was expressed when he said: 'I was disappointed by the Atlantic.'

Even in my own home (which in 1894 was No.5 in the street in which Wilde resided when he was not in London hotels or elsewhere) – even in that thoughtful dwelling Wilde was closely identified with the aesthetic bridegroom, whose intense bride adjured him to 'live up' to their six-mark teapot. He was an iconoclast who passed with the crowd as a comedian.

After 16 Tite Street, Chelsea, had been ransacked and despoiled to pay his creditors, a resident of 5 Tite Street, Chelsea, entered a bookshop in the adjacent Queen's Road. That resident was I. There I bought Wilde's beribboned Bible, some leaves of his MSS., the copy of Shakespeare's Sonnets which he had studied before writing 'Mr. W. H.,' a private copy of *Duchess of Padua* and a corrected copy of *Vera the Nihilist*, a tragedy which he wrote when he was eighteen. The find was a happy one, enabling me to penetrate into his workshop. Among the pencilled marginalia of *Vera* I found this variant on an epigram attributed to Sir Robert Walpole: 'Every man has his price – but he was really quite expensive.' In *The Duchess of Padua* this witticism reappears in blank verse: 'Why every man among them has his price, although, to do them justice, some of them are quite expensive.'

In 1898 I wrote to Wilde, offering him the plays as a gift. His reply[1] reached me in Paris. It told me that his name was henceforth Sebastian Melmoth, and I saw that he had borrowed from a horrible romance which half Europe once admired, but which he was too modern to care much about. I mean *Melmoth the Wanderer*, by Charles Maturin, a connection of Wilde's family.

Wilde's Paris address was Hôtel d'Alsace, Rue des Beaux Arts, and there I delivered *The Duchess of Padua* and some leaves of his MSS.[2] He was staying, however, at l'Idée, Perreaux, Nogent-sur-Marne, and thence he sent me an invitation to breakfast.

On July 5, 1895 – a perfect summer day – I saw for the first time, except in *Punch*, the tall and debonair poet and wit, who, in adversity, had entered my Pantheon. He awaited me at the gate of the courtyard of l'Idée – an unaffected Englishman, stalwart in homespun.

'I am correcting the proofs of a play,' he said, *The Importance of Being Earnest*.'[3] He gave good Irish weight, without roll, to the syllable 'port,' and I was amused, for I knew that he was throwing the play into the title.

We sat *vis-à-vis* at a round table in the courtyard, and I noticed the massiveness of his hair, and thought how different was its thick but not wavy abundance from the operatic idea of flowing locks. I hoped, as my eyes fell on his proofs, on a table near us, that he felt creative and eager for art. I named a man who borrowed his style in affecting to satirise it, and asked if such a person were not enough to irritate him into the mood for writing more novels and plays.

'It is dreadful, is it not?' he said, *à propos* the imitations of him thrown upon the market. 'Of course I can write, but I have lost the joy of writing'.

I praised the future, and he said piously, 'I do not doubt that there are as wonderful things in my future as they are in my past.'

I told him my impression of *The Ballad of Reading Gaol*. 'Ah! I had to write that,' he said, as if it came as naturally as the eloquent letter upon children in Reading Gaol, which appeared in *The Daily Chronicle* after his release.[4] 'I am glad,' I said, 'that you allowed yourself a bad rhyme. "We banged the tins and bawled the hymns" is so perfectly out of tune.' He said he had thought of revising the line, but a friend had persuaded him to retain it. He thought the press had noticed the poem 'very sweetly,' and quoted a phrase by Mr. Arthur Symons – 'the unseen violence upon souls.'[5] 'I should love to have written it,' he said. This unseen violence was the only personal suffering in prison which he spoke about.

'Once,' he said, 'while we were exercising, a man behind me said, "This is a strange place to meet Dorian Gray in!" "Not Dorian Gray," I said, "but Lord Henry Wotton."' Lord Henry, in *The Picture of Dorian Gray*, is Dorian's instructor in pleasure. 'This man,' added Wilde, 'had mastered, as we all had to, the art of talking without moving the lips. He said, 'I was at all your first nights, and I was at your trials.'

Wilde spoke with kindness of the associates of C.3.3., and here and there admired. 'Have you ever noticed a thief's hands?' he asked, 'how beautiful they are? How fine and delicate at the tips? They must be fine and delicate to take the watch from your pocket without your knowing.' His own hands were large and thick, and one of them was adorned by a scarab as big as sixpence. 'They say it is unlucky to wear it,' he said; 'but it is thousands of years old. I kept it when the rest went.'

He told me that, after his release (1897), he went to a palmist in Paris. She looked at his hands and said, 'I am puzzled. By your line of life you died two years ago. I cannot explain the fact except by supposing that since then you have been living on your line of imagination.'

Having some knowledge of the chiromantic art, I looked at his left hand. 'Here,' I said, indicating a horizontal under the little finger, 'is the line of your marriage.'

'That, too, was a fatality,' he murmured.

Of two prison governors with whom he had to do, he said that the former was not able to enjoy his breakfast unless some one was punished before he ate it; of the other he said, 'He was the most Christ-like man I ever met.'

Snatcher, a lively dog lent to him by Mr. Rowland Strong,[6] was present and eagerly snapped up a morsel which Wilde rendered more appetising by christening it Dreyfus. He told me that he knew Esterhazy,[7] and said that that remarkable man had said that at the age of thirteen he had a profound conviction that he would never be happy again as long as he lived. 'And it was quite true; he never was,' Wilde added.

We went for a long walk by the pleasant river Marne; and I was touched when the exile said, 'Might not his be a bit of the Thames?' Delightful residences rose on our right, and at a tall gate, which suggested rather than disclosed one of them, Wilde paused and said, 'That is what I like, just to stand and peep through the bars. It would be better than being in paradise to stand like this, catch a glimpse as now, and want to go in. The reality would sure to be disappointing.'

We talked literature, and he told me stories from Guy de Maupassant with enchanting energy. Thus it was that I heard of the two malcontents who, after all their grumbling, preferred to be shot rather than divulge the password to the besiegers of Paris. He said that he had been struck by the power of a drama he had seen acted in a French theatre patronised both by criminals who wished to see an actor in a criminal rôle and men of letters interested in an artistic production. The point of the drama was the betrayal of a ferocious murderer by a timid light of love with whom he spent his last hours of freedom. There is a reward for his capture, and the girl is pressed by a hag to earn it. The murderer is taken in his sleep, and as, hopelessly overpowered, he is borne away, his hatred of his betrayer goes out in one venomous look. She sees it, and his impotence, the absolute certainty of his doom, are nothing to her. 'J'ai peur, j'ai peur!'[8] she shrieks, and the curtain falls. Wilde delivered these words with a force that went into the marrow of my bones.

The subject of fear made him talk of the guillotine, which he had seen operate in the early morning. 'I have seen the victim look green with fright,' he said. 'They are kind to him up to the last minute. He may smoke a cigarette as he goes to the Place de la Roquette, but once there, what a change! They are on him like tigers, and his head is thrust into the groove under the knife as if he were not a man at all.'

He spoke of the Morgue. 'It is a dignified place. I cannot understand why people should object to go to it. There is nothing horrible in death. Death is solemn. Now waxworks are horrible, if you like. I remember,' he proceeded, 'going to the Morgue after seeing a brilliant function – all colour and music – at Notre Dame. A woman of the lowest class was on one of the slabs. She was having her day. All Paris might look at her gravely. She was no longer despised.'

He grew gay when, in addition to finding a franc for a cannette of beer, I found matches for our cigarettes. 'You are perfect,' he said. 'It was good when you produced money, and now you produce matches. What more can you ask of life?'

More, of course, could be asked, but my requisition waited while he told me of a silver matchbox he once had. It was stolen by a Neapolitan boy.

Taxed with the theft, the culprit confessed. 'You must give it up,' said Wilde. 'I cannot,' was the reply. 'It is too beautiful.' 'Come, come, where is it?' insisted the owner of the matchbox. 'I have hidden it,' said the boy. 'Every night I look at it before I sleep. I have never been so happy.' At last Wilde pleaded that the Matchbox was a souvenir from a dear friend. The boy was sceptical. There must be no fibbins. 'Are you sure?' Wilde was sure, upon his honour, and the boy's heart was moved.

We dined in the courtyard of l'Idée, and talked more literature. 'Do you know,' asked Wilde, 'who destroyed the MS. of Carlyle's *French Revolution*?' 'The servant of John Stuart Mill,' I replied, as informed by biographies. 'It was finer than that,' said he. It was Mrs. Mill. She read it and saw at once that if it was published, the first name in nineteenth century English literature could not be John Stuart Mill. It would be Carlyle. Think of it. What servant could destroy the MS. of a whole volume in lighting a kitchen fire? She could only burn a few pages at a time, and be found out long before the end. No, it was Mrs. Mill. But her heroism was wasted. She had not reckoned on Carlyle's marvellous memory. How great he was! He made history a song for the first time in our language. He was our English Tacitus.'

He spoke with enthusiasm of Dickens. Micawber, Pecksniff, Mrs. Gamp, flitted before us. 'There have been no such grotesques since the Gothic gargoyles,' he said, and he quoted the passage in *Martin Chuzzlewit* which compares the rusty gowns and other garments hanging from Sarah Gamp's bed to 'guardian angels' watching her in her sleep.

He spoke with affectionate amusement of Mr. J. B. Yeats, Sr. 'Do you know how he became a painter? It was so simple and natural. He was a thriving barrister, when one day he came down to breakfast and said, "Children, I am tired of the law, and shall become a painter." They said, "Papa is going to be a painter," and were quite happy.'

'Could he paint?' I asked.

'Not in the least; that was the beauty of it,' said Wilde.

He could, however, as I discovered when I was in the dining-room of Mr. and Mrs. Hickson and saw his portrait of Katharine Tynan's father.

Wilde expressed much amusement at Mr. W. M. Rossetti's family publications. He understood, I know not with what authority, that Christina Rossetti's washing book had been given to the public, and supposed that historical piety could go no further. He diverted me by a parody of Mr. Rossetti's account of his brother's misunderstanding with a bird. The poet, it appears, was much annoyed, and explained that a thrush was saying ill-natured things about him in the garden. 'But as far as I could gather,' Wilde represented Mr. Rossetti as remarking, 'the bird's observations had nothing to do with my brother.'[9]

'Tell me about "Jameson's Ride,"' he said. 'I am told it was very funny,' and I quoted a line here and there from Mr. Austin's refreshing song. He begged for a copy of it, and it is on my conscience that I never sent him one.

By way of conversation I wondered how the laureateship was supportable in a sleet of ridicule. 'Vanity, my dear sir,' he replied. 'Vanity, the invulnerable breast-plate of man.'

'Why didn't they make Kipling the laureate?' he asked. 'It would have been such a change, so artistic. There was Tennyson, with his idyls, his well-bred and dainty muse, and here is Kipling, who makes his muse say, "Go to hell."' He commented sarcastically on Mr. Kipling's encyclopaedic method. 'I object to know all about cod fishing,' he remarked. He spoke with enthusiasm of some of Mr. Kipling's poetry, and quoted two well-known passages for the sake of their metaphor. 'An' the dawn comes up like thunder' was one of them. The other he gave as one who rejoices. 'He trod the ling like a buck in spring, and he looked like a lance in rest.'

Swinburne he termed 'mere froth of the sea,' meaning high praise, perhaps. He said he was the first English poet to sing divinely the song of the flesh. We did not speak of Donne, Carew, Herrick, who were so much more minute in their praise of women. He spoke with aversion of Matthew Arnold's snippety sonnets: the adjective is mine. He said that he read through the whole of Dante's *Divina Commedia* in prison. 'You can imagine,' he said, 'how I tasted every word.' He recommended me to read it with Longfellow's rhymed translation, preferring it to Carey's dull blank verse. I mentioned Verhaaren, and he immediately said, 'Oh! now you mention the greatest living poet.'

He spoke of old friends – of Mr. Frank Harris,[10] a man who does not think that a murmur of 'poor fellow' suffices to attest his sympathy for a friend in trouble; of 'dear Max,'[11] whose caricature of him I cannot imagine. Of Sir Charles Dilke[12] he said: 'I've only one fault to find with Dilke; he knows too much about everything. It is hard to have a good story interrupted by a fact. I admit accuracy up to a certain point, but Dilke's accuracy is almost a vice.'

Of Henley,[13] whom I found a sympathetic critic, he spoke more harshly than of any one except a prison governor. 'Have you noticed,' he observed, 'that if a man has once been an editor he can always be an editor? The fact that a paper has a way of dying when he is on it is of the smallest importance. He is in demand before the corpse is buried. Here is Henley. He kills the *Scots Observer*. Hey presto! he is made editor of the *New Review*. Then the *New Review* dies.'[14]

He had not yet done with the author of *London Voluntaries;* his next remark was a voluntary of sensational vigour: 'The man,' he said, 'is simply eaten up with envy of any man whom he has not discovered. Fame exists on this condition: Henley must have made it.'[15] For me, of whom Henley had written that he read me 'with unwonted interest,' this was simple Esperanto, and I was pleased when Wilde descanted upon envy as distinct from henvy. It is very wrong; it is unintellectual, he said.

The night was warm, and we stayed in the darkened courtyard. The eyes of Oscar Wilde grew very bright and he gazed with devotional rapture into his own day.

'My work was a joy to me' he said. 'I wrote *Dorian Gray* in three weeks. When my plays were on, I drew a hundred pounds a week! I delighted in every minute of the day.'

He told me to read *In Mes Communions*, by George Eekhond, a story of friendship ending in disaster worse than his, and he spoke that story to me in thrilling English, which returned to me when I read its French, and is in me yet.

The implacable Old Bailey rose before me as I looked at him, and again I waited for a verdict which would be upon Art as well as a man. I remembered a verdict which set Wilde free in an atmosphere of dread, and I remembered Lockwood's stentorian oration on a Saturday when I waited alone in a house of the street where he had lived. I remembered the brute force of judgment which banged the books of Scott and Dickens upon this man's writing. I remembered his infernal Sabbath after the second jury had spoken. I remembered a thriving comedy which Mr. Alexander had put on without its author's name, and I remembered, as one remembers rhetoric, that Lockwood was dead and that Mr. Alexander had known what it was to be criminally slandered and to encounter the professionally sceptical gaze of a magistrate.

I gave Wilde the gleams of my thought; he was indifferent. 'When I came out,' he said, 'my friends presented me with a box full of beautiful books – Keats, and so on. They are at Naples. There they lie.' He looked at me. 'You worry too much: never worry'; and he talked again like an habitué of Hatchard's. 'I do not approve of the shape of the *Pseudonym Library*,' he said. 'It is too narrow. It is unjust to a good style to print it on a tiny page. Imagine turning Pater over rapidly. It is violence.'

I reminded him of his relative, the Rev. E. J. Hardy, one of the *Pseudonym* publisher's great successes. 'Ah, yes, he has got on. I reviewed *How to be Happy though Married* for the *Pall Mall*, and I called it "The Murray of Matrimony and the Baedeker of Bliss."[16] I used to say that I should have received a royalty for that phrase.'

I could not refrain from returning to his own work. While we were out I saw him as the big friend of a pretty French child, whom he had bought a toy for at a fair. I knew he was cut off from his own children. I knew that bright work could be a populous world for him in his lonely histrionic life. He told me in response that his work was in his head; he did not write it down. Then he related to me this parable:

'A man saw a being, which hid its face from him and he said, "I will compel it to show its face." It fled as he pursued, and he lost it, and his life went on. At last his pleasure drew him into a long room, where tables were spread for many, and in a mirror he saw the being whom he had pursued in youth. "This time you shall not escape me!" he cried, but the being did not try to escape, and hid its face no more. "Look!" it cried, "and now you will know that we cannot see each other again, for this is the face of your own soul, and it is horrible.'''

The flash of rhetoric over, he grew sympathetic and looked at my fingers persuasively. 'You worry too much,' he said. 'Never worry.' I touched on religion, which I considered a killjoy and painmaker, as I do now. I recalled to him his remark to Wilberforce that the chief argument against Christianity is the style of St. Paul. 'I fear he tempted me,' he said. 'There is really something very artistic about Christianity,' he said. 'You go into Hyde Park, and a wonderful sentence comes to you on the wind. "What shall it profit a man if he gain the whole world and lose his own soul."'

I spoke of life in spirit. He became indignant 'There is no hell but this,' he said; 'a body without a soul, or a soul without a body.'

It was about ten of the night when he went with me to the railway station. I said that his life was a harmony of two extremes, very rare and I thought very valuable. With a level suavity that, like the lawns of Oxford, had centuries of culture behind it, he replied, 'Yes, artistically it is perfect; socially most inconvenient.' We parted on a gay note. 'It does not matter what class you go up into Paris.'

## NOTES

1. This letter is not included in *The Letters of Oscar Wilde*.

2. *The Duchess of Padua* was published by Methuen in 1908.

3. *The Importance of Being Earnest* was published by Leonard Smithers in 1899. Scarcely a review appeared in the press. 'I am sorry my play is boycotted by the press'—*The Letters of Oscar Wilde*, p. 782.

4. Oscar Wilde, 'The Case of Warder Martin', *Daily Chronicle* (London), (28 May 1897) p. 9.

5. Arthur Symons, '*The Ballad of Reading Gaol*', *The Saturday Review* (London), LXXXV (12 Mar 1898) 365–6.

6. For a note on Rowland Strong see p. 359.

7. Commandant Esterhazy (1847–1923), the man who forged the famous document, known as the *bordereau*, for which Captain Alfred Dreyfus was sentenced to exile on Devil's Island.

8. 'I'm scared, I'm scared!'

9. W. M. Rossetti's words are: 'The adjoining house was occupied by a musician, Mr. Malcolm Lawson, and some members of the family (Rossetti) fancied that there was a large and frequent amount of unnecessary noise from that house and its small grounds, audible both in his studio and in his garden, and annoying, and intended to annoy him.

'I remember there was once a thrush hard by, which, to my hearing, simply trilled its own lay on and off. My brother discerned a different note, and conceived that the thrush had been trained to ejaculate something insulting to him. Such is perverted fantasy – or I may rather infer – such is the outcome of chloral dosing.' – see *Dante Gabriel Rossetti: His Family Letters with a Memoir*, by William Michael Rossetti, 1895, Vol. I, p. 339.

10. For a note on Frank Harris see p. 426.

11. For a note on Max Beerbohm see p. 272.

12. Sir Charles Dilke (1843–1911), English writer and politician.

13. W. E. Henley (1849–1903), English man of letters, whose friendship with Wilde was short-lived.

14. The *Scots Observer* was a brilliant paper, keenly relished, though it had a tendency toward vituperativeness. An etymologist's errors would cause the *S. O.* reviewer to invoke the aid of the common hangman and the fire that burns.

15. On the other side: he did not know what jealousy was (James Fitzmaurice Kelly in the *Outlook*, 18 July, 1903.)

16. The title of Wilde's review, however, was 'A Handbook to Marriage', *The Pall Mall Gazette* (London), (18 November 1885) p. 6; reprinted in *Reviews and Miscellanies* (London: Methuen, 1908) pp. 36–8. Wilde said in his review: 'It is a complete handbook to an earthly Paradise, and its author may be regarded as the Murray of matrimony and Baedeker of bliss.' The author of the book reviewed, Rev. Edward John Hardy, was an assistant master at Portora Royal School, where Wilde was educated from 1864–1871. He married Sir William Wilde's niece. Wilde himself is referred to in Chapter xii of the book.

# The Latter Days of Oscar Wilde*

## Chris Healy

The statement that Oscar Wilde was one of the direct instruments in freeing Alfred Dreyfus[1] has been freely criticised. To the commonplace mind only commonplace things are possible. One critic, in particular, 'jibbed' at my remark that Wilde objected to meeting Zola[2] on the ground that the latter was the author of immoral books, and concludes with the remark that 'Wilde is understood to have become a reformed character, but he cannot be believed to have suddenly developed into a Mawworm.'

What the latter may be I do not know, but, perhaps even at the risk of disturbing some of my critic's family traditions, I am impelled to add some further facts about poor Wilde. 'English law is cruel and senseless,' once remarked a well-known barrister to me at the conclusion of a certain *cause célèbre*. 'Few of our judges admit a fact accepted by most medical men – that certain forms of crime should be treated by a lunacy specialist rather

* *Confessions of a Journalist* (London: Chatto & Windus, 1904) pp. 130–8.

than by a judge and jury.' Those who were best in a position to judge
recognised that, despite the splendour of his intellect, Oscar Wilde on one
point was as mad as the proverbial hatter. There are innumerable cases of
men whose sanity, in business and the ordinary walks of life, is beyond
suspicion, and who on one question are completely insane. I have in mind
a dear friend of my own, a brilliant chess-player, a consummate man of
affairs, who, despite his income of but a few hundreds a year, believes that
he could buy up Rothschild, Pierpont Morgan, Mackay, and Rockefeller,
and then have enough money left to repeat the process.

To the many Wilde was an unspeakable person, but to the few he was an
accomplished scholar and gentleman, suffering from one of the most
terrible and loathsome forms of insanity, which two years of prison life
increased rather than diminished. I met him in Paris a few weeks after he
finally left England, and his appearance was burnt in on my memory. A
tall, stalwart figure, with a face scored with suffering and a mistaken life.
The gray, wearied eyes, the mocking curves of the mobile mouth,
reminded me of Charles Reade's description of Thomas of Sarranza at the
time that he sat in the Fisherman's Seat – 'a *gentilhomme blasé*, a high-bred
and highly-cultivated gentleman who had done, and said, and seen, and
known everything, and whose body was nearly worn out.'

Wilde was then living in the Rue des Beaux Arts, under the name of
Sebastian Melmoth. He invited me to lunch, and we had déjeuner at a
little restaurant on the Boulevard St. Michel, where for over two hours he
talked with the same delightful insouciance which had characterized him
in his best days. Wilde detested coarse language or coarse conduct, and I
remember him moving his chair away from the vicinity of some students
who, with their Mimis and Marcelles, were talking in a strain that would
have made Rabelais blush. He talked lightly about his trial, but his face
lighted up with savage indignation when he spoke of his prison treatment.
Of one prison official he said: 'He had the eyes of a ferret, the body of an
ape, and the soul of a rat.' The chaplains he characterized as 'the silliest of
God's silly sheep,' and gave an instance of the kind of reading they select
for the prisoners under their charge. A man had been sentenced to seven
years' imprisonment, six months of which was to be endured in solitary
confinement. The book served out to him by the chaplain at—Prison was
'Sermons Delivered at—Prison to Prisoners under Sentence of Death.' I
had had the advantage of reading 'The Ballad of Reading Gaol' in
manuscript some days before I met the author, and I asked him whether he
intended to write further in the same vein.

'Do not ask me about it!' Wilde said with a sigh. 'It is the cry of Marsyas,
not the song of Apollo. I have probed the depths of most of the experiences
of life, and I have come to the conclusion that we are meant to suffer. There
are moments when life takes you, like a tiger, by the throat, and it was
when I was in the depths of suffering that I wrote my poem. The man's face
will haunt me till I die.'

The conversation drifted on to Aubrey Beardsley, who was then on the point of becoming a Catholic.

'I never guessed,' said Wilde, 'when I invented Aubrey Beardsley, that there was an atom of aught but pagan feeling in him.'

I happened to mention something that Herr Max Nordau had told me the day before on the subject of 'The Degenerates,' and on Nordau's firm belief that all men of genius were mad.[3]

'I quite agree with Dr. Nordau's assertion that all men of genius are insane,' said Wilde, 'but Dr. Nordau forgets that all sane people are idiots.'

He leaned back in his chair, lit a cigarette, and gazed reflectively at the beautiful scarab ring on his finger. 'I shall start working again, and trust to the generosity of the English people to judge it on its merits, and apart from their Philistine prejudices against myself. I do not acknowledge that I have ever been wrong . . . only society is stronger than I. Should the English people refuse my work, then I shall cross to America, a great country which has always treated me kindly. I have always been drawn towards America, not only because it has produced a very great poet – its only one – in Walt Whitman, but because the American people are capable of the highest things in art, literature, and life.'

'Do you not care for Longfellow, then?'

'Longfellow is a great poet only for those who never read poetry. But America is great because it is the only country in the world where slang is borrowed from the highest literature. I remember some years ago, when I was travelling out West, I was passing by a store when a cowboy galloped past. The man with me said: "Last night that fellow painted the town red." It was a fine phrase, and familiar. Where had I heard it? I could not remember, but the same afternoon, when I was taken to see the public buildings – the only ones in this place were the gaols and cemeteries – I was shown a condemned cell where a prisoner, who had been sentenced to death, was calmly smoking a cigarette and reading "The Divine Comedy" of Dante in the original. Then I saw that Dante had invented the phrase "painting the town red." Do you remember the scene where Dante, led by Virgil, comes to the cavernous depths of the place swept by a mighty wind, where are confined those who have been the prey of their passions? Two pale faces arise from the mist – the faces of Francesca da Rimini and her lover. "Who art thou?" cries Dante in alarm, and Francesca replies sadly: "We are those who painted the world red with our sin." It is only a great country which can turn the greatest literature into colloquial phrases.'

He bowed his head for a moment; then he murmured: 'When the greatest literary men of the world petitioned the English Government to treat me with less severity, the prison authorities allowed me, whilst I was lying in a hospital bed, to have one book to read. I chose the "Divine Comedy," and it saved my reason.'

There was one painful incident, however, associated with this petition, that Wilde never knew. François Coppée, the author of 'Pour la Couronne,' was asked to sign the petition. At first he refused, but when he was pressed to give his name to the movement to give Wilde better treatment by a well-known French actor who sincerely believed Wilde to be mad, Coppée grudgingly consented, and signed his name thus: 'François Coppée, member of the Society for the Prevention of Cruelty to Animals.'

Wilde laughed as he began to criticise, good-humouredly, some of his contemporaries. 'I look upon Zola,' he said, 'as a third-rate Flaubert. Zola is never artistic, and often disgusting. As to Flaubert, all I can say is, that whenever I enter a strange town I always order the "Confessions de St. Antoine" and a packet of cigarettes, and I am happy. I have never read any of Huysmans' works, but he must be a great artist, because he has selected a monastery as his retreat. It is delightful to see God through stained-glass windows.'

Then he referred to English writers, and his opinions on these I forbear from quoting, except in the case of Richard Le Gallienne.[4] 'Poor Richard!' he said. 'He is an absurdity, but, then, he is a graceful absurdity.' After a long talk, Wilde concluded: 'It would be useless on my part to tell you what I am going to do with my life. Popular authors – and by popular authors I mean authors who are talked about but never read – are in the habit at certain times of confiding about two columns of their future intentions to the newspapers. I cannot say what I am going to do with my life; I am wondering what my life is going to do with me. I would like to retire to some monastery – to some gray-stoned cell where I could have my books, write verses, and reverently smoke my cigarettes.'

I saw him frequently after this until he left for Naples. It was during this time that he suggested the clue which enabled Zola to successfully defend Dreyfus, and Maître Labori and Mathieu Dreyfus can attest the authenticity of this statement. The last time I saw Wilde he was kneeling in the Church of Nôtre Dame. The sun streamed through the windows, the organ was pealing a majestic chant, and his head was bowed, almost hidden. Perhaps some vision of what his life might have been came to him and scourged his soul anew. I only know that when I left him he was still kneeling before the altar, his face hidden by his hands. I heard of his new play being effusively accepted by Sara Bernhardt, who later on backed out of her offer, and this plunged Wilde into the depths of poverty. I also heard about another play – since produced in London with a well-known person's name attached to it as the author – being offered to an authoress famous for her epigrammatic powers. She was to pay Wilde a certain sum down, and a part of the royalty; but the lady in question indignantly refused, saying that to rob a writer of such a fine piece of work would be monstrous. Others were not so sympathetic – and Wilde never received his share. A few, a very few, of his old-time friends stood loyally by him, but he was a proud man, and suffered his privations in silence, with the same courage he had evinced in court by refusing to betray the high-placed associates of whom he was made the scapegoat.

The end of his meteoric career is too sad to be dealt with here. Suffice it to say that, if his terrible mania made him sin in the eyes of the world, he suffered no less terribly. Apart from this side of his character, he had a rare delicacy in the things of this world, and his remark that Zola was a writer of immoral books, to which my 'Mawworm' critic objected, was made in all sincerity. Those who really knew him made due allowance on his behalf, ignoring the maniac who had fallen under the ban of English displeasure, and recking only of the rare artist, the accomplished scholar, the greatest sonneteer in the world of poetry since the days of Rossetti and John Keats, and the kindly gentleman whose heart was a mine of generosity and good-nature. May his soul rest in peace and his sins be forgiven him!

## NOTES

Chris Healy, then a freelance Paris correspondent. See Wilde's reference to him in *The Letters of Oscar Wilde*, p. 706.

1. Alfred Dreyfus (1859–1935), French army officer who was convicted (1894) of treason and imprisoned (1895). Later investigation, forced (1898) largely by Émile Zola, proved that the papers on which he had been convicted were forged by Major Esterhazy and Lieut. Col. Henry.

2. Émile Zola (1840–1902), French novelist.

3. Max Nordau, 'Decadence and Aesthetes', *Degeneration* (London: Heinemann, 1895) pp. 319–22. On Wilde and Decadence see also William Aspenwall Bradley, 'What Is Decadence?" *The Bookman* (New York), XXXVII (June 1913) 431–8; G. K. Chesterton, 'Writing "Finis" to Decadence', *Independent* (Boston), LXXXIX (15 Jan 1917) 100; Russell M. Goldfarb, 'Late Victorian Decadence', *Journal of Aesthetics and Art Criticism*, XX (summer 1962) 369–73; Shane Leslie, 'Degeneracy or Decadence?', *National Review* (New York), XV (19 Nov 1963) 445–6; Paul Elmer More, 'A Naughty Decade: Oscar Wilde and Other Decadents of the Nineties', *The Nation* (New York), XCVIII (14 May 1914) 566–8 and (21 May 1914), 598–600; Clyde de L. Ryals, 'Toward a Definition of "Decadent" As Applied to British Literature of the Nineteenth Century', *Journal of Aesthetics and Art Criticism*, XVII (Sep 1958) 85–92; and Hugh E. M. Stutfield, 'Tommyrotics', *Blackwood's Edinburgh Magazine*, CLVII (June 1895) 833–45.

4. For a note on Richard Le Gallienne see p. 398.

# My Last Meeting with Oscar Wilde*

Laurence Housman

And so, from the non-popular standpoint, I had sufficient reason for putting on record my last meeting with so conspicuous a failure as Oscar Wilde. Our previous acquaintance, except by correspondence, had been very slight. Only once before had I met him at a friend's house. He was then at the height of his fame and success, and I an unknown beginner, still undecided whether to be book-illustrator or author. But I had recently published a short story,[1] with illustrations of my own, in the *Universal Review*; and a few minutes after our introduction Mr. Wilde turned and, addressing me for the first time, said: 'And when, pray, are we to have another work from your pen?'

Like most of his remarks, the enquiry was phrased with a certain decorative solemnity, in excess of what the occasion required; but the kindness and the courtesy of it were very real, and of course it pleased and encouraged me. I learned later that a certain descriptive phrase, 'The smoke of their wood-fires lay upon the boughs, soft as the bloom upon a grape,' had attracted him in my story; he had quoted it as beautiful, adding that one day he should use it himself, and, sure enough, in *The Picture of Dorian Grey*, I came upon it not long afterwards, slightly altered; and again I was pleased and complimented; for it meant that he had really liked something in my story, and had not praised merely to please.

I did not see him again to speak to, until we met in Paris some seven years later, the year before his death.

Upon his release from prison I had sent him my recently published book, *All-Fellows: seven legends of lower Redemption*, hoping that its title and contents would say something on my behalf, which, in his particular case, I very much wished to convey. A fortnight later a courteous and appreciative letter reached me from the south of France, telling me incidentally that by the same post had come a copy of *A Shropshire Lad*[2], sent with the good wishes of the author, whom he had never met. 'Thus, you and your brother,' he wrote, 'have given me a few moments of that rare thing called happiness.'

* *Echo de Paris; A Study from Life* (London: Cape, 1923) pp. 13–16. Editor's title.

From that time on I sent him each of my books as they appeared, and received letters of beautifully ornate criticism; and as I passed through Paris on my way back from Italy in the autumn of 1899, we met once more in the company of friends.

My memory of him upon that occasion inclines me to believe that those are right who maintain that as a personality he was more considerable than as a writer. The brilliancy of conversation is doubtfully reproduced in the cold medium of print, and I may have wholly failed to convey the peculiar and arresting quality of what, by word of mouth, sounded so well. But the impression left upon me from that occasion is that Oscar Wilde was incomparably the most accomplished talker I had ever met. The smoothflowing utterance, sedate and self-possessed, oracular in tone, whimsical in substance, carried on without halt, or hesitation, or change of word, with the quiet zest of a man perfect at the game, and conscious that, for the moment at least, he was back at his old form again: this, combined with the pleasure, infectious to his listeners, of finding himself once more in a group of friends whose view of his downfall was not the world's view, made memorable to others besides myself a reunion more happily prolonged than this selected portion of it would indicate.

But what I admired most was the quiet, uncomplaining courage with which he accepted an ostracism against which, in his lifetime, there could be no appeal. To a man of his habits and temperament – concious that the incentive to produce was gone with the popular applause which had been its recurrent stimulus – the outlook was utterly dark: life had already become a tomb. And it is as a 'monologue d'outre tombe' that I recall his conversation that day; and whether it had any intrinsic value or no, it was at least a wonderful expression of that gift which he had for charming himself by charming others.

Among the many things he touched on that day (of which only a few disjointed sentences now remain to me), one note of enthusiasm I have always remembered, coming as it did so strangely from him, with his elaborate and artificial code of values, based mainly not on the beauty of human character, but on beauty of form – when, with a sudden warmth of word and tone, he praised Mrs. Gladstone for her greatness and gentleness of heart: 'her beautiful and perfect charity' I think was the phrase he used, adding: 'But then, she was always like that.'

None of us knew her; but from that day on, the warmth and humility of his praise left an impression upon my mind, which a reading of her life only two years ago came to confirm. Perhaps – I like to think that it was possible – an expression of her 'beautiful and perfect charity' had come to him personally, so making her stand differently in his eyes from the rest of the world.

NOTES

Laurence Housman (1865–1959), English writer and illustrator. He first met Wilde at the studio of Ricketts and Shannon.

1. 'The Green Gaffer.'
2. By Laurence Housman's brother, Alfred Edward Housman (1859–1936).

# Oscar Wilde as a Symbolic Figure*

Richard Le Gallienne

My acquaintance with Oscar Wilde began in my pre-London days as a member of an audience in Birkenhead, the sister city to Liverpool, assembled to hear him lecture on his 'Impressions of America,' whence he had recently returned. He had not then published anything except his first volume of poems, and was known only as the 'apostle' of aestheticism, the prototype of Bunthorne in 'Patience,' a ridiculous, posturing figure, a fantastic laughing-stock, whom no one took seriously. And yet I am glad to record to the credit of that Birkenhead audience, that, after its first bewilderment, it forgot to laugh at him, and soon began laughing with him, and I remember how grateful I was to my father, the last man I expected to be impressed, for saying, as the lecture ended: 'Don't make any mistake. That man is no fool.'

At that time Wilde had abandoned his knee-breeches and was dressed in a sort of Georgian costume, with tight pantaloon trousers and a huge stock. His amber-coloured hair, naturally straight, was not very long, and was unashamedly curled and massively modelled to his head, somewhat suggesting a wig. His large figure, with his big loose face, grossly jawed, with thick, sensuous lips, and a certain fat effeminacy about him, suggested a sort of caricature Dionysius disguised as a rather heavy dandy of the Regency period. There was something grotesquely excessive about his whole appearance, and while he was in a way handsome, he made one think of an enormous doll, a preposterous, exaggerated puppet such as smile foolishly from floats at the Nice carnival. But his strong, humorous, haughty eyes, his good brow and fine nose must not be forgotten from the general effect, nor his superb and rather insolent *aplomb*,[1] which early

* *The Romantic '90s* (London and New York: G. P. Putnam's, 1926) pp. 181–200. Editor's title.

dominated his audience. And, of course, his wonderful golden voice, which he modulated with elaborate self-consciousness. Exotic as he was, he was at the same time something entirely different from the dilettante, lily-like 'aesthete' we had expected, and the great surprise about him was his impudent humour and sound common sense. That he should talk sense at all was a complete revelation. Bunthorne, indeed, had not remotely suggested anything like this boyish fun, or such searching yet laughable social criticism, and such reasonable ideas on all possible subjects. There was, too, an unquestionable fascination about the strange popinjay who said things all we youngsters had been dimly feeling, and who even won our parents into the involuntary admission that he was 'no fool.' It was only natural that, when one of these youngsters published a volume of poems of his own, he should send a copy to this friend of dreaming and rebellious youth, suddenly dropped out of the sky into that very British and humdrum Birkenhead; and that the flattering letter of acknowledgement which presently followed, in that exquisite handwriting of Wilde's which made English look beautiful as Greek, and the like of which had certainly never come through the Birkenhead mail before, should have had no little of the quality of a fairy tale. In that letter Wilde had asked me to come and take tea with him and Mrs. Wilde, when next I was in London, and it was not long after my arrival there that I found myself one spring afternoon on my way to '16 Tite Street, Chelsea,' a street that Whistler had already made famous.

I remember that my first feeling at seeing Wilde again was one of boyish disappointment. He didn't seem as 'romantic' as when I had seen him at Birkenhead. His Regency clothes had gone, and he wore a prosaic business suit of some commonplace cloth, tweeds I almost fear. His hair, too, was short and straight, no Dionysiac curls. Also I had a queer feeling of distaste, as my hand seemed literally to sink into his, which were soft and plushy. I never recall those lines in 'The Sphinx' – [2]

> Lift up your large black satin eyes,
> Which are like cushions where one sinks,

without thinking of Wilde's hands. However, this feeling passed off as soon as he began to talk. One secret of the charm of Wilde's talk, apart from its wit and his beautiful voice, was the evidently sincere interest he took in his listener and what he also had to say. It is seldom that a good talker can listen too, and for this reason even great talkers often end in being bores. Wilde was a better artist in this respect, though I am convinced that it was not merely art. With all his egoism, he had an unselfish sympathetic side to him which was well known to his friends, in whose affairs, particularly their artistic projects, he seemed entirely to forget his own. Even in his more elaborate flights of decorated talk, he was never a monopolist. He was always ready to stop and hear someone else. He had none of that impatient patience of some talkers, who seem only waiting till one's remarks are over to resume their own eloquence, as though we had never spoken. Such conversational amenity is a rare grace. With Wilde it came easily, for one reason, because of his intellectual curiosity. His interest in others was not a gossipy interest. What concerned him chiefly was their characters and minds, particularly what they were thinking, or, if they were artists, what they were doing. Naturally, this made him a very agreeable companion, and for a boy from 'the provinces' to have this sophisticated man of letters listening so respectfully to his plans for poems and so forth, on which he immediately began to draw me out, was no little flattering. One of the first things he asked me about was my age. Twenty-three, I told him.

'Twenty-three!' he commented, with a dramatic sigh. 'It is a kind of genius to be twenty-three!'

Who that has long since passed that inspired age will deny that this was as much a truth as a phrase – which, indeed, was usually the case with even Wilde's most frivolous phrases.

After we had talked for a while in his study, we went upstairs to the drawing-room where Mrs. Wilde sat with their two boys.[3] Mrs. Wilde was a pretty young woman of the innocent Kate Greenaway type. They seemed very happy together, though it was impossible not to predict suffering for a woman so simple and domestic mated with a mind so searching and so perverse and a character so self-indulgent. It was hard to see where two such different natures could find a meeting-place, particularly as poor Mrs. Wilde was entirely devoid of humour and evangelically religious. So sweet and pretty and good, how came she by her outrageously intellectual husband, to whose destructive wit little was sacred and all things comedy? When one thinks that Mrs. Wilde's chief interest after her children was – missionaries, and her bosom friend that Lady Sandhurst, who was one of the pillars of British church work . . . !

'Missionaries, my dear!' I remember Wilde once saying at a dinner party. 'Don't you realize that missionaries are the divinely provided food for destitute and under-fed cannibals? Whenever they are on the brink of starvation, Heaven, in its infinite mercy, sends them a nice plump missionary.' To which Mrs. Wilde could only pathetically exclaim: 'Oh, Oscar! you cannot surely be in earnest. You can only be joking.'

No one present remarked that the Reverend Sydney Smith had indulged in a like humour when he spoke of 'a slice of cold missionary on the side-board.' Wilde, like all wits, was occasionally indebted to his forerunners, though the implication of Whistler's famous 'You will say it, Oscar' is, of course, absurd. Wilde was under no necessity of borrowing from Whistler or anyone else, though, like everyone, he would now and again elaborate on ideas which he had rather made his own than originated. For example, that same evening, he was talking of criticism, and saying that a critic of literature should not feel bound down by his subject, but should merely use whatever author he was discussing, or reviewing, as a starting-point for the expression of his own individuality.

On which I innocently asked him if he had read M. Anatole France's 'La Vie Littéraire'! He looked at me with rather haughty surprise:

'You have read Anatole France!' he said.

Who would have expected a provincial young man from Liverpool to be so unseasonably acquainted with a certain *mot* about the adventures of a critic's soul among masterpieces which had then been made only a very short time. It was mean of me, I admit.

But to return to Mrs. Wilde and the children in the drawing room. Wilde was then in the period of his first fairy tales, and those beautifully simple and innocent stories in 'The Happy Prince' volume were shortly to be published.[4]

'It is the duty of every father,' he said with great gravity, 'to write fairy tales for his children. But the mind of a child is a great mystery. It is incalculable, and who shall divine it, or bring to it its own peculiar delights? You humbly spread before it the treasures of your imagination, and they are as dross. For example, a day or two ago, Cyril yonder came to me with the question, "Father, do you ever dream?" "Why, of course, my darling. It is the first duty of a gentleman to dream." "And what do you dream of?" asked Cyril, with a child's disgusting appetite for facts. Then I, believing, of course, that something picturesque would be expected of me, spoke of magnificent things: "What do I dream of? Oh, I dream of dragons with gold and silver scales, and scarlet flames coming out of their mouths, of eagles with eyes made of diamonds that can see over the whole world at once, of lions with yellow manes, and voices like thunder, of elephants with little houses on their backs, and tigers and zebras with barred and spotted coats. . . ." So I laboured on with my fancy, till, observing that Cyril was entirely unimpressed, and indeed quite undisguisedly bored, I came to a humiliating stop, and, turning to my son there, I said: "But tell me, what do you dream of, Cyril?" His answer was like a divine revelation: "I dream of *pigs*," he said.'

Wilde had a charming gift of improvising, or seeming to improvise, fables to illustrate points of view often no less improvised for the occasion. Some of these he afterwards printed, but many others must have lived and died as he created them, out of his fertile picture-making thought. One I recall from that first afternoon that I have not seen or heard of since. He was talking of free will, which he regarded as an illusion. Destiny, from which none could escape, ruled us all, he was saying. And then he went on:

'Once upon a time there was a magnet, and in its close neighbourhood lived some steel filings. One day two or three little filings felt a sudden desire to go and visit the magnet, and they began to talk of what a pleasant thing it would be to do. Other filings near by overheard their conversation, and they, too, became infected with the same desire. Still others joined them, till at last all the filings began to discuss the matter, and more and more their vague desire grew into an impulse.

"Why not go to-day?" said some of them; but others were of opinion that it would be better to wait till to-morrow. Meanwhile, without their having noticed it, they had been involuntarily moving nearer to the magnet, which lay there quite still, apparently taking no heed of them. And so they went on discussing, all the time insensibly drawing nearer to their neighbour; and the more they talked, the more they felt the impulse growing stronger, till the more impatient ones declared that they would go that day, whatever the rest did. Some were heard to say that it was their duty to visit the magnet, and that they ought to have gone long ago. And, while they talked, they moved always nearer and nearer, without realizing that they had moved. Then, at last, the impatient ones prevailed, and, with one irresistible impulse, the whole body cried out, "There is no use waiting. We will go to-day. We will go now. We will go at once." And then in one unanimous mass they swept along, and in another moment were clinging fast to the magnet on every side. Then the magnet smiled – for the steel filings had no doubt at all but that they were paying that visit of their own free will.'

I grew to know Wilde very well, and have many memories of his charming companionship and of the generous friendship he gave me in those early days before the clouds began to settle about his life. Though there were those whom he repelled, most of his acquaintance came under the spell of his extraordinary personality. For all his sophistication, there was in him a great simplicity. Strange as it may sound, he was an unusually natural creature, and what were regarded as affectations and eccentricities came of his being himself as few have the courage to be – 'an art which nature makes.' His poses were self-dramatizations, of which he expected others to see the fun, as he invariably saw it himself. Moreover, there was reality behind them all, and it was only because his way of looking at things was so new to his day that they seemed fantastic. He employed exag- geration merely as a means of conveying his intellectual sincerity, and, as I once said, paradox with him was merely Truth standing on its head to attract attention. Behind all his humorous fopperies there was a serious philosophy, as beneath all the surface sophistication there was the deep and simple heart of a poet. Doubtless, he was weak as well as strong, and wrong as he was right, but, if there was evil in him, there was also a great good. His success developed a dangerous arrogance, and he lost the captainship of his soul, but that his soul was essentially pure and his heart tender, no one who knew him well could for a moment doubt. I knew him well and am proud to have been his friend.

When his downfall came, a tragedy which, when one considers its nature and extent, he bore with remarkable fortitude, I was already in America, and my memories of him are confined to the sunlit days of his early successes. When I think of him it is as a victorious, happy figure, always gay, always with some witty nonsense on his tongue. His gaiety was not so much in his manner, in which it amused him to affect an almost ostentatious gravity, a humorous gravity, however, which none could mistake. It was the unfailing gaiety of his mind that was so captivating. One never left him without carrying away some characteristic *mot*, light as thistledown, yet usually pregnant with meaning.

I think it was Meredith who said that 'some flowers have roots deep as oaks,' and the phrase might be fitly applied to most of Wilde's talk; as, for instance, when he said, in reference to literature as a possible intercessor between rival nations, that he hoped some day, when men had become sufficiently civilized, it would seem natural to say, 'We will not go to war with France – because her prose is perfect,' a phrase which needs little pondering for one to see how deep it goes. But the *mots* of his which I recall at random were mainly happy nonsense, though usually uttered with imperturbable seriousness.

One day, as he stood outside his Tite Street door, preparing to insert his latchkey, a little humble man came up, saying that he had called about the taxes.

'Taxes!' said Wilde, looking down at him from his lordly height. 'Why should I pay taxes?'

'But, sir,' said the little man, 'you are the householder here, are you not? . . . You live here – you sleep here?'

'Ah, yes!' said Wilde, with utter solemnity, 'but then, you see – I sleep so badly!'

On another occasion, as he walked in the Haymarket, a beggar came up and asked for alms. He had, he said, no work to do and no bread to eat.

'Work!' said Wilde. 'Why should you want to work? And bread! Why should you eat bread?'

Then, after an elaborate pause, he continued, putting his hand good-naturedly on the tatter-demalion's shoulder:

'Now, if you had come to me and said that you had work to do, but you couldn't dream of working, and that you had bread to eat, but couldn't think of eating bread – I would have given you half-a-crown.' – Another pause – 'As it is, I give you two shillings.'

So Wilde, with his accustomed generosity, made the poor fellow happy and had his own little joke in the bargain.

The reference to the Haymarket reminds me of Tree's[5] theatre, and the first night of his Hamlet, which, like all Hamlet first nights, was a very serious occasion. Of course, Wilde was there, and went behind to see Tree, who, all excitement, perspiration, and grease paint, eagerly asked, 'Well, Oscar, what do you think of my Hamlet?' Wilde assumed his gravest, most pontifical air, and, spacing out his words with long pauses of even more than his usual deliberation, as though he was almost too impressed to speak at all, he said:

'My dear Tree – I think – your – Hamlet . . . your – Hamlet, my dear Tree . . . I think – your – Hamlet' – Tree, meanwhile, hanging expectant on each slow-dropping word, nervous and keyed up as most actors are on a first night, anxiously filling the pauses with 'Yes, yes, my dear Oscar . . .'

while Wilde continued to keep him on tenterhooks with further preliminary ejaculations of 'My dear Tree,' and 'I think your Hamlet.' At last,
when he could hold the suspended compliment no longer, Wilde ended
with: 'My dear Tree – I – think – your Hamlet . . . is . . . *funny*
. . . *without – being vulgar!*'[6]

In many of his *mots* Wilde had a remarkable skill in making bricks
without straw, or catching up any wind-blown straw for his purpose with
fascinating readiness. It was that skill which gave his wit so incomparable a
levity. His 'Intentions'[7] were published in London by Osgood, McIlvaine
& Co., a new firm that made a point in all their advertisements of the fact
that all their books were 'published simultaneously in London and New
York'[8] That was their 'slogan,' as the advertising men put it. Well, one
morning I happened to meet Wilde in Piccadilly. After our first greetings,
he assumed an air of deep grief: 'Did you see in the papers, this morning,'
he said, 'that Osgood is dead?' He paused for a moment, his manner
deepening in solemnity, and continued: 'Poor Osgood! He is a great loss to
us! However,' he added, as with consolatory cheerfulness, 'I suppose they
will bury him simultaneously in London and New York!'

Another delightfully foolish remark I recall à *propos* Mr. Kipling's
'Captains Courageous,' which, it will be remembered, is concerned
with a lad's adventures among the cod fishers off the Banks of New-
foundland.

'I really don't know,' said Wilde, 'why an author should write a book all
about cod-fishing.' Then, after a pause, in which he seemed to be thinking
it over, he said, as by way of explanation: 'But perhaps it is because – I
never eat cod!' – the possibility of eating cod being too vulgar to
contemplate.

The story of his appearance before the curtain on the first night of 'Lady
Windermere's Fan' is well known – how he stood in front of the stage, in
light evening overcoat, his opera hat in one hand, and the smoke from a
lighted cigarette mounting from the other, and gravely congratulated the
audience on the great success it had made that evening in so intelligently
appreciating his play.[9]

He had sent me two stalls for the occasion, with a characteristic note of
invitation to my wife and myself, which ran: 'DEAR POET – here are two
stalls for my play. Come, and bring your poem to sit beside you.'

Between the acts I went up to the theatre bar for a drink, and there was
Wilde in the midst of a group of his admiring disciples, over whom he
towered head and shoulders. On catching sight of me he left them and
came over to me.

'My dear Richard,' he said, 'where have you been? It seems as if we
hadn't met for years. Now tell me what you have been doing.'

But, before I could answer, he assumed an air of concern. 'Oh, yes!' he
said. 'I remember. I have a crow to pick with you.'

Though I suspected some jest, I, too, affected concern.

'Yes,' he continued, 'you recently published a book called "The Religion of a Literary Man."'

I nodded.

'Well,' he went on, 'you were very unkind to me in that book,' and he put on an air of deep grievance, 'most unkind!'

'My dear Oscar –' I began.

'Oh, yes, you were, and you know it,' he reiterated.

'I unkind to you!' I said, beginning to be really mystified.

'Most unkind. I could not believe it of you – so unkind to so true a friend.'

So he continued to lure me on into the trap he had suddenly improvised for me. I stood pondering what it was I could have done, for I began to think he was serious.

'Why, Oscar,' I said at last, 'I don't know what you mean. Unkind to you in "The Religion of a Literary Man" . . . why, I can't remember that I even mentioned your name in it.'

Then he laughed out, with huge enjoyment of the success of his little stratagem:

'Ah! Richard, that was just it.'

Then, having drunk together, this serious explanation over, he resumed:

'But do tell me, what else have you been writing?' I told him that, among other things, I had been writing an essay on loving my enemies.

'That's a great theme. I should like to write on that, too. For, do you know, all my life I have been looking for twelve men who didn't believe in me . . . and, so far, I have only found eleven.'

It was not till long after that I reflected on the strangely prophetic significance of that lightly uttered speech, the merest badinage of the moment; for, when a friend brought me the news of Wilde's sentence, I said: 'Poor Oscar! he has found his twelfth man.'

Looking back on that tragedy, I sometimes wonder whether it did not mean more to Wilde's friends than it meant to himself. Indeed, inordinately fond of the limelight as he was, so conscious throughout his career of his own drama, one cannot help the suspicion that he rather enjoyed his own tragedy. And in a sense, aside from its social inconvenience, and he being what he was, it is possible to understand his doing so. For he had been condemned at the bar of a Philistine public opinion whose jurisdiction he regally denied. Despising the public, while at the same time its attention was the breath of his nostrils, it was hardly to be expected that he should take its condemnation seriously. It was, doubtless, disagreeable, for the storm he had raised must have seemed more furious and trying to his courage than he had foreseen, but not important. The ostracism from that society at whose pleasant dinner tables he had been the king must have been to him its greatest hardship – the real 'hard labour' of his sentence. Perhaps he sometimes recalled his own phrase that to be in society was a bore but to be outside it a tragedy. It is one's suspicion of this attitude which robs 'De Profundis' of its convincingness, hard as Wilde worked to convey the impression of a broken and a contrite heart. Wilde's heart was probably neither, but his vanity was at once impaled and flattered. How could he regard himself as a criminal when his intellect did not accept the standards by which he had been judged and condemned? No 'conversion' could have taken place in a brain like his. To him his offence would merely represent a difference of taste in morals, with no essential wrong in it. The penalty for this difference was indeed hard, but it was a necessary part of his drama. It left him spiritually and intellectually unchanged, and he probably considered himself a martyr to Philistine stupidity and ignorance of physiology rather than a criminal. He had haughtily defied the lightning, and even when it struck him, he must have examined its bolts with intellectual curiosity and contempt. Indeed, it is not unlikely that he had counted on their inability effectually to strike him, for success, which had become a disease with him, had made him so insanely arrogant that he probably felt himself capable, so to say, of bluffing the British Empire; and when we consider the posthumous triumphs of his personality, it looks very much as if he had not entirely miscalculated.

Wilde once said that he gave only his talent to his writings, and kept his genius for his conversation. This was quite true, but it would have been truer still if he had said that he kept his genius for his life; for his writings, the value of which is less than he thought, and more than some allow, are but one illustrative part of him. They contribute to the general effect he strove to produce, the dramatization of his own personality. From the beginning to the end he was a great actor – of himself.

As that self, for good or ill, summed up so completely the various aspects and tendencies of his time, he has become its symbolic figure. He is, beyond comparison, the incarnation of the spirit of the '90s. The significance of the '90s is that they began to apply all the new ideas that had been for some time accumulating from the disintegrating action of scientific and philosophic thought on every kind of spiritual, moral, social and artistic convention, and all forms of authority demanding obedience merely as authority. Hence came that widespread assertion and demonstration of individualism which is still actively progressing. Wilde was the synthesis of all these phenomena of change. He may be said to have included Huxley and Pater and Morris and Whistler and Mr. Bernard Shaw and Mr. Max Beerbohm in the amazing eclecticism of his extravagant personality, that seems to have borrowed everything and made everything his own. Out of the 1890 chaos he emerged an astonishing, impudent microcosm.

In him the period might see its own face in a glass. And it is because it did see its own face in him that it first admired, then grew afraid, and then destroyed him. Here, said the moralist, is where your 'modern' ideas will lead you, and the moralist, as often, was both right and wrong. Wilde did gaily and flippantly what some men were doing in dead earnest, with humour and wit for his weapons. What serious reformers had laboured for years to accomplish Wilde did in a moment with the flash of an epigram. He was like that *enfant terrible* in Andersen's fairy tale who called out, 'Why, the king has nothing on,' and while his audience laughed, it awakened, and the truth beneath his phrases went home. Indeed, he made dying Victorianism laugh at itself, and it may be said to have died of the laughter.

## NOTES

Richard Le Gallienne (1866–1947), English man of letters. For Wilde's friendship with him see Richard Whittington-Egan and Geoffrey Smerdon, *The Quest of the Golden Boy: The Life and Letters of Richard Le Gallienne* (London: The Unicorn Press, 1960) *passim*.

1. Self-possession; coolness.
2. Oscar Wilde, *The Sphinx*. With Decorations by Charles Ricketts (London: Elkin Matthews and John Lane, 1894).
3. Cyril (1885–1914) and Vyvyan (1886–1967).
4. Oscar Wilde, *The Happy Prince and Other Tales* illustrated by Walter Crane and Jacomb Hood (London: David Nutt, 1888).
5. Sir Herbert Beerbohm Tree (1853–1917), English actor-manager.
6. The comment that Herbert Beerbohm Tree's Hamlet was funny without being vulgar is generally attributed to W. S. Gilbert.
7. Oscar Wilde, *Intentions* (London: James R. Osgood, McIlvaine, 1891).
8. *Intentions*, however, was published in New York by Dodd, Mead.
9. A member of the St James's Theatre staff took Wilde's speech down in shorthand, and so George Alexander, the manager of the Theatre, was able to tell Hesketh Pearson not only what Wilde said, but the actual words he stressed:

'Ladies and Gentlemen: I have injoyed this evening *immensely*. The actors have given us a charming rendering of a *delightful* play, and your appreciation has been *most* intelligent. I congratulate you on the *great* success of your performance, which persuades me that you think *almost* as highly of the play as I do myself.'

– Hesketh Pearson, *The Life of Oscar Wilde* (London: Methuen, 1946) p. 224.

# My Memories of Oscar Wilde*

George Bernard Shaw

My Dear Harris: –

I have an interesting letter of yours to answer; but when you ask me to exchange biographies, you take an unfair advantage of the changes of scene and bustling movement of your own adventures. My autobiography would be like my best plays, fearfully long, and not divided into acts. Just consider this life of Wilde which you have just sent me, and which I finished ten minutes ago after putting aside everything else to read it at one stroke.

Why was Wilde so good a subject for a biography that none of the previous attempts which you have just wiped out are bad? Just because his stupendous laziness simplified his life almost as if he knew instinctively that there must be no episodes to spoil the great situation at the end of the last act but one. It was a well made life in the Scribe sense. It was as simple as the life of Des Grieux, Manon Lescaut's lover;[1] and it beat that by omitting Manon and making Des Grieux his own lover and his own hero.

Des Grieux was worthless rascal by all conventional standards; and we forgive him everything. We think we forgive him because he was unselfish and loved greatly. Oscar seems to have said: 'I will love nobody: I will be utterly selfish; and I will be not merely a rascal but a monster; and you shall forgive me everything. In other words, I will reduce your standards to absurdity, not by writing them down, though I could do that so well – in fact, *have* done it – but by actually living them down and dying them down.'

However, I mustn't start writing a book to you about Wilde; I must just tumble a few things together and tell you them. To take things in the order of your book, I can remember only one occasion on which I saw Sir William Wilde, who, by the way, operated on my father to correct a squint, and overdid the corrections so much that my father squinted the other way all the rest of his life. To this day I never notice a squint; it is as normal to me as a nose or a tall hat.

I was a boy at a concert in the Ancient [sic][2] Concert Rooms in Brunswick Street in Dublin. Everybody was in evening dress; and – unless I am mixing up this concert with another (in which case I doubt if the

---

* Frank Harris, *Oscar Wilde: His Life and Confessions* (New York: Crown Publishing Company, 1930) pp. 387–404.

Wildes would have been present) – the Lord Lieutenant was there with his blue waistcoated courtiers. Wilde was dressed in snuffy brown; and as he had the sort of skin that never looks clean, he produced a dramatic effect beside Lady Wilde (in full fig) of being, like Frederick the Great, Beyond Soap and Water,[3] as his Nietzschean son was beyond Good and Evil. He was currently reported to have a family in every farmhouse; and the wonder was that Lady Wilde didn't mind – evidently a tradition from the Travers case,[4] which I did not know about until I read your account, as I was only eight in 1864.

Lady Wilde was nice to me in London during the desperate days between my arrival in 1876 and my first earning of an income by my pen in 1885, or rather until, a few years earlier, I threw myself into Socialism and cut myself contemptuously loose from everything of which her at-homes – themselves desperate affairs enough, as you saw for yourself – were part. I was at two or three of them; and I once dined with her in company with an ex-tragedy queen named Miss Glynn, who, having no visible external ears, reared a head like a turnip. Lady Wilde talked about Schopenhauer; and Miss Glynn told me that Gladstone formed his oratorical style on Charles Kean.

I ask myself where and how I came across Lady Wilde; for we had no social relations in the Dublin days. The explanation must be that my sister, then a very attractive girl who sang beautifully, had met and made some sort of innocent conquest of both Oscar and Willie. I met Oscar once at one of the at-homes; and he came and spoke to me with an evident intention of being specially kind to me. We put each other out frightfully; and this odd difficulty persisted between us to the very last, even when we were no longer mere boyish novices and had become men of the world with plenty of skill in social intercourse. I saw him very seldom, as I avoided literary and artistic society like the plague, and refused the few invitations I received to go into society with burlesque ferocity, so as to keep out of it without offending people past their willingness to indulge me as a privileged lunatic.

The last time I saw him was at that tragic luncheon of yours at the Café Royal; and I am quite sure our total of meetings from first to last did not exceed twelve, and may not have exceeded six.

I definitely recollect six: (1) At the at-home aforesaid. (2) At Macmurdo's house in Fitzroy Street in the days of the Century Guild and its paper *The Hobby Horse*. (3) At a meeting somewhere in Westminster at which I delivered an address on Socialism, and at which Oscar turned up and spoke. Robert Ross surprised me greatly by telling me, long after Oscar's death, that it was this address of mine that moved Oscar to try his hand at a similar feat by writing 'The Soul of Man Under Socialism.' (4) A chance meeting near the stage door of the Haymarket Theatre, at which our queer shyness of one another made our resolutely cordial and appreciative conversation so difficult that our final laugh and shake-hands was almost a reciprocal confession. (5) A really pleasant afternoon we spent together on catching one another in a place where our presence was an absurdity. It was some exhibition in Chelsea; a naval commemoration, where there was a replica of Nelson's Victory and a set of P. & O. cabins which made one seasick by mere association of ideas. I don't know why I went or why Wilde went; but we did; and the question what the devil we were doing in that galley tickled us both. It was my sole experience of Oscar's wonderful gift as a raconteur. I remember particularly an amazingly elaborate story which you have no doubt heard from him; an example of the cumulation of a single effect, as in Mark Twain's story of the man who was persuaded to put lightning conductor after lightning conductor at every possible point on his roof until a thunderstorm came and all the lightning in the heavens went for his house and wiped it out.

Oscar's much more carefully and elegantly worked out story was of a young man who invented a theatre stall which economized space by ingenious contrivances which were all described. A friend of his invited twenty millionaires to meet him at dinner so that he might interest them in the invention. The young man convinced them completely by his demonstration of the saving in a theatre holding, in ordinary seats, six hundred people, leaving them eager and ready to make his fortune. Unfortunately he went on to calculate the annual saving in all the theatres of the world; then in all the churches of the world; then in all the legislatures; estimating finally the incidental and moral and religious effects of the invention until at the end of an hour he had estimated a profit of several thousand millions: the climax of course being that the millionaires folded their tents and silently stole away, leaving the ruined inventor a marked man for life.

Wilde and I got on extraordinarily well on this occasion. I had not to talk myself, but to listen to a man telling me stories better than I could have told them. We did not refer to Art, about which, excluding literature from the definition, he knew only what could be picked up by reading about it. He was in a tweed suit and low hat like myself, and had been detected and had detected me in the act of clandestinely spending a happy day at Rosherville Gardens instead of pontificating in his frock coat and so forth. And he had an audience on whom not one of his subtlest effects was lost. And so for once our meeting was a success; and I understood why Morris, when he was dying slowly, enjoyed a visit from Wilde more than from anybody else,[5] as I understand why you say in your book that you would rather have Wilde back than any friend you have ever talked to, even though he was incapable of friendship, though not of the most touching kindness[6] on occasion.

Our sixth meeting, the only other one I can remember, was the one at the Café Royal. On that occasion he was not too preoccupied with his danger to be disgusted with me because I, who had praised his first plays handsomely, had turned traitor over 'The Importance of being Earnest.'[7]

Clever as it was, it was his first really heartless play. In the others the chivalry of the eighteenth century Irishman and the romance of the disciple of Théophile Gautier (Oscar was really old-fashioned in the Irish way, except as a critic of morals) not only gave a certain kindness and gallantry to the serious passages and to the handling of the women, but provided that proximity of emotion without which laughter, however irresistible, is destructive and sinister. In 'The Importance of Being Earnest' this had vanished; and the play, though extremely funny, was essentially hateful. I had no idea that Oscar was going to the dogs, and that this represented a real degeneracy produced by his debaucheries. I thought he was still developing; and I hazarded the unhappy guess that 'The Importance of Being Earnest' was in idea a young work written or projected long before under the influence of Gilbert and furbished up for Alexander as a potboiler. At the Café Royal that day I calmly asked him whether I was not right. He indignantly repudiated my guess, and said loftily (the only time he ever tried on me the attitude he took to John Gray and his more abject disciples) that he was disappointed in me. I suppose I said, 'Then what on earth has happened to you?' but I recollect nothing more on that subject except that we did not quarrel over it.

When he was sentenced I spent a railway journey on a Socialist lecturing excursion to the North drafting a petition for his release. After that I met Willie Wilde at a theatre which I think must have been the Duke of York's because I connect it vaguely with St. Martin's Lane. I spoke to him about the petition, asking him whether anything of the sort was being done, and warning him that though I and Stewart Headlam[8] would sign it, that would be no use, as we were two notorious cranks, and our names would by themselves reduce the petition to absurdity and do Oscar more harm than good. Willie cordially agreed, and added, with maudlin pathos and an inconceivable want of tact: 'Oscar was NOT a man of bad character: you could have trusted him with a woman anywhere.' He convinced me, as you discovered later, that signatures would not be obtainable; so the petition project dropped; and I don't know what became of my draft.

When Wilde was in Paris during his last phase I made a point of sending him inscribed copies of all my books as they came out; and he did the same to me.

In writing about Wilde and Whistler, in the days when they were treated as witty triflers, and called Oscar and Jimmy in print, I always made a point of taking them seriously and with scrupulous good manners. Wilde on his part also made a point of recognizing me as a man of distinction by his manner, and repudiating the current estimate of me as a mere jester. This was not the usual reciprocal-admiration trick. I believe he was sincere, and felt indignant at what he thought was a vulgar underestimate of me; and I had the same feeling about him. My impulse to rally to him in his misfortune, and my disgust at 'the man Wilde' scurrilities of the newspapers, was irresistible: I don't quite know why; for my charity to his perversion, and my recognition of the fact that it does not imply any general depravity or coarseness of character, came to me through reading and observation, not through sympathy.

I have all the normal violent repugnance to homosexuality – if it is really normal, which nowadays one is sometimes provoked to doubt.

Also, I was in no way predisposed to like him. He was my fellow-townsman, and a very prime specimen of the sort of fellow-townsman I most loathed: to wit, the Dublin snob. His Irish charm, potent with Englishmen, did not exist for me; and on the whole it may be claimed for him that he got no regard from me that he did not earn.

What first established a friendly feeling in me was, unexpectedly enough, the affair of the Chicago anarchists, whose Homer you constituted yourself by *The Bomb*. I tried to get some literary men in London, all heroic rebels and skeptics on paper, to sign a memorial asking for the reprieve of these unfortunate men. The only signature I got was Oscar's. It was a completely disinterested act on his part; and it secured my distinguished consideration for him for the rest of his life.

To return for a moment to Lady Wilde. You know that there is a disease called gigantism, caused by 'a certain morbid process in the sphenoid bone of the skull – viz., an excessive development of the anterior lobe of the pituitary body' (this is from the nearest encyclopedia). 'When this condition does not become active until after the age of twenty-five, by which time the long bones are consolidated, the result is acromegaly, which chiefly manifests itself in an enlargement of the hands and feet.' I never saw Lady Wilde's feet; but her hands were enormous, and never went straight to their aim when they grasped anything, but minced about, feeling for it. And the gigantic splaying of her palm was reproduced in her lumbar region.

Now Oscar was an overgrown man, with something not quite normal about his bigness – something that made Lady Colin Campbell, who hated him, describe him as 'that great white caterpillar.' You yourself describe the disagreeable impression he made on you physically, in spite of his fine eyes and style. Well, I have always maintained that Oscar was a giant in the pathological sense, and that this explains a good deal of his weakness.

I think you have affectionately underrated his snobbery, mentioning only the pardonable and indeed justifiable side of it; the love of fine names and distinguished associations and luxury and good manners.[9] You say repeatedly, and *on certain planes*, truly, that he was not bitter and did not use his tongue to wound people. But this is not true on the snobbish plane. On one occasion he wrote about T. P. O'Connor with deliberate, studied, wounding insolence, with his Merrion Square Protestant pretentiousness in full cry against the Catholic. He repeatedly declaimed against the vulgarity of the British journalist, not as you or I might, but as an expression of the odious class feeling that is itself the vilest vulgarity. He made the mistake of not knowing his place. He objected to be addressed as

Wilde, declaring that he was Oscar to his intimates and Mr. Wilde to others, quite unconscious of the fact that he was imposing on the men with whom, as a critic and journalist, he had to live and work, the alternative of granting him an intimacy he had no right to ask or a deference to which he had no claim. The vulgar hated him for snubbing them; and the valiant men damned his impudence and cut him. Thus he was left with a band of devoted satellites on the one hand, and a dining-out connection on the other, with here and there a man of talent and personality enough to command his respect, but utterly without that fortifying body of acquaintance among plain men in which a man must move as himself a plain man, and be Smith and Jones and Wilde and Shaw and Harris instead of Bosie and Robbie and Oscar and Mister. This is the sort of folly that does not last forever in a man of Wilde's ability; but it lasted long enough to prevent Oscar laying any solid social foundations.[10]

Another difficulty I have already hinted at. Wilde started as an apostle of Art; and in that capacity he was a humbug. The notion that a Portora boy, passed on to T. C. D. and thence to Oxford and spending his vacations in Dublin, could without special circumstances have any genuine intimacy with music and painting, is to me ridiculous.[11] When Wilde was at Portora, I was at home in a house where important musical works, including several typical masterpieces, were being rehearsed from the point of blank amateur ignorance up to fitness for public performance. I could whistle them from the first bar to the last as a butcher's boy whistles music hall songs, before I was twelve. The toleration of popular music – Strauss's waltzes, for instance – was to me positively a painful acquirement, a sort of republican duty.

I was so fascinated by painting that I haunted the National Gallery, which Doyle had made perhaps the finest collection of its size in the world; and I longed for money to buy painting materials with. This afterwards saved me from starving. It was as a critic of music and painting in the *World* that I won through my ten years of journalism before I finished up with you on the *Saturday Review*. I could make deaf stockbrokers read my two pages on music, the alleged joke being that I knew nothing about it. The real joke was that I knew all about it.

Now it was quite evident to me, as it was to Whistler and Beardsley, that Oscar knew no more about pictures[12] than anyone of his general culture and with his opportunities can pick up as he goes along. He could be witty about Art, as I could be witty about engineering; but that is no use when you have to seize and hold the attention and interest of people who really love music and painting. Therefore, Oscar was handicapped by a false start, and got a reputation[13] for shallowness and insincerity which never retrieved until it was too late.

Comedy: the criticism of morals and manners *viva voce*, was his real forte. When he settled down to that he was great. But, as you found when you approached Meredith about him, his initial mistake had produced that 'rather low opinion of Wilde's capacities,' that 'deep-rooted contempt for the showman in him,' which persisted as a first impression and will persist until the last man who remembers his esthetic period has perished. The world has been in some ways so unjust to him that one must be careful not to be unjust to the world.

In the preface on education, called 'Parents and Children,' to my volume of plays beginning with *Misalliance*, there is a section headed 'Artist Idolatry,' which is really about Wilde. Dealing with 'the powers enjoyed by brilliant persons who are also connoisseurs in art,' I say, 'the influence they can exercise on young people who have been brought up in the darkness and wretchedness of a home without art, and in whom a natural bent towards art has always been baffled and snubbed, is incredible to those who have not witnessed and understood it. He (or she) who reveals the world of art to them opens heaven to them. They become satellites, disciples, worshippers of the apostle. Now the apostle may be a voluptuary without much conscience. Nature may have given him enough virtue to suffice in a reasonable environment. But this allowance may not be enough to defend him against the temptation and demoralization of finding himself a little god on the strength of what ought to be a quite ordinary culture. He may find adorers in all directions in our uncultivated society among people of stronger character than himself, not one of whom, if they had been artistically educated, would have had anything to learn from him, or regarded him as in any way extraordinary apart from his actual achievements as an artist. Tartuffe is not always a priest. Indeed, he is not always a rascal; he is often a weak man absurdly credited with omniscience and perfection, and taking unfair advantages only because they are offered to him and he is too weak to refuse. Give everyone his culture, and no one will offer him more than his due.'

That paragraph was the outcome of a walk and talk I had one afternoon at Chartres with Robert Ross.

You reveal Wilde as a weaker man than I thought him. I still believe that his fierce Irish pride had something to do with his refusal to run away from the trial. But in the main your evidence is conclusive. It was part of his tragedy that people asked more moral strength from him than he could bear the burden of, because they made the very common mistake – of which actors get the benefit – of regarding style as evidence of strength, just as in the case of women they are apt to regard paint as evidence of beauty. Now Wilde was so in love with style that he never reailzed the danger of biting off more than he could chew. In other words, of putting up more style than his matter would carry. Wise kings wear shabby clothes, and leave the gold lace to the drum major.

You do not, unless my memory is betraying me as usual, quite recollect the order of events just before the trial. That day at the Café Royal, Wilde said he had come to ask you to go into the witness box next day and testify that *Dorian Gray* was a highly moral work. Your answer was something like this: 'For God's sake, man, put everything on that plane out of your head. You don't realize what is going to happen to you. It is not going to be a matter of clever talk about your books. They are going to bring up a string of witnesses that will put art and literature out of the question. Clarke[14] will throw up his brief. He will carry the case to a certain point; and then, when he sees the avalanche coming, he will back out and leave you in the dock. What you have to do is to cross to France to-night. Leave a letter saying that you cannot face the squalor and horror of a law case; that you are an artist and unfitted for such things. Don't stay here clutching at straws like testimonials to *Dorian Gray*. *I tell you I know*. I know what is going to happen. I know Clarke's sort. I know what evidence they have got. You must go.'

It was no use. Wilde was in a curious double temper. He made no pretence either of innocence or of questioning the folly of his proceedings against Queensberry. But he had an infatuate haughtiness as to the impossibility of his retreating, and as to his right to dictate your course. Douglas sat in silence, a haughty indignant silence, copying Wilde's attitude as all Wilde's admirers did, but quite probably influencing Wilde as you suggest, by the copy. Oscar finally rose with a mixture of impatience and his grand air, and walked out with the remark that he had now found out who were his real friends; and Douglas followed him, absurdly smaller, and imitating his walk, like a curate following an archbishop.[15] You remember it the other way about; but just consider this. Douglas was in the wretched position of having ruined Wilde merely to annoy his father, and of having attempted it so idiotically that he had actually prepared a triumph for him. He was, besides, much the youngest man present, and looked younger than he was. You did not make him welcome. As far as I recollect you did not greet him by a word or nod. If he had given the smallest provocation or attempted to take the lead in any way, I should not have given twopence for the chance of your keeping your temper. And Wilde, even in his ruin – which, however, he did not yet fully realize – kept his air of authority on questions of taste and conduct. It was practically impossible under such circumstances that Douglas should have taken the stage in any way. Everyone thought him a horrid little brat; but I, not having met him before to my knowledge, and having some sort of flair for his literary talent, was curious to hear what he had to say for himself. But, except to echo Wilde once or twice, he said nothing.[16] You are right in effect, because it was evident that Wilde was in his hands, and was really echoing him. But Wilde automatically kept the prompter off the stage and himself in the middle of it.

What your book needs to complete it is a portrait of yourself as good as your portrait of Wilde. Oscar was not combative, though he was supercilious in his early pose. When his snobbery was not in action, he liked to make people devoted to him and to flatter them exquisitely with that end. Mrs. Calvert, whose great final period as a stage old woman began with her appearance in my *Arms and the Man*, told me one day, when apologizing for being, as she thought, a bad rehearser, that no author had ever been so nice to her except Mr. Wilde.

Pugnacious people, if they did not actually terrify Oscar, were at least the sort of people he could not control, and whom he feared as possibly able to coerce him. You suggest that the Queensberry pugnacity was something that Oscar could not deal with successfully. But how in that case could Oscar have felt quite safe with you? You were more pugnacious than six Queensberrys rolled into one. When people asked, 'What has Frank Harris been?' the usual reply was, 'Obviously a pirate from the Spanish Main.'

Oscar, from the moment he gained your attachment, could never have been afraid of what you might do to him, as he was sufficient of a connoisseur in Blut Bruderschaft to appreciate yours; but he must always have been mortally afraid of what you might do or say to his friends.[17]

You had quite an infernal scorn for nineteen out of twenty of the men and women you met in the circles he most wished to propitiate; and nothing could induce you to keep your knife in its sheath when they jarred on you. The Spanish Main itself would have blushed rosy red at your language when classical invective did not suffice to express your feelings.

It may be that if, say, Edmund Gosse had come to Oscar when he was out on bail, with a couple of first class tickets in his pocket, and gently suggested a mild trip to Folkestone, or the Channel Islands, Oscar might have let himself be coaxed away. But to be called on to gallop *ventre à terre*[18] to Erith – it might have been Deal – and hoist the Jolly Roger on board your lugger, was like casting a light comedian and first lover for *Richard III*. Oscar could not see himself in the part.

I must not press the point too far; but it illustrates, I think, what does not come out at all in your book: that you were a very different person from the submissive and sympathetic disciples to whom he was accustomed. There are things more terrifying to a soul like Oscar's than an as yet unrealized possibility of a sentence of hard labour. A voyage with Captain Kidd may have been one of them. Wilde was a conventional man; his unconventionality was the very pedantry of convention; never was there a man less an outlaw than he. You were a born outlaw, and will never be anything else.

That is why, in his relations with you, he appears as a man always shirking action – more of a coward (all men are cowards more or less) than so proud a man can have been. Still this does not affect the truth and power of your portrait. Wilde's memory will have to stand or fall by it.

You will be blamed, I imagine, because you have not written a lying epitaph instead of a faithful chronicle and study of him; but you will not lose your sleep over that. As a matter of fact, you could not have carried kindness further without sentimental folly. I should have made a far sterner summing up. I am sure Oscar has not found the gates of heaven shut against him. He is too good company to be excluded; but he can hardly have been greeted as, 'Thou good and faithful servant.' The first thing we ask a servant for is a testimonial to honesty, sobriety and industry; for we soon find out that these are the scarce things, and that geniuses[19] and clever people are as common as rats. Well, Oscar was not sober, not honest, not industrious. Society praised him for being idle, and persecuted him savagely for an aberration which it had better have left unadvertized, thereby making a hero of him; for it is in the nature of people to worship those who have been made to suffer horribly. Indeed I have often said that if the crucifixion could be proved a myth, and Jesus convicted of dying of old age in comfortable circumstances, Christianity would lose ninety-nine per cent of its devotees.

We must try to imagine what judgement we should have passed on Oscar if he had been a normal man, and had dug his grave with his teeth in the ordinary respectable fashion, as his brother Willie did. This brother, by the way, gives us some cue; for Willie, who had exactly the same education and the same chances, must be ruthlessly set aside by literary history as a vulgar journalist of no account. Well, suppose Oscar and Willie had both died the day before Queensberry left that card at the Club! Oscar would still have been remembered as a wit and a dandy, and would have had a niche beside Congreve in the drama. A volume of his aphorisms would have stood creditably on the library shelf with La Rochefoucauld's Maxims. We should have missed the 'Ballad of Reading Gaol' and 'De Profundis'; but he would still have cut a considerable figure in the Dictionary of National Biography, and been read and quoted outside the British Museum reading room.

As to the 'Ballad' and 'De Profundis,' I think it is greatly to Oscar's credit that, whilst he was sincere and deeply moved when he was protesting against the cruelty of our present system to children and to prisoners generally, he could not write about his own individual share in that suffering with any conviction or sympathy.[20] Except for the passage where he describes his exposure at Clapham Junction, there is hardly a line in 'De Profundis' that he might not have written as a literary feat five years earlier. But in the 'Ballad,' even in borrowing form and melody from Coleridge, he shews that he could pity others when he could not seriously pity himself. And this, I think, may be pleaded against the reproach that he was selfish. Externally, in the ordinary action of life as distinguished from the literary action proper to his genius, he was no doubt sluggish and weak because of his gigantism. He ended as an unproductive drunkard and swindler; for the repeated sales of the Daventry plot,[21] in so far as they imposed on the buyers and were not transparent excuses for begging, were undeniably swindles. For all that, he does not appear in his writings a selfish or base-minded man. He is at his worst and weakest in the suppressed[22] part of 'De Profundis'; but in my opinion it had better be published, for several reasons. It explains some of his personal weakness by the stifling narrowness of his daily round, ruinous to a man whose proper place was in a large public life. And its concealment is mischievous because, first, it leads people to imagine all sorts of horrors in a document which contains nothing worse than any record of the squabbles of two touchy idlers; and, second, it is clearly a monstrous thing that Douglas should have a torpedo launched at him and timed to explode after his death. The torpedo is a very harmless squib; for there is nothing in it that cannot be guessed from Douglas's own book; but the public does not know that. By the way, it is rather a humorous stroke of Fate's irony that the son of the Marquis of Queensberry should be forced to expiate his sins by suffering a succession of blows beneath the belt.

Now that you have written the best life of Oscar Wilde, let us have the best life of Frank Harris.[23] Otherwise the man behind your works will go down to posterity[24] as the hero of my very inadequate preface to 'The Dark Lady of the Sonnets.'

G. BERNARD SHAW.

## NOTES

George Bernard Shaw (1856–1950), Irish playwright, novelist, and critic. He sent Wilde a copy of his *Widowers' Houses* in 1893. On 6 November 1897 *The Academy* printed a list of suggested members for an Academy of Letters, 'based upon a consensus of opinion gathered from the staff'. This produced a flood of letters in the issue of 13 November. Both Shaw and H. G. Wells suggested the inclusion of Wilde's name. See references to Shaw in *The Letters of Oscar Wilde*; and Hiroshi Hirai, 'Bernard Shaw and Oscar Wilde', *Eibungaku-Kenkyu*, XXVIII (1952) 42–58.

1. In the novel entitled *Manon Lescaut*, by the French novelist the Abbé Prévost (1697–1763).

2. The Antient Concert Rooms was a commodious hall on Brunswick Street (now Pearse Street). The hall was later converted into a cinema. Shaw lectured there, perhaps his first lecture in Dublin, and recalled how he had heard his mother, a fine singer, singing there in oratorio.

3. Sir William Wilde, Oscar's father, was very shabby and careless about his appearance. He used to be spoken of as one of the untidiest men in Ireland. At a dinner-party at which Father Healy was present, and which was held shortly after Sir Wilde had been knighted, an Englishman who had just crossed from Holyhead was complaining of the sea-passage he had been through. 'It was, I think,' he said, 'the dirtiest night I have ever seen.' 'Oh,' said Father Healy, 'then it must have been wild.' Dublin society was amusing itself with the question 'Why are Dr Wilde's nails so black?', the answer to which ran 'Because he has scratched himself.'

4. Mary Travers, an attractive girl of 19 and the daughter of a professor at Trinity College Dublin, called to consult Dr William Wilde one summer day in 1854. The medical consultation led to a friendship between doctor and patient, which quickly ripened to physical intimacy. They went about together and he spent a good deal of money on her. His wife got to know of the affair, but, accustomed to the doctor's habits, treated it as a normal occurrence. Mary, however, felt that hers was a special case and determined to monopolise his affections. Her intention to become a permanent member of his household took the form of a visit to his wife's bedroom, whence she was expelled with some heat by 'Speranza'; and he decided to get rid of her. A law case was tried in December

1864. Although Wilde was acquitted of the charge of seducing Miss Travers, the publicity given to the case had an unfortunate effect on Wilde, who rapidly deteriorated.

5. This oft-repeated story that when the English poet and artist William Morris (1834–96) was dying the only person he could bear to see was Wilde seems to have been invented by Shaw. Wilde had been almost eighteen months in prison when Morris died. The story was denied by Sydney Cockerell, Morris's secretary. See 'William Morris and Oscar Wilde', *The Times Literary Supplement*, (3 Feb 1950) p. 73; William Ruff 'Shaw on Wilde and Morris: A Clarification', *Shaw Review*, XI (Jan 1968) 32–3; and R. Page Arnot, *Bernard Shaw and William Morris* (London: Norwood, 1975).

6. 'Excellent analysis.' – Frank Harris.

7. See G. B. S[haw] 'Two New Plays', *The Saturday Review* (London), LXXIX (12 Jan 1895) 44–5. This includes a review of only *An Ideal Husband*. Shaw, therefore, is inaccurate in saying that he 'had praised his first *plays* handsomely' before turning traitor over *The Importance of Being Earnest*. The review of this last play was included in Shaw's 'An Old Play and a New One', *The Saturday Review* (London), LXXIX (23 Feb 1895) 249–50. In this review Shaw said: 'I cannot say that I greatly cared for *The Importance of Being Earnest*. It amused me, of course; but unless comedy touches me as well as amuses me, it leaves me with a sense of having wasted my evening.'

8. The Rev. Stewart Duckworth Headlam (1847–1924), whose Socialism and religious unorthodoxy cost him his position in the Church. Although he scarcely knew Wilde, he went bail for him in 1895 because he thought the case was being prejudged; and on Wilde's release from prison he offered his house as temporary asylum. See F. G. Bettany, *Stewart Headlam: A Biography* (London: John Murray, 1926) pp. 129–32.

9. 'I had touched on the evil side of his snobbery, I thought, by saying that it was only famous actresses and great ladies that he ever talked about, and in telling how he loved to speak of the great houses such as Clumber to which he had been invited, and by half a dozen other hints scattered through my book. I had attacked English snobbery so strenuously in my book "The Man Shakespeare," had resented its influence on the finest English intelligence so bitterly, that I thought if I again laid stress on it in Wilde, people would think I was crazy on the subject. But he was a snob, both by nature and training, and I understand by snob what Shaw evidently understands by it here.' – F. H.

10. 'The reason that Oscar, snobblish as he was, and admirer of England and the English as he was, could not lay any solid social foundations in England was, in my opinion, his intellectual interests and his intellectual superiority to the men he met. No one with a fine mind devoted to things of the spirit is capable of laying solid social foundations in England. Shaw, too, has no solid social foundations in that country.' – F. H.

*'This passing shot at English society serves it right. Yet able men have found niches in London. Where was Oscar's?'* –G. B. S.

11. 'I had already marked it down to put in my book that Wilde continually pretended to a knowledge of music which he had not got. He could hardly tell one tune from another, but he loved to talk of that "scarlet thing of Dvorak," hoping in this way to be accepted as a real critic of music, when he knew nothing about it and cared even less. His eulogies of music and painting betrayed him continually though he did not know it.' – F. H.

12. 'I touched upon Oscar's ignorance of art sufficiently, I think, when I said in my book that he had learned all he knew of art and of controversy from Whistler, and that his lectures on the subject, even after sitting at the feet of the Master, were almost worthless.' – F. H.

13. 'Perfectly true, and a notable instance of Shaw's insight.' – F.H.

14. For a note on Sir Edward Clarke see p. 284.

15. 'This is an inimitable picture, but Shaw's fine sense of comedy has misled him. The scene took place absolutely as I recorded it. Douglas went out first saying – "Your telling him to run away shows that you are no friend of Oscar's." Then Oscar got up to follow him. He said good-bye to Shaw, adding a courteous word or two. As he turned to the door I got up and said: – "I hope you do not doubt my friendship; you have no reason to."

"I do not think this is friendly of you, Frank," he said, and went on out.' – F. H.

16. 'I am sure Douglas took the initiative and walked out first.' – F. H.

'*I have no doubt you are right, and that my vision of the exit is really a reminiscence of the entrance. In fact, now that you prompt my memory, I recall quite distinctly that Douglas, who came in as the follower, went out as the leader, and that the last word was spoken by Wilde after he had gone.*' – G. B. S.

17. 'This insight on Shaw's part makes me smile because it is absolutely true. Oscar commended Bosie Douglas to me again and again and again, begged me to be nice to him if we ever met by chance; but I refused to meet him for months and months.' – F. H.

18. At full speed.

19. The English paste in Shaw; genius is about the rarest thing on earth whereas the necessary quantum of "honesty, sobriety and industry," is beaten by life into nine humans out of ten.' – F. H.

'*If so, it is the tenth who comes my way.*' – G. B. S.

20. 'Superb criticism.' – F. H.

21. For a note on *Mr. and Mrs. Daventry* see p. 370.

22. I have said this in my way. – F. H.

23. For a note on Frank Harris see p. 426.

24. 'A characteristic flirt of Shaw's humour. He is a great caricaturist and not a portrait-painter.

When he thinks of my Celtic face and aggressive American frankness he talks of me as pugnacious and a pirate: "a Captain Kidd." In his preface to "The Fair Lady of the Sonnets" he praises my "idiosyncratic gift of pity"; says that I am "wise through pity"; then he extols me as a prophet, not seeing that a pitying sage, prophet and pirate constitute an inhuman superman.

I shall do more for Shaw than he has been able to do for me; he is the first figure in my new volume of "Contemporary Portraits." I have portrayed him there at his best, as I love to think of him, and henceforth he'll have to try to live up to my conception and that will keep him, I'm afraid, on strain.' – F. H.

'*God help me!*' – G. B. S.

# Oscar Wilde*

Frank Harris

As a result of nearly twenty years' friendship I have written a life of Oscar Wilde. The publishers of this book of 'Portraits' wish me to sketch him here in a dozen pages. Replicas in art are unthinkable: even a hen cannot lay two eggs exactly alike; but I can take some pages from my book here and there, and so give some idea of the man and his excelling humor, though in such narrow limits I cannot trust myself to speak of his deeper self and tragic fate. Here is a snapshot, so to speak, with apologies to the reader, who will have to use imagination to stuff out the meagre outline.

\*          \*          \*

In the early eighties I met Oscar Wilde continually, now at the theatre, now in some society drawing-room; most often, I think, at Mrs. Jeune's (afterwards Lady St. Helier). His appearance was not in his favor; there was something oily and fat about him that repelled me. Of course, being very young I tried to give my repugnance a moral foundation; fleshly indulgence and laziness, I said to myself, were written all over him. The snatches of his monologues which I caught from time to time seemed to me to consist chiefly of epigrams almost mechanically constructed of proverbs and familiar sayings turned upside down. One of Balzac's characters, it will be remembered, practised this form of humor. The desire to astonish and dazzle; the love of the uncommon for its own sake, were so evident that I shrugged my shoulders and avoided him. One evening, however, at Mrs. Jeune's, I got to know him better. At the very door Mrs. Jeune came up to me:

'Have you ever met Mr. Oscar Wilde? You ought to know him: he is so delightfully clever, so brilliant!'

I went with her and was formally introduced to him. He looked like a Roman Emperor of the decadence; he was over six feet in height, and both broad and thick-set. He shook hands in a limp way I disliked; his hands were flabby; greasy; his skin looked bilious and dirty. He had a trick which I noticed even then, which grew on him later, of pulling his jowl with his right hand as he spoke, and his jowl was already fat and pouchy. He wore a

---

*Contemporary Portraits* (London: Methuen, 1915) pp. 90–118; (New York: Mitchell Kennerley, 1915) pp. 97–126.

great green scarab ring on one finger. He was overdressed rather than well dressed; his clothes fitted him too tightly; he was too stout. His appearance filled me with distaste. I lay stress on this physical repulsion because I think most people felt it, and because it is a tribute to the fascination of the man that he should have overcome the first impression so completely and so quickly. I don't remember what we talked about, but I noticed almost immediately that his grey eyes were finely expressive; in turn vivacious, laughing, sympathetic; always beautiful. The carven mouth, too, with its heavy, chiselled, almost colorless lips, had a certain charm in spite of a black front tooth which showed ignobly.

We had a certain interest in each other, an interest of curiosity, for I remember that he led the way almost immediately into the inner drawing-room, in order, as he said, to talk at ease in some seclusion. The conversation ended by my asking him to lunch next day.

At this time he was a superb talker, more brilliant than any I have ever heard in England, but nothing like what he became later in life. His talk soon made me forget his repellant physical peculiarities; indeed, I soon lost sight of them so completely that I have wondered since how I could have been so disagreeably affected by them. There was an extraordinary physical vivacity and geniality in the man, a winning charm in his gaiety, and lightning quick intelligence. His enthusiasms too were infectious. Every mental question interested him, especially if it had anything to do with art or literature. His whole face lit up as he spoke, and one saw nothing but his soulful eyes, heard nothing but his musical tenor voice; he was indeed what the French call a *charmeur*.

\* \* \*

IN THE WORLD'S SCHOOL. LONDON, 1880–1884.

Before Oscar Wilde left Oxford he described himself as a 'Professor of Æsthetics and Critic of Art.' He had already dipped into his little patrimony to pay for his undergraduate trip to Greece and Italy with Mahaffy, and he could not conceal from himself that he would soon have to live on what he could earn by his pen in London – a few pounds a week. But then he was a poet, and had boundless confidence in his own ability. To the artist nature the present is everything; just for today he resolved that he would live as he had always lived; so he travelled first class to London and bought all the books and papers that could amuse or distract him: 'Give me the luxuries,' he used to say, 'and anyone can have the necessaries.'

Of course, in the background of his mind there were serious misgivings – ghosts that would not be laid. Long afterwards he told me that his father's death and the smallness of his patrimony had been a heavy blow to him. He encouraged himself, however, at the moment by dwelling on his brother's comparative success as a journalist in London, and waved aside fears and doubts as unworthy.

It is to his credit that at first he tried to cut down expenses and live laborious days. He took a couple of furnished rooms in Salisbury Street, off the Strand, a very Grub Street for a man of fashion, and began to work at journalism while getting together a book of poems for publication. His journalism at first was anything but successful. It was his misfortune to appeal only to the best heads, and good heads are not numerous anywhere. His appeal, too, was still academic and derivative. His brother Willie with his commoner sympathies appeared to be better equipped for this work. But Oscar had from the first a certain social success.

As soon as he reached London he stepped boldly into the limelight, going to all 'first nights' and taking the floor on all occasions. He was not only an admirable talker, but he was invariably smiling, eager, full of life and the joy of living, and, above all, given to unmeasured praise of whatever and whoever pleased him. This gift of enthusiastic admiration was not only his most engaging characteristic, but also, perhaps, the chief evidence of his extraordinary ability. It was certainly, too, the quality which served him best all through his life. He went about declaring that Mrs. Langtry was more beautiful than the 'Venus of Milo,' and Lady Archie Campbell more charming than Rosalind, and Mr. Whistler an incomparable artist. Such enthusiasm in a young and brilliant man was unexpected and delightful, and doors were thrown open to him in many sets. Those who praise passionately are generally welcome guests, and if Oscar could not praise he shrugged his shoulders and kept silent; scarcely a bitter word ever fell from those smiling lips. No tactics could have been more successful in England than his native gift of radiant good-humor and enthusiasm. He got to know not only all the actors and actresses, but the chief patrons and frequenters of the theatre: Lord Lytton, Lady Shrewsbury, Gladys, Lady Lonsdale (afterwards Lady de Grey), and Mrs. Jeune; and, on the other hand, Tennyson, Hardy, Meredith, Browning, Swinburne, and Matthew Arnold – all Bohemia, in fact, and all that part of Mayfair which cares for the things of the intellect.

But though he went out a great deal and met a great many distinguished people, and won a certain popularity, his social success put no money in his purse. It even forced him to spend money; for the constant applause of his hearers gave him self-confidence. He began to talk more and write less, and cabs and gloves and flowers cost money. He was soon compelled to mortgage his little property in Ireland.

At the same time, he was still nobly intent on bettering his mind, and in London he found far wiser teachers than in Oxford, Matthew Arnold, and Morris, and in especial Whistler. Morris and Arnold, though greatly overestimated during their lives, had hardly any message for the men of their own time. Morris went for his ideals to an imaginary past, and what he taught and praised was often totally unsuited to modern conditions.

Arnold was an academic critic and dilettante poet, his views of life those of the snobbish goody-goody schoolmaster, his influence a scholarly and cloistered influence, an evil influence for Oscar Wilde confirming his bookish bias. Whistler, on the other hand, was a student of life, a master of ironic persiflage, and a great artist to boot: he had not only assimilated much of the newest thought of the time, but with the alchemy of genius had transmuted it and made it his own. He was, indeed, worth listening to.

Oscar sat at his feet and assimilated as much as he could of the new aesthetic gospel. He even ventured to annex some of the master's theories and telling stories, and thus came into conflict with his teacher.

Everyone must remember one instance of this and Whistler's use of it. The art critic of *The Times* had come to see an exhibition of Whistler's pictures. Filled with an undue sense of his own importance he buttonholed the master and pointing to one picture said: 'That's good, first-rate, a lovely bit of color; but that, you know,' he went on, jerking his finger over his shoulder at another picture; 'that's bad, drawing all wrong . . . bad!'

'My dear fellow,' cried Whistler, 'you must never say that that painting's good or that bad, never! Good and bad are not terms to be used by you; but say, I like this, and I dislike that, and you'll be within your right. And now come and have a whiskey for you're sure to like that.'

Carried away by the witty fling, Oscar cried:

'I wish I had said that.'

'You will, Oscar, you will,' came Whistler's lightning thrust.

Of all the personal influences which went to the moulding of Oscar Wilde's talent, that of Whistler was by far the most important; Whistler taught him the value of wit and the power a consciousness of genius and a knowledge of men lend to the artist, taught him, too, that singularity of appearance counts doubly in a democracy of clothes. But neither his own talent, nor the stories and ideas he borrowed from Whistler helped him to earn money: the conquest of London seemed further off and more improbable than ever. Where a Whistler had failed to win, how could he, or indeed anyone, be sure of success?

A weaker professor of aesthetics would have been discouraged by the monetary and other difficulties of his position, and would have lost heart at the outset before the impenetrable blank wall of English philistinism and contempt. But Oscar Wilde was conscious of great ability and was driven by an inordinate vanity. Instead of diminishing his pretensions in the face of opposition, he increased them. He began to go abroad in the evening in knee breeches and silk stockings, wearing strange flowers in his coat – green carnations and gilded lilies – while talking about Baudelaire, whose name even was unfamiliar, as a world poet, and proclaiming the strange creed that 'nothing succeeds like excess.' Very soon his name was in every one's mouth, fashionable London talked of him and discussed him at a thousand tea-tables. For one invitation he had received before, he now received a dozen; he became a celebrity.

Of course, he was still sneered at by the many as a mere *poseur*; it still seemed to be all Lombard Street to a china orange that he would be beaten down under the myriad trampling feet of English indifference and contempt.

But if the artistic movement was laughed at and scorned by the many as a craze, a select few stood firm, and soon the steadfast minority began to sway the majority, as is usually the case. Oscar Wilde became the prophet of an esoteric cult. But notoriety even did not solve the monetary question, which grew more and more insistent. A dozen times he waved it aside and went into debt rather than restrain himself. Somehow or other he would fall on his feet, he thought. Men who console themselves in this way usually fall on some one else's feet, and so did Oscar Wilde. At twenty-six years of age, and, curiously enough, at the very moment of his insolent-bold challenge of the world with fantastic dress, he had to borrow from his mother and a little later was fain to sell his small patrimony in order to meet the most pressing necessities; but the difficulty was only postponed; what was to be done?

Even as a young man Oscar had a certain understanding of life. He could not make his way as a journalist, but he might as a lecturer; he knew in his heart that he could talk, better than he could write and there was a lot of money in a successful lecture tour. But for the moment he put off this new adventure, having persuaded himself that his book of poems would make him famous and perhaps rich. He had used all his cleverness on the book; he had written sonnets in it to Miss Ellen Terry and other notable persons; they would surely talk about the book and buy copies and get their friends also to buy. His calculation was not mistaken: the book went into four editions in as many weeks and brought in some two or three hundred pounds – tenfold more than Keats's first book. There was a bitter in the sweet, however; the critics would not have him at any price: *The Times, The Saturday Review, Punch* – the bigwigs declared unanimously that his poems were mere echoes and furnished striking proof of their assertions. Oscar Wilde, they all concluded, was anything you like; but not a poet.

In face of the condemnation of the critics Oscar acted at once: he got his brother Willie to announce in *The World* that the unexampled success of the poems had brought Oscar Wilde an offer from the famous impresario, Major Pond, to lecture in the States, and incontinently he betook himself to New York.

On landing he boldly challenged Fortune again by telling the custom officials that he had nothing to declare but his genius. The phrase caught the public fancy and his first lecture in Chickering Hall brought together so distinguished an audience that an impresario volunteered his services and Oscar began his tour under the best auspices. His subjects were 'The English Renaissance' and 'The House Beautiful.' He had what the French call a *succès de scandale* – a success of notoriety in America, but nothing more. People went to see his old-world attire rather than to hear him. One is fain to confess today that his lectures make very poor reading. There is not a new thought in them; not even a memorable expression; though now and then a gleam of humor, an unexpected bird-like flirt of wing and quick change of direction are diverting. The lectures were a half-success. He made some money by them, repaid his mother, and spread his name abroad. But the cash result was not conclusive. In a year or so we find him again in England; grown a little wiser.

*     *     *

It is greatly to his credit that he did not settle down in London. Whistler had studied in Paris, so Oscar went there, too, using the money he had made in America to better his culture. In a few months he learned a great deal of French and got to know most of the younger French writers. On his return he talked of Verlaine as familiarly and admiringly as he had formerly talked of Baudelaire.

Before going to France he had lectured in London to the Art Students of the Royal Academy on art and thereby excited Whistler's anger. Whistler asserted that Oscar had begged him for assistance in composing this address; he had imparted some simple, necessary truths and from a gentleman had naturally looked for the usual acknowledgment. But Oscar had coolly appropriated his ideas, flaunted his feathers and had omitted to give his master the credit. There can be no doubt that Whistler's complaint, though over-shrill and passionate, was justified: whoever compares Oscar's lecture on 'The English Renaissance of Art' with his lecture to the Art Students will have to recognize a change of front. Such phrases as 'artists are not to copy beauty but to create it . . . a picture is a purely decorative thing,' proclaim their author. Oscar himself, when questioned, admitted that there was some truth in Whistler's contention. The newspaper dispute between the two was brought to a head in 1885, when Whistler gave his famous *Ten o'clock* lecture on Art: Whistler's lecture was infinitely better than any of Oscar Wilde's. Twenty odd years older than Wilde, Whistler was a master of all his resources: he was not only witty, but he had new views on art and original ideas. As a great artist he knew that 'there never was an artistic period. There never was an Art-loving nation.'

Again and again, too, he reached pure beauty of feeling and expression. I thought the lecture masterly, the best ever heard in London, and I said so loudly enough. To my astonishment Oscar would not admit the super-lative quality of Whistler's talk: he thought the message paradoxical and the ridicule of the professors too bitter. 'Whistler's like a wasp,' he cried, 'and carries about with him a poisoned sting.' Oscar's kindly sweet nature revolted against the bitter aggressiveness of Whistler's attitude. Besides, in essence, Whistler's lecture was an attack on the academic theory taught in the universities, and defended naturally by a young scholar like Oscar

Wilde. Whistler's view that the artist was sporadic, a happy chance, a 'sport,' in fact, even in 1885, was a new view, and Oscar was not on this level; he reviewed the master in the *Pall Mall Gazette*, a review remarkable for one of the earliest gleams of that genial humor which later became his most characteristic gift: 'Whistler,' he said, 'is indeed one of the very greatest masters of painting in my opinion. And I may add that in this opinion Mr. Whistler himself entirely concurs.'

Whistler retorted in *The World* and Oscar replied, but Whistler had altogether the best of the argument.

A little later we had Whistler's famous and bitter summing up. . . . 'What has Oscar in common with Art? except that he dines at our tables and picks from our platters the plums for the pudding he peddles in the provinces. . . . Oscar – the amiable, irresponsible, esurient Oscar – with no more sense of a picture than of the fit of a coat, has the courage of the opinions . . . of others!'

Oscar Wilde learned almost all he knew of art and of controversy from Whistler, but he was never more than a pupil in either field; for controversy especially, he was poorly equipped: he had neither the courage, nor the bitterness, nor the joy in conflict of his great exemplar. It was only his geniality and high intelligence which saved him from becoming as manifest a butt as Mr. Sidney Colvin or poor 'Arry Quilter.

Ten years later he had become as witty as his master, and a thousand times more humorous, but even then he was a wretched fighter, too kindly ever to be a good disputant.

\* \* \*

Very soon after meeting Oscar Wilde for the first time I confessed to myself that I liked him; his talk was intensely quickening. He had something unexpected to say on almost every subject. His mind was agile and powerful, and he took delight in using it. He was well read, too, in several languages, especially in French, and his excellent memory stood him in good stead. Even when he merely repeated what the great ones had said perfectly, he added a new coloring. And already his characteristic humor was beginning to illumine every topic with lambent flashes.

The first time we lunched together he told me that he had been asked by Harper's to write a book of one hundred thousand words and offered a large sum for it – I think some five thousand dollars – in advance. He wrote to them gravely that he did not know one hundred thousand words in English, so could not undertake the work, and he laughed merrily like a child at the cheeky reproof.

'I have sent their letters and my reply to the Press,' he added, and laughed again, probing me with inquisitive eyes; how far did I understand that self-advertisement was a necessity, notoriety a short-cut to fame?

About this time an impromptu of his moved the town to laughter. At

some dinner-party it appeared the ladies sat a little too long; Oscar wanted
to smoke. Suddenly the hostess drew his attention to a candle on his left:
'Please put it out, Mr. Wilde,' she said, 'it's smoking.'

Oscar turned to do as he was told with the remark: 'Happy candle!'
The delightful impertinence had an extraordinary success. . . .

Early in our friendship I was forced to see that his love of the uncommon,
his paradoxes and epigrams were natural to him, sprang immediately from
his nature and temperament. Perhaps it would be well to define once for all
his attitude towards life with more scope and particularity than I have
hitherto done. It is often supposed that he had no clear and coherent view
of life, no belief, no faith to guide his vagrant footsteps; but such an opinion
does him an injustice. He had his own philosophy, and held to it for long
years with astonishing tenacity. His attitude towards life can best be seen if
he be held up against Goethe. He took the artistic view of life which Goethe
had first stated, and, indeed, in youth had overstated with an astonishing
persuasiveness: 'the beautiful is more than the good,' said Goethe; 'for it
includes the good.'

It seemed to Oscar, as it had seemed to young Goethe, that 'the
extraordinary alone survives'; the extraordinary whether good or bad; he
therefore sought after the extraordinary, and naturally enough often fell
into extravagance. But how stimulating it was in London, where sordid
platitudes drip and drizzle all day long, to hear some one talking brilliant
paradoxes. Oscar's appeal to the artistic intelligence was as quickening as
sunshine.

Goethe did not linger long in the half-way house of unbelief; the
murderer, he saw, may win notoriety as easily as the martyr, but the
memory of him will not be cherished. '*The fashion of this world passeth away*,'
said the great German, 'I would fain occupy myself with that which
endures.'

Midway on life's road Goethe accepted Kant's moral imperative and
restated his creed: 'A man must resolve to live,' he said, 'not only for the
Good and Beautiful, but for the Common Weal.'

Oscar did not push his thought into such transcendental regions.

It was a pity, I often felt, that he had not studied German as thoroughly
as French; Goethe might have done more for him than Verlaine or Balzac,
for in spite of some stodgy German faults Goethe is the best guide through
the mysteries of life that the modern world has yet produced. Oscar Wilde
stopped where the religion of Goethe began; he was as obstinate a pagan
and individualist as Goethe had been in youth; he lived for the beautiful
and extraordinary, but not for the Good, and still less for the Whole; he
acknowledged no moral obligation; *in commune bonis*[1] was an ideal which
never said anything to him; he cared nothing for the common good; he held
himself above the mass of the people with an Englishman's extravagant
insularity and aggressive pride. Politics, religion – everything interested
him simply as a subject of art; life itself was merely material for art. In fine

he had taken Whistler's position, the position most natural to an artist.

The view was astounding in England, and new everywhere in its onesidedness. Its passionate exaggeration, however, was quickening, and there is, of course, something to be said for it. The artistic view of life is often higher than the ordinary religious view; at least it does not deal in condemnations and exclusions; it is more reasonable, more catholic, more finely perceptive.

'The artist's view of life is the only possible one,' Oscar used to say, 'and should be applied to everything, most of all to religion and morality. Cavaliers and Puritans are interesting for their costumes and not for their convictions.'

'There is no such thing as morality; for there is no general rule of spiritual health; it is all personal, individual. . . . I only demand that freedom which I willingly concede to others. No one condemns another for preferring green to gold. Why should any taste be condemned? Liking and disliking are not under our control. I want to choose the nourishment which suits *my* body and *my* soul.'

I can almost hear him say the words with his charming humorous smile and exquisite flash of deprecation, as if he were half inclined to make fun of his own creed.

It was not his views on art, however, which recommended him to the aristocratic set in London; but his contempt for social reform, or rather his utter indifference to it, and his English love of inequality. He never took sufficient interest in politics to state his position clearly or strongly, but his prejudices were the prejudices of the English governing class and were all in favor of individual freedom, or anarchy under the protection of the policeman.

'The poor are poor creatures,' he used to say, 'and must always be hewers of wood and drawers of water. They are really the dunghill out of which men of genius and artists grow like flowers. Their function is to give birth to genius and nourish it. They have no other *raison d'être*. Were men as intelligent as bees, all gifted individuals would be supported by the community, as the bees support their queen. We should be the first charge on the State, just as Socrates declared that he ought to be kept in the Prytanœum at the public expense.

Don't talk to me, Frank, about the hardships of the poor. The hardships of the poor are necessities, but talk to me of the hardships of men of genius, and I could weep tears of blood. I was never so affected by any book in my life as I was by the sordid misery of Balzac's poet, Eugène [*sic*] de Rubempré.'[2]

Naturally this creed of an exaggerated individualism appealed peculiarly to the best set in London. It was eminently aristocratic.

The more I thought the matter over, the more clearly I saw that the only chance of salvation for Oscar was to get him to work, to give him some purpose in life, and the reader should remember here that at this time I had not seen *De Profundis*, and did not know that while in prison Oscar had himself recognized this necessity. After all, I said to myself, nothing is lost if he will only begin to write. A man should be able to whistle happiness and hope down the wind and take despair to his bed and heart, and win courage from his harsh companion. Happiness is no good to the artist: happiness never creates anything but memories. . . . If Oscar would work and not brood over the dead past; but let it bury itself, he might yet come to soul-health and achievement. He could win back everything; his own respect, and the respect of his fellows, if indeed that were worth winning. After all, an artist must have at least the self-abnegation of the hero, and heroic resolution to strive and strive, or he will never bring it far even in his art. If I could only get Oscar to work, it seemed to me everything might yet come right. I spent a week with him, lunching and dining and putting all this before him in every way.

I noticed that he enjoyed the good eating and the good drinking as intensely as ever. He was even drinking too much I thought, and was beginning to get stout and flabby again, but the good living was a necessity to him, and it certainly did not prevent him from talking charmingly. He was getting very deaf, and on that account fell into unusual drifts of silence, but the pauses seemed to set off the brilliance of his talk: his monologues were more interesting than ever, his humor richer and more pervasive. For hours together he would keep his hearers smiling delightedly, interested in all he said, exquisitely amused by the happy verbal radiance playing over his rhythmic speech. He would frequently begin with some little story, or apologue, and then toss witty nothings about like a conjuror playing with colored balls, always ready to seize on the first remark and illumine it with a novel significance, or make it the reason for relating some new and interesting experience. Other men may have talked as well, but surely no one has ever had such wealth of verbal humor. Dozens of the winged words of today were of his coining on the spur of the moment: 'Thick as thieves in Vallombrosa'. 'The woman who hesitates is won'; 'Familiarity breeds consent'; unexpected flirts of gay insight.

I perpetually praised these performances in order to induce him to write: but as soon as I brought up the subject he would shake his head gloomily:

'Oh, Frank, I cannot, you know my rooms; how could I write there? A horrid bedroom like a closet, and a little sitting-room without air or outlook. Books everywhere; and no place to write; to tell the truth, I cannot even read in it. No artist could write in such sordid misery.'

Again and again he came back to this. He harped upon his poverty, so that I could not but see purpose in it. He was already cunning in the art of getting money without asking for it. My heart ached for him; one goes down hill with such fatal speed and ease, and the mire at the foot is so loathsome.

'You ought to work, Oscar. After all, why should anyone help you, if you will not help yourself? If I cannot assist you to save yourself, I am only doing you harm.'

'A base sophism, Frank, mere hypocrisy, as you know: the fatted calf is better than husks for any man.'

'You could easily win thousands and live like a prince again. Why not make the effort?'

'It is harder than you think, Frank. If I had pleasant sunny rooms I'd try. . . . It's harder than you think.'

'Nonsense, it's easy for you. Your punishment has made your name known in every country in the world. A book of yours would sell like wildfire; a play of yours would draw in any capital. You might live here like a prince. Shakespeare lost love and friendship, hope and health to boot – everything, and yet forced himself to write *The Tempest*. Why can't you?'

'I'll try, Frank, I'll try.'

I may just mention here that any praise of what others had done, moved Oscar to emulation. He always compared himself to the greatest. In one of my articles on Shakespeare in *The Saturday Review*, in 1896, I declared that no one had ever given completer record of himself than Shakespeare: 'We know him better than we know any of our contemporaries,' I wrote, 'and he is better worth knowing.' When this appeared Oscar wrote to me praising the article; but condemning the phrase.

'Frank, Frank, you have forgotten me,' were his words, 'surely I am better worth knowing than Shakespeare.'

I did not agree with him, but it didn't matter. I had to go back to England, but I crossed to Paris early in the summer, and found he had written nothing.

I often talked with him about it; but now he changed his ground a little.

'I can't write, Frank. When I take up my pen all the past comes back: I cannot bear my thoughts . . . regret and remorse, like twin dogs, wait to seize me at any idle moment. I must go out and watch life; amuse and interest myself, or I should go mad. . . . You don't know how sore it is about my heart as soon as I am alone. I am face to face with my own soul: the Oscar of five years ago, with his beautiful secure life and his glorious easy triumphs, comes up before me, and I cannot stand the contrast. . . . My eyes burn with tears. If you care for me you will not ask me to write.'

'You promised to try,' I said, somewhat harshly, 'and I want you to try. You haven't suffered more than Dante suffered in exile and poverty; a man as proud as Lucifer forced to be a parasite; yet you know if he had suffered ten times as much he would have written it all down. Tears, indeed! the fire in his eyes would have dried the tears.'

'True enough, Frank, but don't you see that Dante was all of one piece? I am at war with myself. I was born to sing the joy and pride of life, the pleasure of living, the delight in everything beautiful in this most beautiful world, and they took me and tortured me till I learned sorrow and pity. Now I cannot sing the joy, Frank, because I know the suffering and I was never made to sing of suffering. I hate it and I want to sing the love-songs of joy and delight. It is joy alone which appeals to my soul. The joy of life and beauty and love – I could sing the song of Apollo the Sun-God, and they try to force me to sing the lament of the tortured Marsyas. . . . '

This to me was his true and final confession. His second fall after leaving prison had put him 'at war with himself.' That is, I think, the heart of truth about him; the song of sorrow, of pity and renunciation was not his song, and the experience of suffering prevented the great pagan from singing the delight of life and his joy in beauty. It never seemed to occur to him that he should stand with one foot on self-indulgence and with the other on renunciation, and reach a faith which should include both in a completer acceptance of life.

In spite of his sunny nature he had a certain amount of jealousy and envy in him which was always brought to light by the popular success of those whom he had known and measured. I remember his telling me once that he wrote his first play because he was annoyed at the way Pinero was being praised. 'Pinero, who can't write at all: he can make plots and scenes and nothing else. His characters are made of dough: and never was there such a worthless style, or rather such a complete absence of style: he writes like a grocer's assistant.'

I noticed now that this trait of jealousy was stronger in him than ever. One day I threw him an English illustrated paper which I had bought on my way to lunch. It contained a picture of Lord Curzon as Viceroy of India. He was photographed in a carriage with his wife by his side: the State carriage drawn by four horses, with outriders, and escorted by cavalry and cheering crowds – all the paraphernalia and pomp of imperial power.

'Do you see that, Frank?' Oscar cried; 'fancy George Curzon being treated like that. I knew him well; a more perfect example of plodding mediocrity was never seen in the world. He had never a thought or phrase above the common . . . '

* * *

"Now George Curzon plays king in India: Wyndham is a Secretary of State, and I'm hiding in shame and poverty here in Paris, an exile and outcast. Do you wonder that I cannot write, Frank? The dreadful injustice of life maddens me. After all, what have they done in comparison with what I have done?

'Close the eyes of all of us now and fifty years hence, or a hundred years hence, no one will know anything about the Curzons, or the Wyndhams:

whether they lived or died will be a matter of indifference to every one; but my comedies and my stories and *The Ballad of Reading Gaol* will be known and read by millions, and even my unhappy fate will call forth world-wide sympathy.'

'That's your real reward, Oscar, an exceeding great reward; that's what you have labored for, fame and sympathy when you are dead, a longer breath of life than other men can hope to enjoy, and that is why you should write now. Go on, do more, and do it better.'

'Oh, Frank, it's impossible, impossible for me to work under these disgraceful conditions.'

'But you can have better conditions now and more money as you want it if you'll begin to work.'

He shook his head despairingly. Again and again I tried, but again and again failed to move him to any effort. At last one day I said to him:

'The only thing that will make you write, Oscar, is absolute, blank poverty. That's the sharpest spur after all – necessity.'

'You don't know me, Frank,' he replied tartly. 'I would kill myself. I can endure to the end; but to be absolutely destitute would show me that suicide is the open door.'

Suddenly his depressed manner changed and his whole face lighted up:

'Isn't it comic, Frank, the way the English talk of the "open door" while their doors are always locked and barred and bolted, even their church doors? Yet it is not hypocrisy in them; they simply cannot see themselves as they are; they have no imagination.'

There was a long pause, and then he went on gravely:

'Suicide, Frank, is always the temptation of the unfortunate, a great temptation.'

'Suicide is the natural end of the world-weary,' I replied, 'but you enjoy life intensely. For you to talk of suicide is ridiculous.'

'Do you know that my wife is dead?'[3]

'I had heard it,' I replied.

'My way back to hope and a new life ends in her grave,' he went on. 'Everything that happens to me is symbolic and irrevocable.'

He spoke, I thought, with a certain grave conviction.

'The great tragedies of the world are all final and complete; Socrates would not escape death, though Crito opened the prison door for him. I could not avoid prison, though you showed me the way to safety. Some of us are fated to suffer, don't you think? as an example to humanity – 'an echo and a light unto eternity." '

'I think it would be finer, instead of taking the punishment lying down, to trample it beneath your feet, and make it a rung of the ladder.'

'Oh, Frank, you would turn all the tragedies into triumphs, that is the fighter in you.'

'Nonsense,' I cried, 'you love life as much as ever you did; more than anyone I have ever seen.'

'It is true,' he cried, his face lighting up again, 'more than anyone. Life delights me. The people passing on the boulevards, the play of the sunshine in the trees; the vibrating noise, the quick movement of the cabs, the costumes of the *cochers* and *sergents-de-ville*, kings and beggars, princesses and prostitutes all please me to the soul, charm me, and if you will only let me talk instead of bothering me to write I shall be quite happy. Why should I write any more? I have done enough for fame. . . .

'I will tell you a story, Frank,' he broke off, and he told me a slight thing about Judas. The little tale was told delightfully, with eloquent inflections of voice and still more eloquent pauses.

\* \* \*

'The end of all this is,' I said, before going back to London, 'the end of all this is, that you will not write?'

'No, no, Frank,' he said, 'that I cannot write under these conditions. If I had money enough; if I could shake off Paris and forget those awful rooms of mine and get to the Riviera for the winter and live in some seaside village of the Latins or Etrurians with the wine-colored sea at my feet, and the blue sky above, and the scent of rosemary and myrtle at my nostrils, and God's sunlight about me and no care for money, then I would write as naturally as a bird sings, because one is happy and cannot help it. . . . '

But when the occasion was given him, and he spent a whole winter on the Riviera, he composed nothing more than a couple of verses of a ballad on *A Fisher Boy*, verses which were never even written down.

\* \* \*

The will to live had almost left him: so long as he could live pleasantly and without effort he was content; but as soon as ill-health came or pain, or even discomfort, he grew impatient for deliverance.

One day when out driving in the last months Ross remonstrated with him for stopping too frequently to drink:

'You know you shouldn't, Oscar; the doctors said you shouldn't; it is poison to you.'

For one moment the sad eyes held him:

'Why not, Bobbie? What have I to live for?' And his best friend could only bow his head.

But to the last he kept his joyous humor and charming gaiety. His disease[4] brought with it a certain irritation of the skin, annoying rather than painful. Meeting this same friend after some weeks of separation he wanted to apologize for scratching himself:

'Really,' he exclaimed, 'I'm more like a great ape than ever; but I hope you'll give me a lunch, Bobbie, and not a nut.'

At the very last, he asked for champagne and when it was brought declared that he was 'dying beyond his means' – his happy humor lighting up even his death-bed.

## NOTES

Frank Harris (1854–1931), American author born in Ireland. His biography of *Oscar Wilde* (1916) and the autobiographical *My Life and Loves* (1923) excited hostile criticism because of their frankness. On the relationship between Wilde and Harris see Vincent Brome, *Frank Harris* (London: Cassell, 1959) *passim;* Hugh Kingsmill, 'Park Lane and Oscar Wilde', *Frank Harris* (London: Jonathan Cape, 1932) pp. 86–105; E. Merrill Root, *Frank Harris* (New York: Odyssey Press, 1947) chap. VI; A. I. Tobin and Elmer Gertz, 'The "Oscar Wilde" and Its "Villains"', *Frank Harris; A Study in Black and White* (Chicago: Madelaine Mendelsohn, 1931) pp. 275–97; and Samuel Roth, 'Seeing Oscar Through', *The Private Life of Frank Harris* (New York: William Faro, 1931) chap. 12. For Harris on Wilde see Hugh Kingsmill, 'The Intelligent Man's Guide to Oscar Wilde', *The Fortnightly Review*, CXLIV (Sep 1938) 296–303.

   1. For the common weal; for the public well-being.

   2. Wilde says in *De Profundis: 'Voilà où mènent les mauvais Chemins!'* The last five words are the title of Balzac's *Splendeurs et Misères des Courtisanes*, in which the misguided life of Lucien de Rubempré comes to its pitiful and tragic end. Vincent O'Sullivan records Wilde's saying: 'When I was a boy my two favourite characters were Lucien de Rubempré and Julien Sorel [in Stendhal's *Le Rouge et le Noir*]. Lucien hanged himself, Julien died on the scaffold, and I died in prison.'

   3. Constance Wilde, following an operation, died in Genoa on 7 April 1898.

   4. For a note on Wilde's last illness see p. 474.

# Oscar Wilde; An Idler's Impression*

### Edgar Saltus

Years ago, in a Paris club, one man said to another: 'Well, what's up?' The other shook a paper: 'There is only one genius in England and they have put him in jail.'

One may wonder though whether it were their doing, or even Wilde's, that put him there. One may wonder whether it were not the high fates who so gratified him in order that, from his purgatory, he might rise to a life more evolved. But that view is perhaps obvious. Wilde himself, who was the least mystic of men, accepted it. In the 'De Profundis,' after weighing

* *Oscar Wilde; An Idler's Impression* (Chicago: Brothers of the Book, 1917) pp. 13–26.

his disasters, he said: 'Of these things I am not yet worthy.'

The genuflexion has been called a pose. It may have been. Even so, it is perhaps better to kneel, though it be in the gallery, than to stoop at nothing, and Wilde, who had stood very high, bent very low. He saw that there is one thing greater than greatness and that is humility.

Yet though he saw it, it is presumable that he forgot it. It is presumable that the grace which was his in prison departed in Paris. On the other hand it may not have. There are no human scales for any soul.

It was at Delmonico's, shortly after he told our local Customs that he had nothing to declare but genius,[1] that I first met him. He was dressed like a mountebank. Without, at the entrance, a crowd had collected. In the restaurant people stood up and stared. Wilde was beautifully unmoved. He was talking, at first about nothing whatever, which is always an interesting topic, then about 'Vera,'[2] a play of his for which a local manager had offered him an advance, five thousand dollars I think, 'mere starvation wages,' as he put it, and he went on to say that the manager wanted him to make certain changes in it. He paused and added: 'But who am I to tamper with a masterpiece?' – a jest which afterward he was too generous to hoard.

Later, in London, I saw him again. In appearance and mode of life he had become entirely conventional. The long hair, the knee-breeches, the lilies, the velvet, all the mountebank trappings had gone. He was married, he was a father, and in his house in Tite street he seemed a bit bourgeois. Of that he may have been conscious. I remember one of his children running and calling at him: 'My good papa!' and I remember Wilde patting the boy and saying: 'Don't call me that, it sounds so respectable.'

In Tite street I had the privilege of meeting Mrs. Oscar, who asked me to write something in an album. I have always hated albumenous poetry and, as I turned the pages in search of possible inspiration, I happened on this: *From a poet to a poem..Robert Browning.*

Poets exaggerate and why should they not? They have been found, too, with their hands in other people's paragraphs. Wilde helped himself to that line which he put in a sonnet to this lady, who had blue eyes, fair hair, chapped lips, and a look of constant bewilderment.

As for that, Oscar was sufficiently bewildering. He talked infinitely better than he wrote, and on no topic, no matter what, could he talk as other mortals must. Once only I heard of him uttering a platitude and from any one else that platitude would have been a paradox. He exuded wit and waded in it with a serenity that was disconcerting.

It was on this abnormal serenity and on his equally abnormal brilliance that he relied to defeat the prosecution. 'I have all the criminal classes with me,' he announced, and that was his one platitude, a banality that contrived to be tragic. Then headlong down the stair of life he fell.

Hell he had long since summarised as the union of souls without bodies to bodies without souls. There are worse definitions than this which years later I recalled when, through a curious forethought of fate, he was taken, en route to the cemetery, through the Porte de l'Enfer.

But in Tite street, at this time, and in Regent street where he occasionally dined, he was gentle, wholesome, and joyous; a man who paid compliments because, as he put it, he could pay nothing else. He had been caricatured: the caricatures had ceased. People had turned to look: they looked no longer. He was forgiven and, what is worse, forgotten. Yet that tiger, his destiny, was but sharpening its claws.

At an inn where Gautier dined, the epigrams were so demoralising that a waiter became insane. Similarly in the Regent street restaurant it was reported, perhaps falsely, that a waiter had also lost his reason. But Wilde, though a three decanter man, always preserved his own. He preserved, too, his courtesy which was invariable. The most venomous thing that he ever said of anyone was that he was a tedious person, and the only time he ever rebuked anybody was at the conclusion of one of those after-dinner stories which some host or other interrupted by rising and saying: 'Shall we continue the conversation in the drawing-room?'

But I am in error. That was not his only rebuke. On one occasion I drove with him to Tite street. An hour previous he had executed a variation on the 'Si j'étais roi.' 'If I were king,' he had sung, 'I would sit in a great hall and paint on green ivory and when my ministers came and told me that the people were starving, I would continue to paint on green ivory and say: "Let them starve."'

The aria was rendered in the rooms of Francis Hope, a young man who later married and divorced May Yohe, but who at the time showed an absurd interest in stocks. Someone else entered and Hope asked what was new in the City. 'Money is very tight,' came the reply. 'Ah, yes,' Wilde cut in. 'And of a tightness that has been felt even in Tite street. Believe me, I passed the forenoon at the British Museum looking at a gold-piece in a case.'

Afterward we drove to Chelsea. It was a vile night, bleak and bitter. On alighting, a man came up to me. He wore a short jacket which he opened. From neck to waist he was bare. I gave him a shilling. Then came the rebuke. With entire simplicity Wilde took off his overcoat and put it about the man.

But the simplicity seemed to me too Hugoesque and I said: 'Why didn't you ask him in to dinner?'

Wilde gestured. 'Dinner is not a feast, it is a ceremony.'

Subsequently that ceremony must have been contemplated, for Mrs. Wilde was kind enough to invite me. The invitation reached me sometime in advance and I took it of course that there would be other guests. But on the appointed evening, or what I thought was the appointed evening, when I reached this house – on which Oscar objected to paying taxes because, as he told the astonished assessors, he was so seldom at home – when I reached it, it seemed to me that I must be the only guest. Then, presently, in the dreary drawing-room, Oscar appeared. 'This is delightful of you,' he told me. 'I have been late for dinner a half hour, again a whole hour; you are late an entire week. That is what I call originality.'

I put a bold face on it. 'Come to my shop,' I said, 'and have dinner with me. Though,' I added, 'I don't know what I can give you.'

'Oh, anything,' Wilde replied. 'Anything, no matter what. I have the simplest tastes. I am always satisfied with the best.'

He was not boasting. One evening he dined on his 'Sphinx.' Subsequently I supped with him on 'Salome.'

That was in the Regent street restaurant where, apropos of nothing, or rather with what to me at the time was curious irrelevance, Oscar, while tossing off glass after glass of liquor, spoke of Phémé, a goddess rare even in mythology, who, after appearing twice in Homer, flashed through a verse of Hesiod and vanished behind a page of Herodotos. In telling of her, suddenly his eyes lifted, his mouth contracted, a spasm of pain – or was it dread? – had gripped him. A moment only. His face relaxed. It had gone.

I have since wondered, could he have evoked the goddess then? For Phémé typified what modern occultism terms the impact – the premonition that surges and warns. It was Wilde's fate to die three times – to die in the dock, to die in prison, to die all along the boulevards of Paris. Often since I have wondered could the goddess then have been lifting, however slightly, some fringe of the crimson curtain, behind which, in all its horror, his destiny crouched. If so, he braved it.

I had looked away. I looked again. Before me was a fat pauper, florid and overdressed, who, in the voice of an immortal, was reading the fantasies of the damned. In his hand was a manuscript, and we were supping on 'Salome.'

As the banquet proceeded, I experienced that sense of sacred terror which his friends, the Greeks, knew so well. For this thing could have been conceived only by genius wedded to insanity and, at the end, when the tetrarch, rising and bundling his robes about him, cries: 'Kill that woman!' the mysterious divinity whom the poet may have evoked, deigned perhaps to visit me. For, as I applauded, I shuddered, and told him that I had.

Indifferently he nodded and, assimilating Hugo with superb unconcern, threw out: 'It is only the shudder that counts.'

That was long before the crash. After it, Mrs. Wilde said that he was mad and had been for three years, 'quite mad' as the poor woman expressed it.

It may be that she was right. St. George, I believe, fought a dragon with a spear. Whether or not he killed the brute I have forgotten. But Wilde fought poverty, which is perhaps more brutal, with a pen. The fight, if indolent, was protracted. Then, abruptly, his inkstand became a Vesuvius of gold. London that had laughed at him, laughed with him and laughed colossally. A penny-a-liner was famous. The international hurdle-race of the stage had been won in a canter and won by a hack. A sub-editor was top of the heap.

The ascent was perhaps too rapid. The spiderous Fates that sit and spin are jealous of sudden success. It may be that Mrs. Wilde was right. In any event, for some time before the crash he saw few of his former friends. After his release few of his former friends saw him. But personally, if I may refer to myself, I am not near sighted. I saw him in Paris, saw too, and to my regret, that he looked like a drunken coachman, and told him how greatly I admired the 'Ballad,' – that poem which tells of his life, or rather of his death, in jail. Half covering his mouth with his hand, he laughed and said: 'It does not seem to me sufficiently vécu.'[3]

Before the enormity of that I fell back. But at once he became more human. He complained that even the opiate of work was denied him, since no one would handle his wares.

The Athenians, who lived surrounded by statues, learned from them the value of silence, the mystery that it lends to beauty, in particular the dignity that it gives to grief. In their tragedies any victim of destiny is as though stricken dumb. Wilde knew that, he knew everything, in addition to being a thorough Hellenist. None the less he told of his fate. It was human, therefore terrible, but it was not the tragic muse. It was merely a tragedy of letters.

Letters, yes, but lower case. Wilde was a third rate poet who occasionally rose to the second class but not once to the first. Prose is more difficult than verse and in it he is rather sloppy. In spite of which, or perhaps precisely on that account, he called himself lord of language. Well, why not, if he wanted to? Besides, in his talk he was lord and more – sultan, pontifex maximus. Hook, Jerrold, Smith, Sheridan, rolled into one, could not have been as brilliant. In talk he blinded and it is the subsiding wonder of it that his plays contain.

In the old maps, on the vague places, early geographers used to put: Hic sunt leones – Here are lions. On any catalogue of Wilde's plays there should be written: Here lions might have been. For assuming his madness, one must also admit his genius and the uninterrupted conjunction of the two might have produced brilliancies such as few bookshelves display.

Therein is the tragedy of letters. Renan said that morality is the supreme illusion. The diagnosis may or may not be exact. Yet it is on illusions that we all subsist. We live on lies by day and dreams at night. From the standpoint of the higher mathematics, morality may be an illusion. But it is very sustaining. Formerly it was also inspirational. In post-pagan days it created a new conception of beauty. Apart from that, it has nothing whatever to do with the arts, except the art of never displeasing, which, in itself, is the whole secret of mediocrity.

Oscar Wilde lacked that art, and I can think of no better epitaph for him.

## NOTES

Edgar Evertson Saltus (1855–1921), American author. He gave Wilde a copy of his *Mary Magdalen* (1891). His writings on Wilde include 'Introduction,' *Intentions*, vol. v of *The Complete Works of Oscar Wilde*, (New York: A. R. Keller, 1907) pp. ix–xvii; 'Introduction', *Salomé; The Importance of Being Earnest; Lady Windermere's Fan, By Oscar Wilde* (New York: The Modern Library, [1919]), pp. i–iv; and 'Introduction', *The Plays of Oscar Wilde* (New York: The Modern Library, [1933]) pp. i–iv.

    1. When he went to America on a lecture tour in 1882.

    2. *Vera* was first produced at the Union Square Theatre, New York, on 20 August 1883.

    3. Alive.

# Without Apology*

## Lord Alfred Douglas

To sum up all I have said about him, I will say that I think that he was a man of enormous genius, and that his work is quite certain to survive indefinitely, and will be read and loved by countless thousands in the future, long after the very names of his present-day detractors are forgotten. I will also say that in spite of his sad moral lapses he was essentially a man "of good will," because he was kind and charitable, in the Catholic sense, and generous and loyal to his friends, and never really an enemy of the light. His constant love for his mother, who always neglected him and preferred to him his younger brother Willie,[1] was a touching feature of his character. He adored his mother and spoke of her always with a reverence which was really quite excessive considering her character and achievements. As to his wife, he married her solely for love, and if she had treated him properly and stuck to him after he had been in prison, as a really good wife would have done, he would have gone on loving her to the end of his life. I always liked Mrs Wilde and she liked me, though I never saw her again after the catastrophe. She was a charming, pathetic and pretty little thing. Obviously she suffered a great deal and deserves every sympathy, but she fell woefully short of the height to which she might have risen, and while I fell very deeply for her, I cannot but blame her for the attitude she took up after his conviction.[2] She was far from generous to him in the matter of money, and apart from that, she wrote to him a letter which he received very soon after he left prison which was calculated, as she must have known perfectly well (knowing his character as she did), to exasperate and embitter him and to make

* *Without Apology* (London: Martin Secker, 1938) pp. 219–23.

impossible the reunion which she professed to desire. She offered to 'take him back' on certain conditions. Oscar did not show me the letter (I did not see him for the first time since his imprisonment till some time after he received it), but he told me that her 'conditions' were insulting, and he turned pale and trembled with anger when he spoke to me about her letter. That letter finished all chance of reconciliation and finally killed all that was left of his love for her. In his *De Profundis* letter he praises her kindness and nobility; at my expense, of course, since what we wrote was in his letter to me which was full of reproaches and abuse. Yet it was the abused and be-rated friend and not the 'kind and noble' wife who stuck to him and would not be driven away even by his own abuse and railing. If Oscar had accepted her conditions (one of which was that he was never to see me), there is no doubt that our reunion at Naples would not have taken place and I would probably never have seen him again. From my point of view, looking at it in the purely material aspect, this would have been enormously to my advantage. My father had more than once offered to 'forgive' me and to give me back the substantial allowance, of which he had deprived me, if I would give up Wilde. The reproving and hostile attitude of 'Society' in general and King Edward VII (then Prince of Wales) in particular towards me was greatly accentuated when it became known that I had resumed my friendship with him, and all my friends told me that I was 'cutting my own throat' when I asked him to come to stay with me at Naples. So that if Mrs Wilde (whether merely because she had no tact or because she deliberately imposed conditions which she knew he would not accept) had not made it impossible for him to rejoin her, I would certainly not have been able, even if I had wished it (which I was very far from doing), to stand in their way.

I have long got past the stage in which I consider that I have anything to defend or apologise for in my conduct to and about Wilde after his release from prison. The plain truth is that if I had been the Archangel Gabriel I could not possibly have acted better towards him than I did. I gave everything and received nothing, except abuse from *soi-disant*[3] friends. People who do not approve of what I did are welcome to do the other thing. I care no more for their opinion now than I did at the time. I am not defending myself, I require no defence; I am defending Oscar and trying to show that it was no fault of his that there was no reunion with his wife. The blame for this rests entirely on Mrs Wilde. It was not till after she had written him the letter to which I have referred that he seriously considered the idea of coming to stay with me at Naples, and I only asked him to come then because by that time I knew that he had nowhere else to go and that I was the only person in the world who had the pluck to take him in.

The cruelty of the world was then what it always is and always will be. I was the only person in the world who wanted him, out of pure friendship and compassion, and the world, having driven him out of every other refuge, proceeded to smoke him out of this last asylum also.

The prime mover in all the intrigue to separate us was Robert Ross. He was, in this, as in everything else connected with Wilde, the villain of the piece. I believe this fact will emerge more clearly when Mr A. J. A. Symons publishes his book on Wilde which is due very soon,[4] and which will contain a number of Wilde's hitherto unpublished letters, most of which I myself have never read.

## NOTES

1. Willie Wilde, Oscar's *elder* brother, was born in 1852.

2. The friends and relations of Constance Wilde had been urging her to obtain a divorce, but Wilde's friend Robert Sherard felt that this would be the last straw, and at length managed to persuade her to visit Oscar in prison. Constance also changed her name to Holland, her maiden name.

3. So-called.

4. This book was never published. The only writings on Wilde by A. J. A. Symons are 'Wilde at Oxford', *Horizon*, III, no. 16 (April 1941) 253–64 and no. 17 (May 1941), 336–48; and 'The Diner-Out', *Horizon*, IV, no. 22 (Oct 1941) 251–8.

# Oscar Wilde*

### Ella Hepworth Dixon

The first time Oscar Wilde loomed on my horizon I was painting, together with Charlotte McCarthy and my sister, a portrait of Justin McCarthy the younger, in their hospitable house in Bloomsbury. Our model had got himself up in mediaeval finery and we had chalked in our outlines, when an announcement came, somewhat pontifically, from a tall, stout young man, leaning with his back to the window. What he said, very deliberately, was the strange phase, 'I can *never* consent to be led by – a bacon merchant!'

Irish politics bored even the youngest of us in those days (if we were English), but the 'bacon merchant,' it appeared, was Mr. Biggar, who was then a power as a leader, and, more important, as a supplier of funds to the Irish Parliamentary Party. The voice of the young man in the window was remarkable; I am sure now it was one of Oscar Wilde's principal assets. It made everything he said sound not only impressive but distinguished.

* *As I Knew Them; Sketches of People I Have Met on the Way* (London: Hutchinson, 1930) pp. 34–6.

Otherwise he had not an engaging personality, being too much occupied with his own personal appearance and his carefully prepared paradoxes. Wilde was too fat and puffy to be good-looking, but his wit was formidable, and he enjoyed a real fashion in London for a time; hostesses intrigued to get him; a woman, to whom he offered a verbal bouquet in passing, felt uplifted for the rest of the evening. I often met him at parties, including those brilliant gatherings at West House, Campden Hill, by Mr. George Boughton, R. A., and his vivacious wife.

At one time Oscar Wilde edited a magazine of splendid appearance called the *Woman's World*, and I have a most flattering letter from him about a story I contributed to it called 'Murder or Mercy,' to which he gave that unstinted praise which is so rare in Editors. I had also contributed a few 'interviews at home' of some personal friends, when Wilde decided, very wisely, to end the series. 'People,' he wrote, 'are beginning to tire of the silver ink-pot, the Persian rug, the brass paper-weight, the palms in pots. . . .' He was right. Made attractive at first by Edmund Yates in the *World*, this kind of journalism had become passably absurd.

Yet with all his assurance, Wilde, in a literary sense, was timorous enough. He knew what he could do; the essay, the fanciful story, he had accomplished with marked success. His lecture tour in America was triumphant. But when Sir George Alexander commissioned him to write a play for the St James's Theatre, Oscar was all diffidence. He did not, he declared, know how to begin. Time went on and at length he had to be bullied into writing his comedy. The result was *Lady Windermere's Fan*, at once a triumphant box-office success, and a play which even the severest critics were bound to praise for its wit and construction.

Oscar Wilde had no more devoted friend than Robert Ross[1] – that universal favourite in London – who stuck to him in his fame and in his disgrace, and to whom he left his masterpiece, *The Ballad of Reading Gaol*. Robert Ross, who came from a most distinguished family in Toronto, 'commenced author,' as the phrase goes, by writing in the *Saturday Review*. I had never met him then, but in that well-known paper he reviewed my first book (published anonymously by Chatto and Windus), and announced that 'a new humorist had arisen.' The little volume certainly had a vogue among such formidable critics as Heads of Oxford Colleges and the like, while I remember the late Chief Justice Coleridge stopping me at a party, on my way to eat an ice, to tell me what he thought of it. As it had a foolish title (suggested for publishing reasons) I never owned to its authorship, but I am sure its success (two editions) was largely due to the delightful illustrations by Mr. (now Sir Bernard) Partridge of *Punch*. Robbie Ross was not only a good literary critic, but was an expert on Art, and after he started a gallery in London he was often invited to the (country) seats of the mighty to give advice about Old Masters, and he told me, with great glee, that on one occasion he was shown into housekeeper's room and offered a glass of beer, an episode which must have diverted him enormously. There was no trace of the snob in his charming personality. Among his great friends was Mrs. Asquith – now Lady Oxford and Asquith – and I recollect his witty *mot* in 1916, when I asked him to meet, at luncheon, Mrs. Lloyd George and the wives of three other members of the new Government, Lady Cowdray, Lady Mond and Mrs. Ian Macpherson: 'I cannot come. I am going to lunch with the Fallen! '

Robert Ross, to the day of his sudden death in his beautiful rooms in Half Moon Street, was devoted to the literary fame of Oscar Wilde. This cost him much sorrow, and expense over libel suits, and I feel sure it hastened his end. The reputation of Oscar Wilde is higher on the Continent than here; Epstein's[2] strange Egyptian tombstone to the poet at Père Lachaise[3] is a place of piligrimage for foreigners, even though English people are chary of mentioning his name.

A few years ago, Robert Ross came and asked me, as a favour, to attend a wedding of a young friend of his in Sloane Street. It was that of one of Oscar Wilde's sons, Mr. Holland.[4] I went.

### NOTES

Ella Nora Hepworth Dixon (d. 1932), English novelist and journalist.
1. For a note on Robert Ross see p. 341.
2. For a note on Epstein see p. 477.
3. For a note on Père Lachaise see p. 477.
4. Vyvyan Holland (1886–1967), Wilde's younger son.

# The Last Days of Oscar Wilde*

### Elisabeth Marbury

Probably the most conspicuous figure in England with whom I came in contact during the formative period of my business was Oscar Wilde. I had met him in America while he was there on his first lecture tour. He was dressed, as has often been described, in brown velvet knickerbockers, a soft

* *My Crystal Ball; Reminiscences* (New York: Boni & Liveright, 1923) pp. 97–103. Editor's title.

silk shirt with a Byronic collar, a flowing scarlet tie and a huge white boutonnière in the lapel of his coat. His appearance seemed ridiculous, but nevertheless it was well conceived, and of value in stimulating curiosity and in providing copy for the press.

I met him at the house of Professor Doremus, holding a cup of tea which he courteously offered me. At the time I felt little interest in the poet, and it was not until I really began to know him in later years, that I realized Wilde's intellectual potentialities. Like many others I fell under the thrall of his gifts as a conversationalist and could listen with delight to the brilliancy of his talk. His wit scintillated incessantly. His joy in the phrases he compiled was always evident though never offensive.

Wilde's egotism, which eventually wrecked his life, was far too deep rooted to be of any passing importance. It was so obvious as to be beyond comment. It was so fundamental that it had become assimilated and an integral part of his being. It was such a magnificent gesture that it frequently inspired one to admiration. Nothing could exaggerate the importance of his rule in London society over a period of several years. There he reigned supreme, flattered, honored, sought after and imitated. His sway over the imagination of the British public was undisputed. He was literally without a rival. His self-confidence was abnormal. The atmosphere in which he lived supplied the virus, of which he, its victim, was sublimely unconscious. Nothing short of an upheaval such as he finally experienced would ever have torn Oscar Wilde from his social moorings. While mocking and excoriating society, it was his very life. The adulation and servility which it exhaled was his daily diet. He reached the zenith of his success when his first modern play was produced, 'Lady Windermere's Fan.' This paved the way to a long line of dramatic triumphs. One comedy after another glittered from his pen. Epigrams became the keynote of conversation. From the very offset I was his representative in this country. The plays reproduced here echoed his London fame. Their first nights were eagerly anticipated. Daniel Frohman[1] was presenting 'An Ideal Husband' at the moment of Wilde's downfall.[2]

At the St. James' Theatre, where this play was then running,[3] the manager, George Alexander, determined that he would withdraw it shortly after Wilde's arrest. He lacked the courage to continue, for like many others he was afraid of public opinion and dared not be classed with the few friends who stood loyally by Wilde even in his darkest moments. Frohman, on the contrary, kept 'An Ideal Husband' at the Lyceum until the play no longer attracted patronage.

Although I had heard incessant innuendoes as to the flagrant offenses of Wilde's private life, nevertheless knowing as I did that he was the centre of a circle which was powerful in its connections and influence, I never believed that Wilde would be the scapegoat of this band, yet such was the case. I could not reconcile myself to the fact that he alone was signalled out to pay the penalty; he, who from his prison cell was able to give the world

'The Ballad of Reading Gaol,' and 'De Profundis.' Oscar Wilde was incarcerated in a common prison until his brain power was crushed and his spirit broken. Upon the testimony of science, he should have been sent to a sanatorium and not to a penitentiary. His was a clear case of psycho-perversity. Long before the final blow was struck it would have been a more humane thing to have placed him under the care of physicians rather than to have delivered him over to jailers. But British justice was appeased when Oscar Wilde was condemned to pick okum in a prison yard.

Directly after he was taken to Pentonville, [4] I became troubled about his royalties which had been accumulating, and which were in my hands. I was waiting until I could communicate with him, for I thought that at least these sums might be saved from the wreck in order to keep his wife and his two boys. Wilde had spent lavishly and without any recognition of his family responsibilities, therefore his list of creditors was long. When interrogated in court as to his assets, he referred to me as his American agent, stating that doubtless I had funds which could be appropriated toward the liquidation of his debts. I was soon notified that from that time on all money collected for Wilde would have to go through the legal channels. I confess to a sneaking disappointment at this turn of affairs, for sentimentally I felt the deepest sympathy for that wife and those little lads upon whom the sad fate of the husband and father had fallen. How well I recall that house on Tite Street, Chelsea, full of charm and infinite taste. It was there before his own friends that Wilde was at his best. Many were the plots of plays which he thought out aloud. He almost wrote them as he talked. I remember one terrible tragedy, brutally conceived, which revolved around a most revolting theme. It took me many days before I could prove to him that despite the dramatic value of the story that the managers and public would never tolerate the motive. Wilde was so totally devoid of any ethical sense that, while he accepted my verdict, he was not in the least convinced by it. Form and treatment were everything to him. Matter and morals meant nothing. I once complained that I had spent a dreary evening at dinner in the society of some dull but eminent people, saying that the neighbor on my right was a member of the City Council, and that I had failed utterly in my attempt to interest him.

'Bless my soul,' exclaimed Wilde, 'it isn't possible that you care whether you interest your neighbor or not. The only thing of consequence when one dines out is whether one interests oneself!'

How often in life I have been reminded of this. Again when I was sending him letter after letter urging him to come to New York to attend the rehearsals of a certain play which required most careful direction, he refused to sail. Afterward, in London, when I reproached him for not realizing the logic of my arguments that I should have brought him over to this country, he remarked that in my logic lay the whole difficulty, that I was so convincing and impelling that it made him stuff cotton in his ears, and put blinders on his eyes, and that after each appeal from me he had become more and more determined not to allow so reasonable a human being as myself to become his mentor. I never again tried to make Wilde reasonable. Heaven knows that all of the stupid blunders of which he was guilty during the last days of his liberty could have been avoided, and his freedom assured, had he not wallowed in the morass of conceit, wilfulness and lack of common sense.

From time to time he wrote to me from prison; then one day I received from him a roll of manuscript in his own handwriting. It was the 'Ballad of Reading Gaol.'[5] He said he had scribbled it down and wondered whether I would be his good angel and get him a few pounds for it, as he needed some personal articles which the sale of this poem might supply.

As I read it, it seemed like a voice from the dead. I remember that the tears rolled down my cheek. Then I realized that to sell it might, after all, be difficult. My fears were justified, for after peddling it about unsuccessfully, as no editor was willing to revive Wilde's memory in his magazine, I sold it to the New York World, which paid me $250.00 for it. This money I sent to Wilde, together with the manuscript which he wished returned. I have often wondered whether this original is still in existence. Then came the moment of his liberation. The story has been too often told. Shortly afterwards he sought me out in Paris unkempt, forlorn and penniless. He told me that he had just staged a miracle play in the Latin Quarter.

I knew that Charles Frohman[6] stood ready to commission a comedy from him, and had even authorized me to prepare the contract, and to advance Wilde $500.00 on account, which I did. But when I presented the agreements to him for signature, his hand trembled and he wrote 'Sebastian Melmoth,' a fanciful name he had chosen to conceal his identity. I looked at him fixedly and said, 'This contract is being made with Oscar Wilde, who alone has the talent to fulfill it. I will accept no understudy, my friend. This is to be your recall to honor and to fame.' His tears blotted the page. The first name was erased, and with firmness his own was affixed to that contract, which alas, was never productive, as he died shortly after its execution.

The last time I ever saw him was in Paris, living in a wretched room in the attic of a squalid little hotel, and the last letter I ever received from him was written to warn me against a youthful adventurer who was then exploiting stray Americans.

The bed on which his bulky form was stretched was covered with a hideous brown blanket. The furniture was of the ugliest and plainest description. Not a creature comfort of any sort was visible. I recalled the house in Tite Street. The contrast was appalling.

His few remaining friends had given until they could give no more. They at least had kept the roof over his head and had provided him with the necessities of life.

He barely recognized me. The memory of that visit is still painful.

One of the Fathers from St. Joseph's Church, in the Avenue Hoche, was with him at the end, but whether Oscar Wilde was finally a convert to that faith, in which even in his most clouded moments he had a mystical belief, will always remain an unsolved problem until the day when the secrets of all hearts shall be revealed. It was said that when the priest leaned over to hear his dying confession, he found that the throat had become contracted, and that the lips had lost all power of speech. It seems a sinister fact that he who had revelled in irresponsible volubility all his life was unable at the end to proclaim a broken and a contrite heart.[7]

Yet possibly at no time in his career had this poor soul been so near the recognition of truth which is eternal, as at this bitter moment of his physical disintegration and of his final detachment from that world from which he had been outcast.

I have always maintained that 'De Profundis' was his masterpiece and a rich contribution to the treasure house of English literature.

It was conceived and written *in* the depths. It was given to the world as Oscar Wilde's last message to save others *from* the depths.

## NOTES

Elisabeth Marbury (1856–1933), leading American play agent who represented both American and foreign dramatists. She was twice decorated by the French government for services rendered to French authors. See references to her in *The Letters of Oscar Wilde*; and Karl Beckson, 'A New Oscar Wilde Letter', *English Language Notes*, VII (June 1971), 284–7.

1. Daniel Frohman (1851–1940), American theatrical manager; brother of Charles Frohman (1860–1915), also a theatrical manager.

2. *An Ideal Husband* was produced at the Lyceum Theatre, New York, on 12 March 1895.

3. This is a misstatement by Elisabeth Marbury. *An Ideal Husband* was presented by Herbert Beerbohm Tree at the Haymarket Theatre, not at the St James's Theatre, on 3 January 1895. She means *The Importance of Being Earnest*, which was produced by George Alexander at the St James's Theatre, London, on 14 February 1895.

4. For a note on Pentonville Prison see p. 343.

5. This is another misstatement by Elisabeth Marbury. Robert Ross, in his preface to the first edition of *De Profundis*, says, '*The Ballad of Reading Gaol* was not planned or even composed until after he [Wilde] had regained his liberty.' The ballad was begun at the Chalet Bourgeat, Berneval, near Dieppe, in the summer of 1897. Wilde's letters of this period make frequent mention of it: one, the earliest reference, being on 19 July. In her preface to *My Crystal Ball* Elisabeth Marbury says, 'Having neither record nor note-book, these pages from memory were written in long hand.' Her memory is evidently not infallible.

6. Charles Frohman (1860–1915), American theatrical impresario; brother of Daniel Frohman.

7. For a note on Wilde's conversion to Catholicism see p. 326.

# 'Mark This Man'*

Richard Best

I remember another curious meeting with Synge in Paris. We were walking down the Avenue de L'Opéra one sunny day and I saw a man coming towards us whom I recognised – a portly man, with a bowler hat and a plain suit. I had just time to say to Synge, 'Mark this man,' because he was on us almost. Synge looked at him, and I looked at him, and this man looked at us very closely, and I said, 'Oscar Wilde,' and Synge said, 'Oh, how interesting, let us go back and meet him again.' I hated this, but Wilde had stopped I remember, and was looking into a big window with Greek vases in it and bronzes. So we turned around and we met him again, a minute afterwards, and Wilde looked at us hard, and I knew Wilde was thinking, 'These two men know who I am.' He was living under the name Sebastian – he had been pointed out to me some months before in the street, that's how I knew him. So I took him in, but I lowered my eyes and I noticed his brick-coloured complexion and his stained teeth which have been described. Well, Synge was immensely impressed by this appearance of Wilde.

* *Irish Literary Portraits*, ed. W. R. Rodgers (London: British Broadcasting Corporation, 1972) p. 99.

## NOTE

Dr Richard Irvine Best (1872–1959), distinguished Gaelic scholar and linguist who was long associated with the National Library of Ireland. A well-kown Dublin character and friend of James Joyce, he appears under his own name in *Ulysses* (the National Library episode). J. M. Synge, the Irish dramatist, met Best in Paris and became his friend.

# Oscar Wilde – A Reminiscence*

Bernard Thornton

In the last year of Oscar Wilde's life I was treasurer of the Grand Opera House of New York. In that capacity I was sent to Europe to conclude some theatrical contracts. The name Grand Opera House meant a great deal more in Paris than it did in New York. To most people I was not the humble traveling clerk of a second-class New York theatre, but the incarnation of metropolitan opera. In fact, many people mistook me for the direct representative of the Metropolitan Opera Company, and treated me as such.

I recall a most amusing coincidence which happened in this connection. On leaving London, where I had graciously been tendered the entrée of all the theatres, the idea presented itself to experiment with Paris. Accordingly I sent a brief request to Mme. Sarah Bernhardt, enclosing my card, which read 'Treasurer Grand Opera House, N. Y.', to see her production of 'L'Aiglon' for any performance that was convenient – business permitting. I had hardly posted the letter when a special uniformed messenger presented himself. He brought a heavily embossed official-looking envelope on which was engraved the words 'Théâtre Sarah Bernhardt,' enclosing, with Mme. Bernhardt's compliments, a stage box for the subsequent Sunday night. Sunday night in Paris is *the* swagger social event of the theatrical week – which needless to say added to my bewilderment. I could arrive at no satisfactory conclusion as to why I had been accorded such distinction.

The eventful evening arrived. During the *entr'acte*, in casually looking over the audience, much to my amazement, I saw David Belasco and Charles Frohman hanging over the front row in the balcony. It seemed so incongruous for two of America's most successful managers to be occupying such modest seats while I – a poor, humble box-office treasurer, was seated in state in a private proscenium box.

Just as I rubbed my eyes to reassure myself that I was awake, the curtain

* *Theatre Magazine* (New York), xxvii (June 1918) 370.

rose on the third act. My attention was divided between the superb acting of Mme. Bernhardt and my sub-conscious brain trying to deduct an explanation of all the honor bestowed upon me. The curtain fell and as the house lights went up – a very distinguished gentleman, who spoke English fluently, came to the box and introduced himself as Mme. Bernhardt's secretary. He implored me to visit her dressing-room. I went. The confusion that followed was perhaps the most embarrassing moment of my life. It appears that Bernhardt was coming to America the following year under the management of Maurice Grau, at that time the impresario of the Metropolitan Opera House. The secretary had confused the Metropolitan Opera House with the Grand Opera House and with the customary Parisian diplomacy, had sent me the box.

Mme. Bernhardt took the situation good-naturedly, giving me a cordial handclasp on departing and a cheery '*Au revoir*.'

At the Théâtre Sarah Bernhardt I was introduced to Mme. Mickauleff, a wealthy Frenchwoman of Russian ancestry and a liberal patron of the fine arts. At numerous receptions at Mme. Mickauleff's house I became acquainted with the most noted personages in Paris of that day. Mme. Mickauleff said that I must meet the famous Oscar Wilde. She mentioned the name as one might speak of a martyr.

I was not over-enthusiastic about the suggestion, but curiosity won over everything. I made my time suit the convenience of Mr. Wilde, and we met at Mme. Mickauleff's – not under the bright glare of the gaslight which was still the vogue in Paris, nor in a tropic atmosphere of palms and bare shoulders. Instead, he came quite early in the morning, and the servant showed no unusual interest in the caller as he announced his solitary entry.

My heart almost stood still as this once celebrated personage crossed Mme. Mickauleff's threshold. I could not believe that this was the man about whom the whole world had been talking. He was bent with a weight not of years. He had an old man's obesity. His cheeks were flabby and sagging, his eyes were dull. His manner of speech was like a blow to me, for his words came very slowly, and his sentences were timorous. He seemed grateful for the least consideration.

I met Wilde several times after that occasion and the thing that touched me most was his manner of deep respect. He was almost servile to me, who in former years would, likely enough, not even have gotten a nod. He was waiting, as I could see very well, for me to advance some hope of an American redemption.

Finally he spoke of America. It was afternoon, and he addressed Mme. Mickauleff and myself. The roseate rays of the sunset took away very much of the age and ruin in his face.

'They tell me that in Western America,' he said, 'a man is a man to-day, and yesterdays don't count – that a desperado can make a reputation for piety on his current performances. What a country to live in! Your Western

America must be like the Greece of the days before the Parthenon, or Italy before the Consulate!'

'Why don't you go to America?' I asked him this question later, when, casually, we spoke of travel. The query alarmed him, and furiously embarrassed him. 'I – perhaps I shall go to America – as soon as I've settled some business matters in Paris, but not before – not before!'

Poor chap, he assuredly had no business to attend to, for he was living on charity even then. As soon as he had said this, he left the room, and I didn't see him again that evening.

But as Mme. Mickauleff told me, it was very evident that America constantly obsessed him. It was his promised land, a refugee from the world of humiliation and shame which he felt surrounded him. Yet, as was plainly to be seen, his courage was gone and his spirit broken. Even had one paid his passage and furnished him with plenty of money, I doubt if he would have had the courage to go.

I last saw him one wonderful afternoon when he walked with Mme. Mickauleff and myself, through Père la Chaise Cemetery. He used a stick, not for style but for support, and I could not but notice, in the bright sunlight, his shabby, spotted clothes. No longer was he the 'Lily of Piccadilly,' but a wretched, broken-down outcast. Still there were flashes and brilliant sallies, that afternoon, of the old Oscar Wilde.

He drew us before the humble grave of Marie du Plessis, the friend of Alexander Dumas, and original of Marguerite Gautier, the lady of the Camellias. He told of her life, of Dumas' careless affection for her, and of her great love for Dumas, and of her death from tuberculosis – unlike Camille though, in that she held Dumas' regard and protection to the end.

My own final picture of Wilde is not a pleasant one, but no doubt it was a characteristic one of the poet in the last days of his life. He sought oblivion in the glass. He had no money in his pockets, but at the drinking suggestion of any stranger he would run eagerly and swallow greedily a great glass of absinthe. He forgot me, he forgot everyone in his glass. Absinthe was his one remaining emotion, and for absinthe he would have hobnobbed with a porter. Pride, ambition, self-respect – all these had disappeared. Oscar Wilde at this time eked out his existence, I am informed, on money put in his way by an actress.

On returning to America about two months later I was not surprised to read of his death. He had been in a coma some time before and while the landlord, physicians and numerous creditors were wrangling about fees and bills, his eyes slowly opened. Turning to those present he said: 'Gentlemen, it seems I'm dying beyond my means.'

Those were the last words of Oscar Wilde.

# My Recollections of Oscar Wilde*

Henri Mazel

## I.

The first time that I saw Oscar Wilde was in Paris, in 1892, at the house of Stuart Merrill[1] – the French poet of American extraction. It is now twenty years ago, but I can recall him clearly – tall and heavy, fair and freshly coloured, with a monocle in his eye and a hot-house flower in his buttonhole, dressed in clothes of an irreproachable cut, and speaking in a slow, quiet manner – slightly affected perhaps, but altogether pleasing – his English accent adding a further charm.

There were present, besides Stuart Merrill, several of our friends from among the circle of symbolical poets – then in the first flush of achievement.

We were all greatly interested in the uncommon personality of this writer, whose reputation was then so great in London literary circles, and I spent the whole evening listening to him, as he was talking with his spicy wit and his good-tempered charm.

Oscar Wilde loved talking before a picked audience, and yet he wanted it to be a fairly large one, for as it seemed to me it pleased and flattered him when those people who were talking amongst themselves in the recess of the window would stop their own conversations and join the circle which had gathered round him.

## II.

Oscar Wilde spoke French very well, and when he did stop for a word it was not like a foreigner unfamiliar with the vocabulary, but as a stylist who brings to conversation the same desire for picturesque and imaginative expression which he shows when writing at his desk. Many among us, the poet Laurent Tailhade, for instance, had this same slightly slow method of expression, which added to the value and relish of the right word when it was found. Although he was very familiar with our language, and capable of appreciating its most subtle shades of meaning, Oscar Wilde could not

*Everyman* (London), I, 1 (18 Oct 1912) 14.

write French with the perfect style of a Beckford or a Hamilton. The first draft of 'Salomé,' according to what I was told, was full of colour, but from the point of view of grammatical correctness needed a good deal of revision. Those amongst us who corrected it limited themselves entirely to this grammatical correction; they modified nothing, and 'Salomé' is truly the work of the English poet, and not, as some evil tongues have said, that of his French friends.

He did not gesticulate much – at least that evening he was restrained in his movements. Fat and heavy as he was, he sat at ease in the arm-chair, which he entirely filled. The thing I remember as most characteristic of him was his happy, friendly laugh, which made us like him immediately, for his attitude, a trifle too languid, and his somewhat affected carriage did not seem to suit the manly breadth of shoulder of this giant of the north.

## III.

I saw him again in 1901,[2] but without having an opportunity of speaking to him. He was seated on the terrace of the Café de la Paix, on the Boulevard, with someone I did not know, and I did not go up to him, as I should have done if he had been alone. Although I had not then read his admirable 'De Profundis,' I was sure that Oscar Wilde, in spite of his inexcusable moral faults, was better than his reputation, and it was a profound satisfaction to me when I read that book and the 'Ballad of Reading Gaol' to find that the soul of Wilde had indeed benefited, like that of Paul Verlaine, from the severe but well-merited experience which they were both condemned to undergo.

This last time that I saw Oscar Wilde he was but a shadow of his former self. I recognised him. One could hardly fail to recognise him – he was so tall and broadly built – but what a change from the radiant lover of beauty that I had known. What a change in his appearance, his manner, and even in his clothes.

## IV.

There had already grown up a kind of Oscar Wilde legend, which people will always hesitate to repeat, simply because it is a legend, and because many of its features were invented afterwards, but he himself was indulgent towards this kind of literary embellishment. 'Legends are often more true than reality,' he used to say. But I shall only recall those anecdotes characteristic of him which have been told me as authentic by his friends in Paris, and chiefly by Stuart Merrill, who knew him so intimately.

One day some visitors calling on Oscar Wilde found him gazing ecstatically at some rare Chinese porcelain. They spoke to him – he gave no answer – they shook him, saying 'Have you gone mad?' He answered gravely, '*I am trying to live up to my china.*'

Another time he seemed suffering from great depression. 'What is wrong?' 'It is sad,' he said; 'one half of the world does not believe in God, and the other half does not believe in me.'

During his tour in America, the inhabitants of Griggsville, in Kansas, sent him a telegram asking him to come and give them a lecture on aesthetics. Oscar Wilde telegraphed back, 'Begin by changing the name of your town.'

It was probably at the Theatre du Moulin Rouge that he conceived the idea of putting on the stage the drama of Salomé, who obtained the head of St. John the Baptist from Herod the Tetrarch. On the stage a Roumanian acrobat was dancing on her hands. Oscar Wilde, who up to that moment had been paying little attention to what was going on, sat up. 'I must see that woman,' he said to Stuart Merrill, who was with him. 'She must play the part of Salomé in a play which I shall write for her. I want her to dance on her hands, as in the tale of Flaubert.'

## V.

The greater number of his Parisian friends remained loyal to him. I remember the incredulity with which they heard the first rumours tending to prove the truth of the accusation which the Marquis of Queensberry had brought against him. Nothing in the talk of Oscar Wilde had ever supported these accusations. He never used expressions that were too free, and he blamed his friends from the *Quartier Latin* for their taste for a Rabelaisian fashion of speech.

Among those whom I have already named, André Gide, Henry Davray, Edouard Julia, and many others did not desert him in his troubles; thanks to them, Oscar Wilde still enjoyed some happy days in Paris, especially during the Exhibition of 1900. But it was no longer the triumphant Oscar Wilde of former days. He thus describes the change. 'My life,' said he, 'is like a work of art. An artist never repeats himself. My life before going to prison had achieved harmonious success; now it is a thing of the dead past.'

Perhaps one day I shall write some recollections of 'Oscar Wilde after his prison days,' from the memories of those who remained faithful to him. Just now I only wish to recall the hero of fashion, the arbiter elegantiarum, the successor at one and the same time of Brummel and Ruskin, he whom his friends delighted to compare to a grand priest of the Moon Goddess in the days of Heliogabalus.

## NOTES

Henri Mazel (b. 1864), French writer.
1. For a note on Stuart Merrill see p. 468.
2. This is evidently a misstatement, as Wilde died in 1900.

# 'I Have Lived'*

### Anna, Comtesse de Brémont

The autumn of the year of the great Paris Exhibition[1] I passed in Paris in order to explore its wonders at my leisure. During the month of August I was the guest of an American friend, whose only interest in the Exhibition consisted in viewing the illuminations and enjoying the dinners at the famous cafés. One night she gave a dinner party at the Spanish café. The feature of the place was the exhibition of Spanish dances given on a small stage erected at one end of the resaurant. Seats were provided for those who wished to enjoy the represenation without dining, while for the diners, tables were arranged in alcoves behind the seats where a good view of the stage was offered. We were a party of eight, including the sons of the hostess. During the dinner my attention strayed often to the music and the very characteristic dances of the performers on the gaudy little stage. I found the pose of the principal danseuse more interesting than the menu, despite its recherché character, and, when I should have been enjoying a particularly choice soufflé, I was lost in a delightful reverie over the haunting motif of the dance music. My hostess had grown weary of chiding me for neglecting the dinner, and left me to my reveries. By some strange coincidence my thoughts wandered to Oscar Wilde's Salome, suggested, no doubt, by the semi-barbaric fierceness of that old Spanish dance with its grotesque attitudes and passionate expression of hatred and love, jealousy and vengeance portrayed by the pantomine of the dancer. The sad minor chords of the music awakened memories of the unhappy author of Salome. Where was he? What had become of Oscar Wilde? I let my gaze roam across the small auditorium, and, suddenly, to my intense surprise, I saw him advancing slowly along the entrance of the café. He was greatly changed, had grown very stout, and the rich waves of hair had given place to a close-cut coiffure that seemed to accentuate the coarseness of his face. A small white straw hat added to the grotesque outline of his once beautiful head. He was clad in a suit of grey tweed, the short coat increasing the heavy lines of his figure and giving an impression of over weight to the upper part of his body. Every vestige of the dandy had disappeared. His eyes were heavy and the pallor of the skin added to the look of ill-health

* Extracted from *Oscar Wilde and His Mother; A Memoir* (London: Everett, 1911; New York: Haskell House, 1972) pp. 176–88. Editor's title.

despite his robust figure. I caught my breath in surprise. It seemed incredible that it was really Oscar Wilde who was coming towards me with such slow ponderous steps. I saw that he was not alone; the faithful friend accompanied him. They both stopped to survey the room in search of seats, and had evidently come to see the dances. I half rose to meet him and just as I did so he turned and looked in another direction. Then it flashed upon me that the meeting might be an awkward one before my friends. They were society people and might resent the encounter. I felt hot and cold with nervous anxiety. I could not snub the son of my dear friend, Lady Wilde, neither could I expose him to the cruel test of being received coldly or insultingly by my hostess, who was an American with all the prejudices and insolent pride of her class towards those who had descended the social ladder. In my dilemma I raised my fan to shield my face and held it there until I heard his footsteps recede as he walked slowly past our table.

'Why do you hold your fan to your face?' enquired my hostess.

I lowered the fan and glancing over my shoulder saw that Oscar Wilde and his companion had taken seats by the stage, near the orchestra. I made some excuse about the light hurting my eyes, but my hostess was not deceived.

'You wished to avoid seeing someone,' she cried. 'Tell me who it was?'

I knew it would be useless to prevaricate as she would have given me no peace in her curiosity. Therefore I thought it best to tell her.

'It was a friend, a son of a very old and dear friend whom I did not wish to greet, as I happen not to be alone.'

'Tell me, who was it, and why did you not wish to speak to him – tell me who is this friend.' She spoke with some heat and, being her guest, I could not very well refuse to tell her.

'It was Mr. Oscar Wilde!' I answered, whereupon ensued a perfect hubbub of exclamations, an exhibition of vulgar curiosity that aroused my secret indignation and convinced me of the wisdom of my act in avoiding the meeting.

'Where is he – point him out,' they cried, much as they would have clamoured to see some monstrosity, but knowing that my poor friend was well hidden in the crowded seats around the stage I directed their attention towards the entrance, where I told them quite truthfully I had seen him standing. There was a craning of necks towards the great doors of the café, and some of the party mounted their chairs to search for him amid the audience. Needless to relate, I had no further appetite for dinner that evening.

When the dinner was at an end and we were driving home, my hostess observed.

'You showed great tact in avoiding that meeting, but all the same I should not have been offended if you had spoken to him, as I was curious to see what sort of a monster he really is.'

I made no reply, my heart was too full and my soul too sad for words.

A thunder storm swept over Paris that night. The electric wave cleared the air and brought an exquisite dawn, fresh and rosy with just a touch of coldness in its breath that was highly welcome to sun-baked, dusty Paris. I rose early after a restless night, full of thoughts of the past evoked by the scene in the Spanish café, my nerves were overstrung by too great an indulgence in retrospect and the tears that had kept me company through that long night of sorrowing over the unhappy fate of the son of my dear friend. I longed for the solitude of the open air; the room seemed peopled with a crowd of memories; I breakfasted and left the house quickly.

*       *       *

The little bateau-mouche was nearing the picturesque heights of St.Cloud, when I awoke from my day-dreams to realize that someone was speaking to me. I was so completely under the lulling influence of the peace and beauty of the scene that I felt no annoyance at the awakening. It seemed, that amid those perfect surroundings, on that perfect river, nothing could break that harmony of repose and beauty: not even the presence of a stranger could disturb that ideal morning sail on the smooth emerald waters of the picturesque Seine. A voice very low, yet distinct in its rich quality was addressing me. I raised my eyes to assure myself that I was not still dreaming, since it seemed impossible that the owner of that unforgettable voice could be there, beside me, on the bench where I sat on the deck of the boat. But there could be no doubt, it was Oscar Wilde upon whom I gazed in astonishment.

'Good morning,' he was saying, 'are you surprised to see me? – Surely not – You are not the only restless spirit in this great Paris. I, too, rose early to seek solace from these beautiful waters and the repose denied me in my stuffy hotel.'

He sank on the seat, and leaning back with a sigh of comfort removed his ugly little white straw hat to enjoy the air more fully.

Somehow, my amazement melted into a feeling of reality under his natural manner; it seemed that there was nothing strange in that meeting. It was quite natural that he also should seek the pleasure of a sail up the river on that lovely morning. I was filled with a sense of thankfulness at the lucky fate that had guided my steps to that particular boat, for now I could say all that was in my soul and open my heart to my poor friend, show him the deep sympathy and high regard that had survived all the evil that the world had heaped upon his unhappy head. I sought for words to explain in the most delicate way my apparent avoidance of him the night before, but he relieved me of the difficult duty.

'I saw you last evening and, believe me, Contessa, I was inexpressibly glad, and would have come to you, but I don't care to meet strangers. Had you been alone it would have been a great pleasure to talk with you over the past,' he paused and sighed. 'I see so few of my old friends now, and when I do, the meeting is too much for me. I passed a sleepless night – a night of watching – and—' He paused.

'I, too, watched and prayed through the night,' I hastened to say in answer to his unfinished sentence.

'Thank you,' he replied simply. I waited for him to speak; there was something indefinable about him that impressed me more than all his former charm and elegance. An atmosphere of spirituality that shone through his changed appearance like the glitter of gold that has been through the refiner's furnace. I felt that he had indeed been refined through suffering.

After an interval, during which we both watched the gliding shores, our souls filled with reminiscent thoughts, he spoke again.

'I have lived – yes – I have lived', he said musingly. 'I have lived all there was to live. Life held to my lips a full flavoured cup, and I drank it to the dregs – the bitter and the sweet. I found the sweet bitter, and the bitter, sweet – yes, I have lived.'

Again he paused. I was silent. What word had I in answer to that mournful admission – could I probe the sorrows of that suffering heart? No! Therefore I waited in silence, forbearing to ask questions, as one who understood him less would have done.

Then his mood changed. With a smile as wan as moonlight breaking through the shadows he looked at me and began to speak of ordinary things, the weather, the Exhibition and books. Finally I ventured to ask a question.

'Why do you not write now?' I said, feeling how inane a question it really was, how almost impertinent in the face of his broken career, his helplessness.

'Because I have written all there was to write. I wrote when I did not know life, now that I do know the meaning of life, I have no more to write; life cannot be written, life can only be lived. I have lived.'

The reiteration of that phrase sank into my heart like the tolling of a bell. It seemed to knell the passing of a soul.

'I have no time to write – if I willed. My time is short – my work is done – and when I cease to live, that work will begin to live. Ah! my work will live as long as men live to read it; my work will be my great monument!'

His face glowed with the enthusiasm of that prophecy. Then his mood again changed and with an air of mystery, he said:

'Would you know my secret? I will tell you – and the river,' pointing to the smooth waves now glittering with the gold of the fully risen sun.

'I have found my soul. I was happy in prison.' He said the word softly, reverently. 'I was happy there because I found my soul. What I wrote before I wrote without a soul, and what I have written under the guidance of my soul, the world shall one day read, it shall be the message of my soul to the souls of men!'

Again there was a pause. The revelation of that solemn moment was overpowering. I closed my eyes and pressed my hands to them to keep back the tears of real joy that filled my heart. God had been indeed merciful, God had rewarded that stricken genius beyond the power of man – yes, God was Good. God had given him back his soul.

'Contessa,' he said. 'Don't sorrow for me, but watch and pray – it will not be for long – watch and pray.'

His voice sank into silence. There was a long pause, broken only by the grating sound of the boat as it touched the landing pier. I strove to compose myself and waited for him to speak. Then I uncovered my face and turned to look at him – but he was gone.

## NOTE

1. 1900.

# My Last Meeting with Oscar Wilde*

Robert Harborough Sherard

At my last meeting with him, however, Wilde was his old self. Not long after Ernest Dowson's[1] death[2] I was in Paris, and I went to the Hôtel d'Alsace,[3] because I thought Wilde would like to hear about it, as he had always had a regard and high esteem for Ernest Dowson. I also remembered how, on a previous occasion, he had written to me to blame me for not going to see him. 'I am glad you are so busy,' he wrote; 'but sorry that you are too busy to come and see me.' It was the injustice of a peeved soul.

It pleased me to see with what deference I was received at the Hôtel d'Alsace as a caller on 'Monsieur Melmoth.' Access to the great man was, however, not a matter of course. 'I will send up and see if Monsieur Melmoss receives,' said the landlord, and a waiter was despatched. When the man returned and, with a 'thousand regrets,' informed me that

---

* *The Real Oscar Wilde* (London: T. Werner Laurie, [1915]) pp. 417–20. Editor's title.

Monsieur was *très fatigué*, far too tired to receive anybody, I wrote a message on a card and sent it up. I was then asked to *monter*. When I reached Oscar's door I found him waiting for me. He caught hold of my two hands and drew me into his room. 'I really *am* too tired to speak to anybody to-day,' he said: 'but I don't like to send *you* away.'

The room was a small and gloomy bedroom, which opened out, however, on to a larger chamber, where there was the sun. Oscar was in a dressing-gown, and reminded me of himself seventeen years previously, at the Hôtel du Quai Voltaire. Here again the table was littered with papers; the bowl containing cigarette ends and ashes was not wanting. Some books were heaped up in disorder in a corner. On the mantelpiece was a pile of letters. 'I hope you weren't offended,' he said, 'because I at first refused to see you. I am never any good in the mornings.' 'I wasn't offended at all,' I said. 'Monsieur Champfleuri either receives or does not receive.' This reference to a famous French *lever de rideau*[4] brought us at once to literary matters. 'I see you have here the *Emaux et Camées*,' I said, picking up a book; 'and there,' I added, pointing to a bottle of Pernod absinthe that stood on the washhandstand, 'is the Pierian spring that inspired them.' 'The "Pernodian" spring, you mean,' he said, with a laugh. 'But you are quite wrong, for it was de Musset who used absinthe, and these exquisite poems are by Théophile Gautier.' It came as quick as lightning, this correction of my mistake, for indeed at the moment I had thought of Alfred de Musset as the author of the poems.

Absinthe and poetry brought me to Ernest Dowson, but Wilde did not seem to care to hear about him. 'It is all so sad,' he said. 'Ernest was an *enfant voué au noir*.'[5] Then he added: 'Much of what he has written will remain.' 'You are working too, I see,' I said, pointing to the litter on his table. He answered: 'One has to do something. I have no taste for it now. It is a penance to me, but, as was said of torture, it always helps one to pass an hour or two.' I then said: 'If you never wrote another line, Oscar, you have done enough to ensure your immortality.' And when I said that I knew nothing about *De Profundis*. He seemed really pleased, and brightened. But then his face went all grey again, and I saw him glance towards the stimulant and I was reminded of poor Alphonse Daudet, in the moments just before the morphine syringe was produced and the injection taken. He went and threw himself on the bed, exhausted it seemed, and I rose. 'Come and see me again,' he said, 'though I hardly like to ask people to see me in this room.' He was referring to the poverty of our surroundings. 'Why, I had never noticed it,' I said. 'What does the *mise-en-scène* matter?' '*Qu'importe le verre, pourvu qu'on ait l'ivresse*,'[4] he said. 'You have become reconciled to Sully-Prudhomme, then?' I said. I think now that the word *ivresse* was the last word that I heard Oscar Wilde say.

## NOTES

For a note on Robert Harborough Sherard see p. 339.

1. Ernest Dowson (1867–1900), English poet. He had met Wilde in 1890, and with Robert Sherard visited him at Oakley Street between his trials. He also visited him in Berneval. Wilde lent him £20 when he was in straits. On Wilde's friendship with Dowson see Mark Longaker, *Ernest Dowson* (Philadelphia: University of Pennsylvania Press, 1944) pp. 233–41.
2. Dowson died in a cottage owned by Sherard in Catford on 23 February 1900.
3. For a note on the Hôtel d'Alsace see p. 455.
4. Curtain raiser.
5. A child doomed to darkness.
6. The glass is immaterial, provided you get the intoxication.

# Oscar Wilde Died in my Arms*

Michelle De Royer

M. Dupoirier[1], former proprietor of the Hôtel d'Alsace, tells us:

'One evening, someone came and told me "There is a tenant at the Hotel at 4, Rue des Beaux Arts who wishes to lodge with you in future. You ought to go and get his things". I went round to this gentleman's place. He told me his name was Sebastian Melmoth. He was a big English chap, tall and heavy in proportion. He weighed easily 100 kilos.

'I took the two valises, one of which, in yellow, which I still possess, was stamped with the initials S M; and his stick and umbrella, and I carried them to the 3rd floor of the Hôtel d'Alsace, which I ran with my wife.'

So spoke M. Dupoirier, who had the honour to lodge the great writer Oscar Wilde for 3½ years.

'This tenant,' he continued, 'was not at all pleasant. He installed himself in the two rooms which I let to him for 70 francs a month. He used the first as an office, and the second as a bedroom.

'He never opened his mouth to the servant, Jules Patuel, and if he wanted anything he only spoke to me.

' "Jean" he used to say "You will have to go to the Avenue de l'Opéra and fetch me some cognac." It was an astonishing cognac, which cost 25,

---

* *L'Intransigeant* (Paris), (30 November 1930) pp. 1–2. This is the first appearance in English.

then 28 francs a bottle; and in the early days Sebastian Melmoth took four or five (bottles) a week.

'I also served him his breakfast each day, and, around 2 p.m., a chop of best mutton and 2 hard-boiled eggs. He never changed his menu.

'Towards evening he would go out, but first he used to read, or else he would write for about a couple of hours. And then he would go to the café. We would never hear him come in until about 2 or 3 in the morning.

'His last illness?' M. Dupoirier remembers it perfectly. He even remembered that one day, he helped Sebastian Melmoth down to a little room on the ground floor. The invalid lay down, and Dr Tucker operated. Afterwards, he needed care. And M. Dupoirier acted as nurse.

'Was he patient, your invalid?'

'Yes. When he suffered too much pain I gave him injections of morphine. I've still got the syringe that I used.

'At night, I used to sleep in an arm-chair facing his bed. He preferred my company to that of a nurse, right up to the day when the priest from Germain-des-Près came to see him. That was when he converted to the Catholic religion, and two nuns came to watch over him in turn. He got on very well with them.

'His illness got worse. Three or four days before his death, his sight failed. The nun had to read poetry to him.

'And then one night, I was sleeping in a chair, the nun came and woke me. Our invalid was restless. About nine in the morning he gave three or four sighs. He was gone.

'With the help of the nun, I washed and laid him out, and put on his nice light maroon suit. In fact, I took care of him as if he were one of my own family.'

M. Dupoirier remembers it all. It is, after all, only 30 years since these happenings, for Oscar Wilde died on 30th November 1900. And he remembers the interment, too, which was of the 6th class.[2] Two wreaths decorated the hearse, one from Stuart Merrill, and the other from 'The owner and staff' of the Hôtel d'Alsace. And Oscar Wilde so loved flowers.

Forty people followed the cortège: Douglas, Stuart Merrill, Jean Dupoirier and Jules Patuel, the servant. But many sightseers watched the passing of the funeral procession, and police guarded the door of the Hôtel d'Alsace. The people continued on foot from the church to the Bagneux cemetery.

When I asked M. Dupoirier if Oscar Wilde owed him money, he said with embarrassment, 'The writer's friends clubbed together to pay what he owed me. One sent me 300 francs, another 500, another 1000.

'Why did I give him credit? Well you know, in those days, people never paid regularly, and then, besides, the gentleman was ill. He was confined to bed for 6 months at the Hôtel d'Alsace. I couldn't throw him into the street.

'What souvenirs have I still got of him? Wait, I'll show you.' M.

Dupoirier went to a narrow desk, opened a drawer, and unwrapped on the table a little package wrapped in a large sheet of tissue paper. There appeared a set of false teeth, in gold. On the upper jaw, only the large molars were replaced. His hand trembles as he holds this piece of prosthetic (equipment).

'This is ours,' said M. Jean Dupoirier.

### NOTES

1. For a note on Dupoirier see the foot of this page.
2. A funeral of the 7th class is still French idiom for something extremely poor. 6th class is presumably not quite, but nearly, a pauper's funeral.

# Oscar Wilde Worked All Night Long*

Jean Dupoirier

He used to work at nights, all night long. As a rule he would come in at one o'clock in the morning and sit down to his table, and in the morning he would show me what he had written, and 'I have earned a hundred francs to-night' he would say. And he seemed pleased and proud to think that he had earned one hundred francs in one night. But the man who employed him was very irregular about sending him his money, and this used to vex Monsieur Wilde very much. He was always *inquiet*[1] until the payment came, and used to rail against his employer. Towards the end it became very difficult for him to write, and he used to whip himself up with cognac. A *litre* bottle would hardly see him through the night. And he ate little and took but little exercise. He used to sleep till noon, and then breakfast, and then sleep again till five or six in the evening.

* Robert Harborough Sherard, *The Real Oscar Wilde* (London: T. Werner Laurie, [1915]) p. 410. Editor's title.

### NOTES

Jean Dupoirier was the proprietor of the Hôtel d'Alsace, in which Wilde spent the latter days of his life and died. In a letter to Robert Ross postmarked 28 March 1898 Wilde said: 'My new address is at Hotel d'Alsace, Rue des Beaux-Arts. Much better and half the price.' When Wilde moved, his clothes and other belongings had been left behind at his previous hotel because of his inability to pay his bill there. Dupoirier eventually paid Wilde's debt and recovered his clothes. After Reginald

Turner had visited Wilde at this hotel, he wrote a letter to Robert Ross on 26 November 1900 saying that 'The *patron* is awfully good to him.' When Wilde died Dupoirier supplied a pathetic bead trophy, inscribed 'A mon locataire' [To my lodger], and there was another of the same kind from the 'service de l'hôtel'. See Paul Wiegler, 'Hôtel d'Alsace', *Genius in Love and Death* (New York: Albert & Charles Boni, 1929) pp. 116–25; Mlle Dupoirier, 'Un Dentier à Vendre', *Adam International Review* (London) nos. 241–3 (1954) 15, and 'Rue not Ave', *Princeton University Library Chronicle*, VIII, no. 4 (June 1974) 191.

    1. Uneasy; restless.


# Was Oscar Wilde Granted a Pension by Queen Victoria?*

## Immanuel De Rudbeck

Almost everything is known about those last sad years the famous English poet spent in Paris. What remains unknown is the tale of those who helped him in the last few days of his life. It gives us great pleasure to be able to publish this story.

On the wall of the little Alsace Hôtel in the Rue des Beaux-Arts in Paris there is a marble plaque on which one can read the following inscription: 'Oscar Wilde, poet and playwright, died in this house on November 30, 1900.'

In that little street with its uneven paving-stones and its old-fashioned houses one is surrounded by throngs of young art students with their put-on airs and models with their carelessly graceful manners. It is easy to imagine for a moment what the Rue des Beaux-Arts was like at the close of the last century. At that time people who made their way along the street might now and then have met a man of about 40, prematurely grey and bent, who hid his haggard but scornful features behind the huge lapels of his fur-collared overcoat. For the man in the street this man was Sébastien Melmoth; but for those few people in the know he was Oscar Wilde.

I have passed by that marble plaque on numerous occasions without stopping. However, one day I decided to go into the hotel. I was greeted by a very nice woman, and with old-fashioned politeness she took me up to the second floor to see room number eight which consists of two adjoining

* 'Oscar Wilde, fut-il pensionné par la reine Victoria?', *Les Annales Politiques et Littéraires* (Paris), C (5 May 1933) 518–19. This is the first appearance in English.

rooms. It is here that Oscar Wilde died. The first room was his study, and the second with its perfect full bow window was his bedroom. For these two rooms he paid (or rather, should have paid) 65 francs a month.

On his arrival Oscar Wilde lived on the fourth floor in a room exactly the same as the one on the second floor. I owe the rest of my story to Mr. Dupoirier, the former proprietor of the hotel, who now lives in retirement on the Right Bank.

– In the beginning I didn't realize that my guest was Oscar Wilde. He registered as Sébastien Melmoth and his luggage had the initials S. M. on it. We agreed on a rate of 65 francs a month for the two rooms. It was only a short time later that I learned his real identity. At first he hardly spoke, but after a while he became more open and we often talked together. He wasn't always easy to get along with, but I never forgot that he had suffered a great deal and for that I forgave him many things.

– What did he live on? I asked.

– Several of his friends regularly sent him money once a month. He also got a small grant of money from the Court of England. I learned that it was the Queen herself who sent him the money he received each month. In addition he wrote articles and sold them.

– Did he write every day?

– I don't think so. He didn't seem very busy, but it's hard to know what to believe. You can never tell with writers. . . .

– How did he use to spend his days?

– I was in the habit of bringing his breakfast up to him at 11 o'clock: coffee and a roll with butter. He couldn't stand hot chocolate. Then he would get up and write letters or read a bit. At 1:30 or 2:00 I would bring him his lunch, which was quite simple: a lamb-chop and two eggs, usually soft-boiled. He used to eat the same thing every day, but always insisted that I bring the food myself. He seemed very mistrustful. At 5 o'clock he used to go across the Seine to the Régence Café where he took his aperitif. In the winter time he always took care to wrap himself up in a vast overcoat which even covered his ears. Dressed like that he seemed enormous. Yet he wasn't very fat, just tall and broad-shouldered, which explains why he weighed 200 kilos. From the Régence Café he used to go to the Café de Paris where he had dinner.

– That must have cost him a lot of money.

– Yes, it's a very fancy place, but Oscar Wilde was always invited to dinner by someone.

– Did he have a lot of friends?

– Yes, he was on very friendly terms with a good number of French and English writers. He moved in the same circles as Sarah Bernhardt, and was often to be found at the home of Verlaine, or Pierre Louÿs or André Gide. Robert Ross and Lord Alfred Douglas, among others, often came from England to see him.

– What were your impressions of Lord Douglas?

– He was very much the nobleman, much too proud for me to be able to get a word out of him. He would never have wanted to speak to a common, ordinary fellow like me. He was content to hand me his card. Ross was quite different. He was a pleasant, obliging fellow. I believe he was Oscar Wilde's best friend.

– Do you think Wilde was terribly unhappy?

– I don't think so. He seemed completely resigned to his way of life and accepted what happened with good humour. But he drank a tremendous amount. Here, just in the hotel, he went through four bottles of brandy in a week. Besides, it wasn't just ordinary brandy, it was a very good and very old Courvoisier that he sent me to the Avenue de l'Opéra to buy. At that time it cost 28 francs a bottle, but I doubt very much that you could find the same thing nowadays for under 200 francs. In any event, I couldn't afford to buy it for myself. Almost every evening Wilde would go to the café and stay there until 2 or 3 in the morning. Besides, his habits were very, very regular.

– Do you remember his death?

– How could I forget it! At the end he had become very ill and had to have an operation. But you could tell already that it was all over. So he begged me to keep him company; he didn't want anyone else by him. But he was so heavy that I couldn't get him out of his bed all by myself. So I resorted to engaging the services of a Sister to care for him. At the end he converted to Catholicism and the priest of St. Germain-des-Prés came to see him. I had got into the habit of spending the night seated in an armchair beside him, for he didn't want me to leave him. He was very long-suffering in spite of his pain. Now and then I gave him an injection of morphine. The last few days he lost his sight and we read him poetry out loud. Then, one morning at 9 o'clock on the 30th of November 1900 he died. I laid him out and arranged for the funeral. At Saint-Germain-des-Prés he had a modest funeral (6th class). There were 35 people present. Lord Douglas was there. On the coffin were two wreaths – one from Stuart Merrill and the other from the proprietor and staff of the Alsace Hôtel. You can see that I rather liked him.

– He owed you a rather large amount of money, didn't he?

– I don't really like to talk about things like that. He owed me 2,600 francs, but I knew he was very poor. He had been confined to bed for six months, and I couldn't just throw him out in the street.

– Didn't hé leave you anything you could sell?

– No, but his friends talked amongst themselves and sent me a certain sum of money. One gave me a thousand francs, and others gave smaller amounts. But even if they hadn't done so, I wouldn't have regretted helping him even more than common decency demanded. He had become so alone at the end.

# Oscar Wilde*

Gustave Le Rouge

I had caught a glimpse of the great English writer at the parties given by Stéphane Mallarmé which he never failed to attend each time he made a trip to Paris. The two poets sincerely admired one another and held each other in mutual esteem. At that time Oscar Wilde was at the height of his brilliant and yet disrespectful triumph. *Hérodiade* had just been put on and had been acclaimed by all the young writers. He was said to be a millionaire, and publishers snatched up his slightest literary efforts, their hands filled with banknotes. Lastly he was received with open arms and lionized by that very exclusive social sphere that is the English aristocracy. The greatest ladies of the land took pride in being singled out by Oscar Wilde. He could do anything he liked.

In the modest drawing room of his house in the Rue de Rome he seemed a prince of writers. His whole manner was so dazzling that he overshadowed everything surrounding him. His waistcoats with their buttons of precious stones presented brilliant hues to the eye: apple-green, pale yellow, delicate blue. Fantastic rings made his hands sparkle with light. His ties, which he had specially woven for him according to detailed instructions, reflected the colours of the rainbow in all their iridescence. When he moved he resembled a saint ascending to heaven surrounded by a cloud of glory for all to see. When you saw him you thought of those 16th-century tyrants whose portraits show us them dressed in sumptuous doublets of velvet and pearls.

His impeccable dandyism also called to mind Barbey d'Aurevilly or Brummel, Sheridan or the Chevalier d'Orsay. He had his own very personal kind of nonchalant insolence which he managed to turn into yet another one of his charms. They say Jean Lorrain used to copy Wilde's manners and his ties that were 'the colour of Indian poison and dotted with gold spangles', but nothing seems less likely to us than this. The author of *Monsieur de Bougrelon* never possessed the calm arrogance and the icy, complete disdain of public opinion which was perfectly natural with Oscar Wilde.

– 'My greatest pleasure is making enemies,' he claimed. 'At the first

* *Nouvelles littéraires*, (3 Nov 1928) p. 5; (10 Nov 1928) p. 5. This is the first appearance in English.

performance of *Lady Windermere's Fan* the audience was calling for the author so I went up on stage, but I didn't think it necessary to put down the cigarette I was smoking. One has to conclude that my face didn't show an expression of gratitude equal to the appreciation shown by the audience, for they became angry and their applause turned to booing.'

He added with a smile born of complete indifference:

– 'It's very amusing.'

Oscar Wilde expressed himself in French without trace of an accent and with a purity and correctness that were disconcerting. He spoke slowly, emphasizing his words, and with a certain affectation when he was reciting poetry designed to underline its rhythm. He would launch into the most shocking of paradoxes in a quiet, even voice, as if he were explaining something utterly simple.

Who could have foreseen then that this lofty literary fortune which seemed built on rock and which made so many envious of the poet would collapse like a house of cards? Oscar Wilde fell victim to his overwhelming pride which had driven him to defy the opinion of all England. As one of his biographers has noted, he could easily have escaped from the revenge of the Marquis of Queensbury. But he had the audacity to stand up to him, maintained all his customary insolence during the public trial, and was broken by being condemned to spend three whole years[1] at hard labour without even a day's grace. While he was undergoing this painful tribulation his enemies did not lay down their arms. His publishers brought suit after suit against him. When he came out of Reading Gaol he was a ruined man.

The papers of the day portrayed him walking along the edge of the station platform at Clapham Junction beneath the December rain, dressed in the grey prison jacket. They showed him dragged into prison by the police, and exposed to the jeers of London's rabble who lined the streets as he passed by and insulted him with their stares and their gibes. Overcome at last, the haughty poet wept copiously and bitterly. It is out of this despair and these tears that came forth that masterpiece: *The Ballad of Reading Gaol*.

Some years went by and I found Oscar Wilde in company with Maurice du Plessys and Ernest La Jeunesse at the bar of the Calisaya in the Boulevard Montmartre. The poet had lately arrived from England to which he had sworn never to return, and was recovering little by little from the terrible ordeal he had recently undergone. He had recovered, if not his former arrogance, at least all his equanimity and serenity. We were surprised by his sincere good spirits and by his laughter which rang true, revealing his teeth which were nearly all capped with gold and which gave him a vague resemblance to an idol.

– You don't realize, he said to us, how stimulating the air of Paris is. Besides, I have become a neurasthenic. Here in this frantic atmosphere it's as if one were breathing liberty and tolerance, something one finds nowhere else and especially not in that hateful London.

'In Paris all my friends have welcomed me with the same eagerness they showed when I was at the height of my fame.'

Contrary to what one might have expected, he did not avoid alluding to his misfortunes, and spoke of them without a trace of bitterness and with such an air of indifference that he might have been referring to some other person.

– There was a time in my life, he told me, when I had really nothing more to wish for. I was rich, held in great affection, famous, and in perfect health. At that time I was resting at Sorrento in a delightful villa whose garden was filled with orange trees. The sea lapped at the base of the terrace. From it my eye could follow the delightful, undulating curves of a countryside as sensuous as the body of a young girl.

'On this terrace I was absentmindedly contemplating the white sails which studded the sea at its horizon. Suddenly I began to reflect, with a secret feeling of terror, that in reality I was too happy, that such improbable bliss could only be a trap set by my evil genius. For a long time this idea haunted me.

'In the end I recalled the adventure of that tyrant of antiquity – Polycrates I think was his name – who had thrown a highly esteemed precious ring into the sea to ward off misfortune.

'I resolved to imitate Polycrates. It's true that his sacrifice had proved vain, but perhaps I would prove more fortunate. As far out into the sea as I could I flung a ring set with a huge diamond that I kept in memory of a very dear friend. I thought I had appeased the hostile gods with this sacrifice and I regained my composure. . . .

– Is there any need to add, interrupted Ernest La Jeunesse in his falsetto voice, that the ring was brought back to you, like Polycrates's, discovered by a fisherman in the belly of an eel?

– You won't believe it, continued Oscar Wilde with a strange smile, but the unfortunate thing about it is that it was a little fisherman, far too handsome a fellow, who brought it back to me.'

The poet had sunk again into silence and was drinking through a straw one of those champagne and whisky cocktails he preferred to any other drink. Ernest La Jeunesse and du Plessys, who detested one another, had begun a bitter quarrel. I hastily withdrew from the scene.

A few days later I unexpectedly encountered Wilde in the Café Procope. He was staying in a little hotel in the Street of Beaux-Arts and he loved exploring the Latin Quarter. In a short time he was familiar with the literary cafés, the wine-cellars frequented by amateur songwriters and even the dens of ill-repute. He greatly enjoyed the company of these as yet unpublished poets. He would take long strolls with them along the quiet streets near the Place Saint-Sulpice, gladly stopping before antique dealers' windows to study the trinkets whose price and origin he knew wonderfully well.

He had quickly become popular with the people in the wine-cellars because of his generosity in offering drinks to first-comers. He displayed none of his arrogance with these humble companions, and was keenly interested in what they wrote.

When I came upon him in the Procope he had just left the songwriter Marcel Legay whom he praised highly.

– Legay is a true poet, he said to me, and some of his songs are masterpieces of words and music. Yet there are certain things he is unaware of. . . .

Oscar Wilde had begun to laugh.

– Just a moment ago he was telling me something really funny. Did you know Legay once had the singular idea of setting a page of your Renan's *Life of Jesus* to music and going to offer it to him? Someone once said that Renan was the pleasantest of cruel men. He never got angry. Faced with any trying circumstance he was all gentleness.

– 'Ah, my child,' he said to Legay, 'how good of you to think of this little trifle and how grateful I am. And yet, see where human error can lead. You have set my sentences to music. Alas! I thought I had done so myself.'

I had known the story for a long time, but I didn't want to deprive the poet of the pleasure of having told it to me.

*       *       *

Suddenly Oscar Wilde died on 30 November 1900. . . .

Everyone remained convinced that Oscar Wilde had resorted to suicide because he was utterly ruined and, more to the point, discouraged and disheartened. The truth is far more tragic because of its terrible simplicity. Exhausted by the work, the pleasures, and especially the sufferings of a life lacking in moderation, Oscar Wilde died of natural causes, completely worn out. He died in his little room in the Rue des Beaux-Arts in conditions that are hard to imagine.

Right up to the last day he had shown himself full of gaiety and generous down to the last penny, for he was too spirited and proud not to hold money in contempt. Yet the circumstances surrounding his death offer a kind of horror which is truly Shakespearean. While he was struggling in his death-throes, the doctors, Tucker and Kleiss, and the hotel-keeper were discussing the matter of money. At first they spoke in hushed tones, then loudly enough for the dying man to hear every word. They were anxiously wondering how they would be paid.

– With a supreme effort the poet came out of his coma to speak with a ghostly smile to his friend Robert Ross that terrible sentence J.-J. Renaud has quoted in that eloquent page from which we borrow it:

– I see I am dying beyond my means! . . .

He died shortly after. Then the hotel-keeper with the aid of his wife and some pliers hastened to tear out the gold bridge from the deceased man's mouth before rigor mortis set in. With a shiver of horror and disgust one can't help but think of the famous engraving by Goya showing the old hags tearing out the teeth of a man who has been hanged. Thus died he who had been called the 'Lord of Speech'.

His body was flung into a common grave in the Bagneux cemetery. Only five or six people followed his casket. Amongst them were Robert Ross, J. -B. de Bucé, director of a small literary paper, and two other regular customers of the Procope. Utter oblivion soon shrouded the name of the poet who had been surrounded by such clouds of glory during his lifetime. Yet now the memory of Oscar Wilde has been almost cleared of the hateful accusations which had sullied it. Several enquiries have established that he was sent to prison on the false testimony of professional sodomites who had been paid by the Marquis of Queensbury, father of Lord Alfred Douglas. Once more the works of this poet who died in poverty enrich his publishers and heirs.

### NOTE

1. Wilde was imprisoned for only two years, from 1895 to 1897.

# Oscar Wilde*

### Henri de Régnier

Today, to mark the 25th anniversary of Oscar Wilde's death, his friends are unveiling a commemorative plaque at the house where he died in Paris: 13 Rue des Beaux-Arts. For this reason we are publishing the following article in which Henri de Régnier vividly recreates for us Oscar Wilde, dandy, conversationalist and raconteur.

The story of Oscar Wilde, the English poet, is too well-known for me to relate it here. Everyone knows how a scandalous trial followed by a harsh sentence hurled him from the height of his fame as a splendid writer and conversationalist to the depths of a prison where he toiled at 'hard-labour'. For two years this splendid, elegant gentleman who had been a favourite of the drawing rooms of Paris and London became a convict with shaven head and roughened hands. When he regained his freedom he no longer had the strength to live, and, a broken man, finished his days in an obscure hotel in the Latin Quarter. It is from this hotel that a few friends

* *Les Annales Politiques et Littéraires*, LXXXV (29 November 1925), 563. This is the first appearance in English.

accompanied his remains to the Bagneux Cemetery on the 30th of November, 1900.

I do not wish to remember that Oscar Wilde who hid behind the name of Sebastien Melmoth, and yet I cannot forget the last time I saw him. It was at the Exhibition in the pavilion where the Spanish dancers were performing their ardent, wanton dances to the sound of guitars and castanets.

He was sitting alone at a table: slouched over, huge, half asleep. I was going over to him when he got up, passed by without noticing me and disappeared. As I watched Wilde leave I thought of the arrogant man who had been acclaimed by all a few years previously. He would stand surrounded by the curious as well as his admirers. As they stared at his broad, clean-shaven face whose regular features resembled those of a Roman proconsul or Greek god he would arrogantly and melodiously offer one by one his stories and his paradoxes. At the same time he would idly tap the ash from his gold-tipped, Egyptian cigarettes with a ringed finger. The setting of this ancient ring held the rounded back of a pharoah's scarab. I also thought of the Oscar Wilde who on his arrival in America replied to the customs officer that he had nothing to declare but his genius.

It was not to his 'genius' that Oscar Wilde owed the welcome he received when he came to Paris in 1893, but rather to his fame and his great reputation as an esthete. His arrival was preceded by a series of anecdotes which portrayed him as a sort of 'pleasure seeker' who looked for only the sensations of beauty and pleasure in life. He was portrayed as a kind of Epicurean of Oxford and Plato of Piccadilly who was crowned with the laurel of the poets as well as the roses of the Sybarites. Besides, rather little was known about Oscar Wilde the poet, and just as little about Oscar Wilde the writer, for his works were, so to speak, unknown in France at that time. There was no translation of them, thus people in France knew practically nothing whatsoever about his literary genius. However, Oscar Wilde had other means to gain recognition than those open to the man in the street. He had his monumental presence which he clothed richly in frock coats from whose button-holes peeked sprigs of green carnations. He had his fame as an eccentric and dandy. Above all he brought with him his wonderful gift as a conversationalist and storyteller.

Oscar Wilde's conversation was little suited to dialogue. He needed more someone to listen to him, than someone to speak with. One felt he could even have managed without the former. The ability to tell stories was so natural to him that Wilde spoke for his own benefit. Of their own account his thoughts would take the form of a story or fable, and he would abandon himself to their inexhaustible inspiration. Wilde would tell stories and he would tell them indefinitely. He used to relate pleasant, ingenious, paradoxical, profound stories which seemed to be invented as he went along. He did it so well that one had the flattering illusion that one had indeed merited this expense of imagination and energy. He seemed to offer to you what he had not yet offered anyone else. He did so generously and as if no one would be worthy after you of hearing those wonderful stories that he, the artful magician, poured out with such royal profusion. On more than one occasion I have witnessed this astonishing bit of acting. There was no one there who was not enchanted, even the most recalcitrant. In vain did one tell oneself it was mere pretence; one derived pleasure from being taken in. Without fail his spell would work and one's reservations would disappear. After all, of what importance was the element of truth in the works of this astonishing magician? What were his poetry, novels, essays and plays really worth? What was the use of even inquiring too closely about the individual who appeared to us in all the prestige of his legend? What was the point of listening to certain troublesome rumours which were beginning to be heard? Why listen to gossip, perhaps ill-founded, instead of enjoying the poetic, sumptuous inventions created by the storyteller in his slow, even, melodious voice; that endless incantation whose sweet-sounding, witty beauty was soon to be interrupted by a disaster of tragic proportions?

Wilde had keen insight into his age. It is this clearsightedness which led him to create the character he portrayed so completely and with such outstanding success; thereby astounding his contemporaries with his words and attitudes. He had discovered that the curiosity one raises is one of the ingredients of fame. What he desired was no less than to embody in the eyes of his fellow men a conception of life founded in the worship of beauty and pleasure. Consequently he declared his own life a work of art, and intended to carry out its realisation with contempt for the objections raised by the excesses of his hedonism.

Out of this attempt to live a life free of any rule and his claim to be above rules came scandal and disaster for Oscar Wilde. Disaster did not come from what he had written but rather from the realization of these theories on his own person. It was not the wonderful storyteller, nor the ingenious essayist, nor the novelist, nor the celebrated dramatist who was attacked, but the representative through his example of a philosophy of life for which he assumed social responsibility and for which he was severely called to account. Wilde paid dearly for his experiment. Let us forget all that, and remember only the witty and curious writer who loved France, and who was lionized in the literary circles of Paris thirty years ago.

## NOTE

Henri de Régnier (1864–1936), French poet, critic, and novelist.

# Oscar Wilde*

### Stuart Merrill

Oscar Wilde, who took delight in his own tales, used to wear two rings, one of which he claimed brought good fortune, and the other, ill luck. 'For,' he would add, 'Unlike most people, I have never mixed my shares of fortune and misfortune. For a long time I was the happiest of men, now I well deserve to be the most unhappy. At the moment I am under the influence of the evil ring.'

A fatalist and a stoic, he would then smile sadly at some ghastly memory or other. But he would soon forget his troubles by inventing a tale whose hero was invariably a king or a god whose adventures unfolded in a marble palace amidst flowers, standards and music. The dream made up for his life.

I knew Oscar Wilde in London at the height of his fame. He used to go about the city surrounded by his followers, astonishing the common herd, sought out by the elite. Three theatres were putting on his plays at one time.[1] *Dorian Gray*, which was to shock the public, was about to make its appearance. Wilde had just published *Intentions*, a book of saucy paradoxes in which he amused himself by turning around the favorite maxims of the middle class. Assailing these cherished beliefs with his wit, he used to entertain the public at the same time as he frightened them. I even believe that between two glasses of champagne Wilde would willingly profess himself an anarchist. Already he had opponents who attacked him from the depths of their vicarages, but few enemies in the world of literature, for at bottom he was a good man. He, who was to know all the bitterness of human ingratitude, never took advantage of his authority to harm an opponent. Wilde only tried his strength against his equals.

Besides, this same man who could appear a little too naïvely proud of himself used to cringe before those he recognized as his superiors. One night at the Garrick Club I saw him tremble like a mere beginning writer in the presence of Walter Pater, the incomparable stylist of *Marius the Epicurean*. Wilde was a respectful frequenter of the presence of Burne-Jones, Walter Crane, Swinburne, Ruskin, Rossetti and Robert Browning. In short, in terms of the ideas of this world, Oscar Wilde was perfectly happy, and, which is rare, knew it and said so.

* *La Plume* (Paris), (15 December 1900), 738–739. This is the first appearance in English.

A lawsuit foolishly brought by him against the Marquis of Queensberry was all that was required for this too beautiful dream to collapse. Oscar Wilde woke up one morning in a prison cell, amidst the ruins of his life and work. His plays were withdrawn from the stage and his book reduced to pulp. His friends pretended never to have known him. He was no longer even Oscar Wilde: he was prisoner C.3.3. It is with this number that he signed the English edition of the *Ballad of Reading Gaol*.

However, he had not suffered enough. He was still to be punished by what happened to his family. It is at Reading that he learned of the death of his mother. After being set free he lost his wife. Lastly, his brother was recently taken from him. The only surviving relatives of his name are, I believe, his two sons whom he dared to see only in secrecy in Geneva.

Oscar Wilde withstood all these disasters. He had challenged destiny, he had sacrificed the remotest hope for happiness, and very nobly without much to do, he bravely faced Life while wishing for Death. Even Death was cruel to him, and only took him after a long wait. At last he is at peace. Before his body I ask the wits and the hypocrites to lay down their arms. This man has paid his debts in full.

We are living in an era where charity is much talked about, and little practised. We live according to social conventions instead of soundly judging an individual act by its causes and consequences. We are especially unjust in sexual matters, and without much consideration we label what is often only a wretched illness as a moral perversion that must be punished. Thus the unsoundness of mind from which Oscar Wilde suffered outweighed, according to public opinion, an entire life of exalted thought, honest hard work, and noble feelings.

Surely this prudishness of public opinion is inspired by the hatred of art? With no fear of punishment scientists can devote themselves to the study of depravities a professional pornographer would blush at. As proof I only have to sight those innumerable treatises on unusual sexual behaviour which stock our bookshop windows. How many of these are truly scientific? Yet the police do not dare to interfere in the case of a book carrying the official stamp of the Faculty of Medicine. But let an artist who is filled with mercy, like Baudelaire or Georges Eekhoud, show sympathy for those poor souls who suffer because of their tastes in love, and immediately the 'moralists' raise a hue and cry from their vicarages and little shops. They denounce the artist to the vindication of society and only cease when they have dishonoured his good character.

Oscar Wilde, who struggled all his life against his folly, died a victim of these moralists. Yet he had written beautiful verses like his *Poems* and *The Sphinx*, criticism in *Intentions*, stories like *The Happy Prince* and *The House of Pomegranates*, a novel, *Dorian Gray*, plays like *Salome* and *Lady Windermere's Fan*. What do these works matter to shopkeepers and clergymen? Such things do not count when a man has spent two years in prison.

Before the death of the most unhappy man of our time, I beg for mercy and I call for forgiveness. He who was convict C.3.3. is forever prisoner of the great Jailor. May the work of Oscar Wilde appear to us henceforth in the serene beauty of anonymity. Let us at least be as merciful as the tomb.

## NOTES

Stuart Merrill (1863–1915), American poet who resided in Paris and wrote in French. He first met Wilde on his way through London to America in 1890. When *Salomé* was nearly finished, Wilde sent it to Merrill for possible linguistic improvements. In November 1895 Merrill drew up a petition to Queen Victoria begging for Wilde's release from prison, but it came to nothing as hardly any French literary figure agreed to sign it.

　1. This seems to be an inaccuracy as only *An Ideal Husband* and *The Importance of Being Earnest* ran simultaneously in London in 1895.

# Some Unpublished Recollections of Oscar Wilde*

### Stuart Merrill

I have written the following in *La Plume*: (i) an article on Oscar Wilde in 1893 which includes a pen-and-ink sketch by Albert Sterner at the time of Wilde's previous stay in Paris;[1] (ii) an article on the petition drawn up by Léon Deschamps and myself demanding Oscar Wilde's release from prison – there I singled out for criticism several well-known men of letters who refused their signatures for more or less spiteful and hypocritical reasons;[2] (iii) a very brief article on his death with a translation by me of his short story, *The Nightingale and the Rose*.[3]

　The best biography is that of Arthur Ransome which has been published by Stephen Swift (?).[4] The material for the chapter 'Oscar Wilde in Paris' has been largely supplied by me.[5] An excellent article by Jacques Dourelle in *Le Gaulois* introduced Wilde to Parisians.[6]

　I made Wilde's acquaintance in London in 1890, during a visit which I paid with Jonathan Sturges, the American novelist and translator of Maupassant, and Clarence McIlvaine, who is now associated with the

　* *Adam International Review* (London), nos. 241–3 (1954) 10–12. Translated and partially edited by H. Montgomery Hyde.

great publishing house of Harper Brothers.[7] At that time Oscar, as he was called by his friends, was so to speak the king of London. In spite of his glory and of our obscurity he was charming to us without displaying the least pose or arrogance. I maintain my assertion that there was nothing either in his conduct or even in his conversation which could give rise to the least suspicion. He actually displayed an extreme modesty, reproaching me in a friendly way for my rabelaisian tastes. I was never inclined to believe the accusations brought against him before his trial.

Wilde has been reproached for his vanity. However I have seen him as meek as a little child before Walter Pater at a dinner given for us by a friend at the Garrick Club. With a playful deference he called him 'Sir Walter' and he proudly recognized him as his master.

Oscar had made a lecture tour of America about 1888 or 1889.[8] Along with the aesthetic school he had recently been held up to ridicule in the Gilbert and Sullivan opera *Patience*, which had had an enormous success at the time. Moreover his lectures, which were extremely interesting (I do not know whether they were republished in his *Complete Works*[9]) attracted that section of the public which was more disposed to jeer than to listen to him. The students of Harvard behaved themselves towards him like cads. I remember that some of the inhabitants of Griggsville in Arkansas telegraphed Oscar asking him for a lecture on the aesthetics. He replied: 'Change the name of your town'. The name Griggs in fact sounded somewhat disagreeable and even a little ridiculous in English.

Other stories occur at random. One day Wilde was discovered at home contemplating with an air of ecstasy his rare Chinese porcelain and making no reply to the questions that were being put to him. At length on someone enquiring whether he had gone mad he answered: 'I am trying to live up to my china'. His expression is almost untranslatable in French. 'J'essaie de me rendre digne de ma porcelaine' is about the nearest rendering but it does not express the precise moral effort involved by the verb 'live up'.

On another occasion Wilde was discovered in very low spirits. 'What's the matter?' 'Ah, my friend', he said, 'one half of the world does not believe in God and the other half does not believe in me'.

He did not always have the laughs on his side, particularly when he pitted himself against Whistler, the other 'lion' of English society. One day Whistler displayed a flash of wit in Wilde's company. 'Oh', said Wilde, 'how I wish I had said that'. 'You will!' retorted Whistler sarcastically. Wilde was much accused of having plagiarised in his *Dorian Gray*.

I have told a number of stories about Wilde in my *Souvenirs sur le Symbolisme*, several chapters of which appeared in *La Plume*.[10] So as to put an end to inaccurate statements it will be of advantage to repeat that *Salomé* was written in French by Wilde, then revised and corrected by me, Retté,[11] and Pierre Louys[12] in that order, but solely from the point of view of the language. Schwob corrected the proofs.[13] Wilde was thus the sole author of *Salomé*, any corrections that were made being only for the purpose of drawing attention to the faults in his French.

Also, Ida Rubinstein has been criticized for having given too much importance to the dance in *Salomé*. But after Flaubert's story, it was this dance above all that interested Wilde. Salmon in *Gil Blas* has repeated what I have said on this subject.[14] One day I happened to be at the Moulin Rouge walking round with Oscar and he stopped in front of the stage where a Roumanian acrobat was dancing on her hands. There was fat Oscar all wrapped up in this spectacle and trying to send the dancer his card inviting her to supper. 'I want to see this woman,' he said. 'I particularly want to see her to make her an offer to play or still more to dance the part of *Salomé* in a play that I am going to write. I want her to dance on her hands like in Flaubert's story.'

Wilde's last days were miserable. After the closing of the Exhibition of 1900, where he had amused himself like a big child, he got bored. He had never been exactly sober; he now gave himself to drinking beyond measure. He used to be so overcome that he could scarcely stagger from the Madeleine to the Opera. His financial resources dried up. It is probable that some of his English friends who remained faithful to him sent him remittances, seeing that he could write nothing more. If he had published *De Profundis* during his lifetime, it would have attracted universal sympathy towards him. Moreover, whether from bravado or genuine inclination he frequented quarters where his presence was extremely disagreeable to those who considered themselves to be compromised in such company.

Incidentally Oscar Wilde was introduced to Jean Lorrain.[15] Someone asked Oscar for his impressions. 'Lorrain is a poseur,' he declared. Lorrain was asked what he thought of Wilde. 'He is a faker,' declared Lorrain. Each had tried to outdo the other. Being confined to bed with the influenza I assisted neither at Wilde's last moments nor at his funeral. I must not omit to mention Robert Ross who showed himself a devoted friend during his last agony and also was appointed his literary executor.

Wilde's hotel keeper has likewise been derided – Jean Dupoirier, who sent a wreath bearing the words, 'To my lodger' (*A mon Locataire*). Not long ago he was summoned to appear in court over some case and the good man declared that he had had the great poet Oscar Wilde as a lodger. 'There is no need for you to boast about it,' interrupted one of the imbecile judges.

And that is about the sum of my stock of reminiscences.

St[uart] M[errill]

Rochfort, September 20, 1912.

## NOTES

For a note on Stuart Merrill see p. 468.

1. *La Plume*, 15 March 1893 'La Jeune littérateure anglaise: Oscar Wilde'. The

drawing is reproduced in L. C. Ingleby's *Oscar Wilde: Some Reminiscences* (1912), p. 64. A drawing of Merrill by the same artist appeared in the supplement to *La Plume*, 13 October 1891.

2. id. January 1896, 'Pour Oscar Wilde: Epilogue'. Léon Deschamps was editor of *La Plume*.

3. id. 15 December 1900, 'Oscar Wilde'; reprinted in Stuart Merrill, *Prose et Vers: Oeuvres Posthumes* (Paris, 1925) pp. 239–43.

4. Ransome's *Oscar Wilde* was published by Martin Secker in London and by La Mercure de France in Paris. The French translation was by Gabriel de Lautrec and Henry-D. Davray.

5. This chapter was not included in the English edition. It was originally published as an article in *The Bookman* (May 1911) and also in *T. P.'s Magazine* (June 1911).

6. This article was by Maurice Sisley, not by Jacques Dourelle. It appeared in *Le Gaulois*, (20 June 1892) p. 1.

7. At the time of this meeting McIlvaine was a member of the firm of James R. Osgood, McIlvaine & Co., which in 1891 was to publish three of Wilde's books: *Intentions, Lord Arthur Savile's Crime and Other Stories* and *A House of Pomegranates*. On Osgood's death a short time afterwards the firm was amalgamated with Harper Brothers.

8. This is incorrect. The lecture tour took place in 1882.

9. Three of Wilde's American lectures were subsequently republished in *Miscellanies* which forms Volume XIV in the First Collected Edition of Wilde's works, appearing in 1908.

10. Reprinted in Stuart Merrill, *Prose et Vers: Oeuvres Posthumes* (Paris 1925). See particularly pp. 142–5 for his remarks on Wilde.

Here is a characteristic anecdote. 'At dessert, Wilde bent his tall body toward Moréas and asked him to recite some verse. "I never recite," replied Moréas, "but if you would like it, our friend Raynaud will recite us something." Raynaud stood up, and resting his redoubtable fists on the table announced, "Sonnet to Jean Moréas". He received our applause and then Wilde again pressed Moréas to recite. "No; but our friend La Tailhède—" In his turn La Tailhède rose, and, eyeglass fixed, launched in a clear voice: "Ode to Jean Moréas". Wilde grew visibly unquiet at the worship paid to its chief by the Ecole Romane; none the less he continued by courtesy his insistence. "Du Plessy, let ue hear your latest verses", commanded the master. Leaping up, Du Plessys trumpeted in vibrant tones: "The tomb of Jean Moréas". Oscar Wilde choked, conquered, routed, he who had silence about him in the salons of London, asked for his hat and coat and fled into the night. It was certainly the first time that all the incense round a dinner table had not been reserved for himself.'

11. Adolphe Retté (1863–1910), French symbolist writer. He claims that in his corrections to *Salomé* he suppressed a considerable number of 'purple patches' put into the mouth of Herod, though he was soon replaced as an adviser by Pierre Louÿs (see n. 12), in whose judgement Wilde had more confidence. See his *Le Symbolisme: Anecdotes et Souvenirs* (1903) pp. 211–13 for further remarks on Wilde. 'The last time I met Wilde', he wrote, 'was at the Rodin Dinner in June, 1900. There was something humble and contrite about his demeanour which concerned me. He took hold of my hand timidly as if he were afraid that I would not grasp his. This attitude made me feel badly and I judged that his misadventure had crushed him.'

12. Pierre Louÿs (1870–1925), French writer and friend of Oscar Wilde. The French edition of *Salomé* was dedicated to him. See H. P. Clive, 'Pierre Louÿs and Oscar Wilde: A Chronicle of Their Friendship,' *Revue de Littérature Comparée*, XLIII (1969), 353–84.

13. Marcel Schwob (1867–1905), French symbolist writer. Translated Defoe's *Moll Flanders* and adapted *Hamlet* for the French stage. Authority on François Villon and his times. Married the actress Marguerite Moreno of the Comédie Française. Wilde's poem *The Sphinx*, also written in Paris, was dedicated to him. He made only two corrections to the proofs of *Salomé*.

14. André Salmon (b. 1881), French poet and critic. He attacked the Epstein memorial to Wilde in an article in *Gil Blas*, 3 February, 1913.

15. Jean Lorrain (1855–1906), French journalist and novelist of the decadent and 'curious' school.

# The Death of Oscar Wilde*

## Wilfrid Scawen Blunt

10*th Dec* [1900] – Oscar Wilde is reported dead. He was without exception the most brilliant talker I have ever come across, the most ready, the most witty, the most audacious. Nobody could pretend to outshine him, or even to shine at all in his company. Something of his wit is reflected in his plays, but very little. The fine society of London and especially the 'Souls'[1] ran after him because they knew he could always amuse them, and the pretty women allowed him great familiarities, though there was no question of love-making. Physically, he was repellent, though with a certain sort of fat good looks. There was a kind of freckled coarseness in his colouring I have seen at times in other Irishmen. I was never intimate with him, though on superficially cordial terms when we met. He had been two or three times at our Crabbet parties and was a member of our Club, but only attended one regular meeting. The last time I saw him was at that brilliant luncheon party at Asquith's in Upper Grosvenor Street which I have already described. His poetry, though nothing very wonderful, was good, especially his 'Ballad of Reading Gaol,' as was also a protest he wrote on leaving prison against prison treatment, and if he had then begun a decent life people would have forgiven him, but he returned to Paris and to his dog's vomit and this is the end. I see it said in the papers that he was received into the Catholic Church on his deathbed, a strange ending, and yet not strange!

*       *       *

* *My Diaries; Being A Personal Narrative of Events 1888–1914* (London: Martin Secker, 1932) Part 1, p. 375; and Part 2, pp. 121–22.

16*th Nov.* [1905] – I have become reconciled to my fate, the more so because the rest has done me good, the pain is less and I have lost all inclination to get up. Numbers of friends have been with me. Yesterday I saw Ross,[2] Oscar Wilde's friend, who was with him in his last hours. I was curious to know about these and he told me everything. Ross is a good honest fellow as far as I can judge, and stood by Oscar when all had abandoned him. He used to go to him in prison, being admitted on an excuse of legal business, for Ross managed some of Mrs. Wilde's affairs while her husband was shut up. He told me Oscar was very hardly treated during his first year, as he was a man of prodigious appetite and required more food than the prison allowance gave him, also he suffered from an outbreak of old symptoms and was treated as a malingerer when he complained of it. Ross's representation got attention paid to these things, and in the last eight months of his imprisonment, Wilde had books and writing materials in abundance and so was able to write his 'De Profundis.' I asked him how much of this poem was sincere. He said, 'As much as possible in a man of Oscar's artificial temperament. While he was writing he was probably sincere, but his "style" was always in his mind. It was difficult to be sure about him. Sometimes when I called he was hysterical, at other times laughing. When Oscar came out of prison he had the idea of becoming a Catholic, and he consulted me about it, for you know I am a Catholic. I did not believe in his sincerity and told him if he really meant it, to go to a priest, and I discouraged him from anything hasty in the matter. As a fact, he had forgotten all about it in a week, only from time to time he used to chaff me as one standing in the way of his salvation. I would willingly have helped him if I had thought him in earnest, but I did not fancy religion being made ridiculous by him. I used to say that if it came to his dying I would bring a priest to him, not before. I am not at all a moral man, but I had my feeling on this point and so the matter remained between us. After he had been nearly a year out of prison he took altogether to drink, and the last two years of his life were sad to witness. I was at Rome when I heard that he was dying and returned at once to Paris and found him in the last stage of meningitis.[3] It is a terrible disease for the bystanders, though they say the sufferer himself is unconscious. He had only a short time to live, and I remembered my promise and got a priest to come to him. I asked him if he would consent to see him, and he held up his hand, for he could not speak. When the priest, an Englishman, Cuthbert Dunn, came to him he asked him whether he wished to be received and put the usual questions, and again Oscar held up his hand, but he was in no condition to make a confession nor could he say a word. On this sign, however, Dunn allowing him the benefit of the doubt, gave him conditional baptism, and afterwards extreme unction but not communion. He was never able to speak and we do not know whether he was altogether conscious. I did this for the sake of my own conscience and the promise I had made.' Wilde's wife died a year after he left prison. She would have gone to see him at Paris but he had already taken to drink, and Ross did not encourage her to do so. Ross made £800 by the 'De Profundis.' He had intended to pay off Oscar's Paris debts with £400 of it and devote the rest to the use of the boys, but just as he was going to do this the whole sum was claimed by the bankruptcy court and the affair is not yet settled.

## NOTES

Wilfrid Scawen Blunt (1840–1922), English poet and traveller. He first met Wilde in 1883. See William T. Going, 'Oscar Wilde and Wilfrid Blunt: Ironic Notes on Prison, Prose, and Poetry', *Victorian Newsletter*, XIII (1958) 27–9.

1. Cf. 'Though this circle prided itself on being intellectually avant-garde, and though it boasted the fiery spirits like Margot Tennant, Herbert Asquith and George Curzon, it was adamant in its exclusion of Oscar Wilde. Nevertheless, while the members kept their social distance, they admired Wilde from an intellectual point of view.' – Welford Dunaway Taylor, 'A "Soul" Remembers Oscar Wilde', *English Literature in Transition*, XIV (1971) 43–8.

2. For a note on Robert Ross see p. 341.

3. See Terence Cawthrone, 'The Last Illness of Oscar Wilde', *Proceedings of the Royal Society of Medicine* (London), LII, no. 2 (February 1959) 123–7; and Macdonald Critchley, 'Medical Reflections on Oscar Wilde', *Medico-Legal Journal*, XXX (1962) 73–84.

# Exit Oscar Wilde*

## Horace Wyndham

The announcement of Mr. Oscar Wilde's death, which took place in a small hotel[1] in the Latin Quarter of Paris, is accompanied by tidings that tend to soften the regrets that such an event must awaken. Mr. Oscar Wilde, whose meteoric appearance in the world of *belles lettres* was succeeded by moral oblivion, belonged to a group of young men, rebels born, whose conventional Protestantism could not hold back from a relapse into paganism. According to report, Mr. Wilde attributed his catastrophe to the fact that his father would not allow him, when he was a youth, to submit himself to the discipline of the Catholic Church. Be that as it may, Mr. Wilde's reception into the Church, during his last illness, by one of the Passionist Fathers in Paris, constitutes his one act of public and voluntary repentance.[2]

A correspondent adds: The last time I saw the name of Oscar Wilde

* *This Was the News* (London: Quality Press, 1948) pp. 162–4.

was in a letter, written about a quarter of a century ago by Father Matthew Russell, S. J., who was asking prayers for him as a brilliant young Irishman, then an undergraduate at Magdalen College, Oxford.

*The Tablet*: December 8th, 1900.

Father Russell did his best, but that in this particular instance his prayers were not entirely efficacious is a matter of history. At any rate, where Oscar Wilde was concerned, something seems to have gone wrong with them.

There have been many scandals in the literary, artistic, and social worlds, but none that caused such a sensation as this one. Of Oscar Wilde, it may be said that 'when he fell, he fell like Lucifer.' After bringing an unsuccessful action for criminal libel against the Marquess of Queensberry, he was himself arrested under Section XI of the Criminal Law Amendment Act. The charge was heard at the Old Bailey, where, on May 25th, 1895, he was convicted and sentenced to two years' imprisonment with hard labour. On November 30th, 1900, he died in Paris (where he had been living, down at heels and poverty stricken, as 'Sebastian Melmoth'), and was buried in Bagneux cemetery. Nine years later his remains were exhumed and reburied at Père Lachaise.[3] As the result of an anonymous gift of £3000 a monument, carved by Epstein,[4] has been erected above his grave. Pious pilgrimages are still made there on the anniversary of his death.

'The two great turning-points in my life,' wrote Oscar Wilde, in his *De Profundis*, 'were when my father sent me to Oxford and when Society sent me to prison.'

But he had only himself to thank for this latter experience.

'He first,' says Thomas Plowman,[5] 'developed his aesthetic proclivities at Oxford, where, for a time, he was an ardent follower of Ruskin; and was one of the band of undergraduates who, at the professor's bidding, devoted themselves (between the intervals of study) to road-making. It has been authoritatively stated that he "had the honour of wheeling Mr. Ruskin's special barrow, and that it was the author of *Modern Painters* who taught him to trundle it." '

Notwithstanding his florid compliments, and habit of inscribing books and poems to them, Oscar Wilde seldom had much success with what journalists called (and still call) the 'fair sex.' As a rule, they were served by their instinct, and took his measure very promptly.

'His appearance,' says Lady Augusta Fane, 'was revolting. He had a fat, clean-shaven, pallid face, a head covered with long fair hair, brushed off his forehead and falling on to the collar of his velvet coat, heavy stooping shoulders and enormous white hands, similar to the hands of Epstein's "Rima," which he waved about the whole time he was talking. If one had not seen him, and only remembered his brilliant conversation and wit, the memory would have been a rare treasure.'

Gertrude Atherton,[6] who had been asked to meet him (and declined to do so when she saw his photograph) was similarly uncomplimentary about his personal appearance:

'His mouth covered half his face, the most lascivious, coarse, repulsive mouth I had ever seen. I might stand it in a large crowded drawing-room, but not in a parlour, eight by eight, lit by three tallow candles. I should feel as if I were under the sea, pursued by some bloated monster of the deep.'

Nor did Mrs. Langtry,[7] who knew him well, go out of her way to hurl bouquets in his direction:

'Vividly do I recall my first meeting with Oscar Wilde, and how astonished I was at his strange appearance. Then he must have been not more than twenty-two. . . . His face was large, and so colourless that a few pale freckles of good size were oddly conspicuous. He had a well-shaped mouth, with somewhat coarse lips and greenish-hued teeth. . . . There were times when I found him too persistent in hanging round the house, or running about after me elsewhere; and I am afraid that I often said things which hurt his feelings, in order to get rid of him. After a frank remark that I made on one occasion, I happened to go to the theatre. As I sat in my box I noticed a commotion in the stalls—it was Oscar, who, having perceived me suddenly was being led away in tears.'

Considering that Oscar had dedicated a poem, 'The New Helen,' to her, and had also offered her a play, this was just a little unkind of the 'Jersey Lily.'

'Even in declaring himself a decadent,' says somebody else, 'Oscar Wilde was a man to be loved. As "Heart's Brother," he was known to the favoured few who were admitted into the inner circle of his life.'

Among those to be thus favoured was, apparently, Walt Whitman.[8] 'Have you,' he wrote to a friend, 'read about Oscar Wilde? He is a fine, large, handsome youngster, and had the good sense to take a great fancy to me!'

A somewhat younger admirer,[9] who has revealed this hitherto un-suspected confidence, once called on 'Heart's Brother' in Paris, and afterwards recorded his impressions in an odd little volume, *Osric, the Self-Sufficient*:

'When I hunted up the poet, whose wild (query Wilde?) fancies had filled my years of adolescence with dreams, at his rooms in the Rue des Beaux Arts, a year after his release, I found him still the gentlemanly man of Letters he had always been. . . . When I left him, he was crooning softly over the fire, a cigarette between his lips.'

According to this authority, the evening was not wasted, since his host pronounced critical judgments (Labelled *bon mots*), upon a number of his contemporaries. They do not sound very penetrating. Thus, Arthur Symons was 'too sickly, and given to panting on the breasts of his loves'; and George Moore struck him as 'a grocer temporarily installed in the place of an artist. His novels are unbearable to a sensitive spirit.'

Oscar must have been caught in petulant mood.

When the news of Wilde's death reached him, Dr. Garnett's[10] comment was: 'This is the death-blow to English poetry, because it will cast odium upon the pre-Raphaelites.' Oscar, had he heard him, would probably have retorted, 'Then I shall not have died in vain.'

## NOTES

Horace Wyndham's writings on Wilde and his family include *Speranza; A Biography of Lady Wilde* (London: T. V. Boardman, 1951); 'Lady Wilde', *Notes and Queries*, CLXXVIII (10 Feb 1940) 98; 'A Chelsea Recamier: Oscar Wilde's Mother', *The Catholic World* (New York), CLVII (May 1943) 142–8; 'Oscar Wilde as Editor', *World Review* (London), (Aug 1946) 46–7; 'Speranza and Her First Editor', *English*, VI, no. 31 (1946) 73; 'When Wilde Was Editor', *Life & Letters*, LV (Dec 1947) 201–4; and 'Edited by Wilde', *Library Review*, XVII (1949) 214–16.

1. For a note on the Hôtel d'Alsace see p. 455.
2. On Wilde's conversion to Catholicism see p. 326.
3. See Herman Scheffauer, 'The Monument to Oscar Wilde', *The International* (New York), VII (Oct 1913) 292, 306.
4. Sir Jacob Epstein (1880–1959), British sculptor of Russo-Polish descent. See his Letter to the Editor, 'The Oscar Wilde Monument', *The Times* (London), (8 Nov 1913) p. 7.
5. Thomas F. Plowman, 'The Aesthetes; The Story of a Nineteenth Century Cult', *The Pall Mall Magazine* (London), V, no. 21 (Jan 1895) 27–44.
6. Gertrude Atherton (1857–1948), American novelist.
7. For a note on Lillie Langtry see p. 264.
8. Walt Whitman (1819–1892), the American poet, whom Wilde met during his American lecture tour in 1882.
9. John M. Stuart-Young.
10. Richard Garnett (1835–1906), English librarian and author.

# Oscar Wilde*

## Ernest La Jeunesse

Wilde in exile remained always English. Irishman by birth, an Italian in his inclinations, Greek in culture and Parisian in his passion for paradox and *blague*,[1] he never could forget London. . . . London, in whose fogs he

* *La Revue Blanche* (Paris), (15 December 1900) 589–96. Translated by Percival Pollard.

had found all his triumphs; London, into which he had brought all exotic civilizations; London, that in his vanity he had transformed into a monstrous garden of flowers and palaces, of subtlest suggestion and discreetest charm. His impertinences toward the English had been those of a benevolent monarch. When he came late into a salon, without greeting to anyone, accosted the hostess and asked, quite audibly: 'Do I know anybody here?' that was nothing but his singular gallantry; he had by no means the intention of slighting this one or that one, but wished merely to avoid the appearance of knowing all the world, inasmuch as the hostess herself probably knew only a small number of her guests. He has been accused of a green carnation and a cigarette; it was for that, perhaps, that for twenty-four months he was deprived of all tobacco and all flowers. He has been reproached with having spent twice the 150,000 francs his plays brought him in; he was declared bankrupt. His name was erased from the hoardings and from the memories of men; his children were taken away from him; all this because the public wished to amaze him with its cruelty.

Still this was not the end. From the moment that he set foot on our soil we were witnesses to a horrible tragedy: his effort to pick up the thread of his life. This giant, whom lack of sleep, of nourishment, of peace and of books, had been unable to destroy and scarcely to weaken, asked for the sea, of Paris and of Naples, that they harbor the dawn of a new era in his art.

He failed.

At forty, confident in the future, he failed. He could but reach out with impotent arms into the past, lose himself in bitter memories. American managers clamored for a new play of his; all he could do was to give Leonard Smithers 'An Ideal Husband,' 1899, to print, a play several years old.

His heavy lids drooped upon cherished dreams: his successes; he walked slowly, in short paces, so as not to disturb his memories; he loved the solitude one gave him, since it left him alone with what he had once been. Yet still the evil habit was on him of haunting, with some companion, the obscurest streets, dreaming of similar adventures in London . . . always London!

He had to have that oblivion which alcohol denied him. For even in the bars it was London he sought. There was left for him nothing but the American bars, which were not to his liking. One evening at Chatham's he had been told his presence was unwelcome. There on the térrace he had tried to distract his incurious eyes, but the passers-by gazed at him too curiously; he gave up even that.

All his face was furrowed by tears. His eyes seemed caverns hollowed out by pale tears; his heavy lips seemed compact of sobs and oozing blood; and everywhere was that horrible bloating of the skin that signals human fear and heartache corroding the body. An unwieldy ghost, an enormous caricature, he cowered over a cocktail, always improvising for the curious, for the known, and for the unknown – for anyone – his tired and tainted paradoxes. But mostly it was for himself he improvised; he must assure himself he still *could*, still *would*, still *knew*.

He knew everything.

Everything. The commentaries on Dante; the sources of Dante Gabriel Rossetti; the events and the battles of history – of all he could talk as a stripling talks, smiling sometimes his smile that was of Purgatory, and laughing – laughing at nothing, shaking his paunch, his jowls, and the gold in his teeth.

Slowly, word for word, he would invent in his feverish, stumbling agony of art, curious, fleeting parables: the story of the man who, having received a worthless coin, voyages forth to meet in combat the ruler whose doubly counterfeit presentment he has found. . . . But he lacked, for the setting down of these tales, the golden tablet of Seneca.

He wasted himself in words; perhaps he tried to lose himself in them. He sought scholars that he might find in them an excuse for finding himself again, for living anew, for being born again, and to keep him from overmuch thinking about ungrateful plagiarists.

Wilde once told a tale of a king and a beggar, and said at close: 'I have been king; now I will be a beggar.' Yet he remained to the very last day the perfect, well-groomed Englishman – and did not beg.

That would indeed have been a new life, this life that fate denied him.

Words fail to paint properly the chaos of hope, of words and laughter, the mad sequence of half-concluded sentences, into which this poet plunged, proving to himself his still inextinguished fancy, his battling against surrender, his smiling at fate; or to suggest the grim dark into which he always must turn, daily fearing death, in the narrow chamber of a sordid inn.

He had been in the country, in Italy, and he longed for Spain, for the Mediterranean; there was nothing for him save Paris, – a Paris gradually closing against him, a deaf Paris, bloodless, heartless, a city without eternity and without legend.

Each day brought him sorrows; he had neither followers nor friends; the direst neurasthenia tortured him. Want clutched at him; the pittance of ten francs a day allowed him by his family was no longer increased by any advances from his publishers; he must needs work, write plays that he had already contracted to undertake, – and he was physically unable to arise from his bed before three in the afternoon!

He did not sour under all this; he simply let himself run down. One day he takes to his bed, and pretends that he has been poisoned by a dish of mussels in a restaurant; he gets up again, but wearily, and with thoughts of death.

He attempts his stories all over again. It is like nothing save the bitter, blinding brilliance of a superhuman firework. All who saw him at the end of his career, still spraying forth the splendor of his wit and his invention, whittling out the golden, jeweled fragments of his genius, with which he was to fashion and embroider the plays and poems he still meant to do – who saw him proudly lifting his face to the stars the while he coughed his last words, his last laughter, – will never forget the tremendous, tragic spectacle as of one calmly damned yet proudly refusing utterly to bend the neck.

Nature, at last kind to him who had denied her, gathered all her glories together for him in the Exposition. He died of its passing, as he died of everything. He had loved it, had drunk it in large measures, greedily, as one drinks blood on the battlefield. In every palace of it he built again his own palace of fame, riches and immortality.

For this dying man it was a long and lovely dream. One day he passed out through the Porte de L'Alma to look at Rodin's work. He was almost the only wayfarer thither. That, too, is tragedy; and the master showed him, quite near by, the *Porte de L'Enfer*!

But enough of details; on to the end.

Thirteen persons, in a bedroom out by the city limits, remove their hats before a coffin marked with a No. 13; a shaky hearse with shabby metal ornaments; two landaus instead of a funeral coach; a wreath of laurel; faded flowers; a church that is not draped for death, that tolls no death-note, and opens only a narrow side-entrance for the procession; a dumb and empty mass without music; an absolution intoned in English, the liturgic Latin turned to a nonconformist jumble; the glittering salute of a captain of the guard on the Place Saint Germain-des-Près; three reporters counting the participants with cold-blooded precision – that is the farewell that the world takes from one of its children, from one who had wished to illuminate and spread far the splendor of its dreams; – that is the knell of a life of phantasms and dreams of impossible beauty; – that is the forgiveness and the recompense; – that, on a false dawn, is the first rosy light of immortality!

Wilde, who was a Catholic, received but two sacraments: the first while in a coma, the last in his last sleep. The priest who looked after him was bearded and English; seemed himself a convert. In all justice I would assert here that Wilde was sincerely enough a Catholic not to have need of the last rites; that he devoutly loved all the Romish pomp and ceremony, even to the color-effects of the stained windows and the notes of the organ; and that some of all this might rightly have been his due, rather than this stolid farce, this hasty burying, this oppressive absolution, in which the vicar seemed to be washing his hands clean of this taint of unrighteousness.

I cannot judge, cannot praise, Oscar Wilde here. Properly to seize and set forth his curious genius were a greater task. One will not find that genius in his writings. Witty and sublime it is, there; but, for him, too piecemeal. His work is the shadow of his thoughts, the shadow of his illuminating speech.

One must conceive him as one who knew everything and said everything in the best way. A Brummel, who was a Brummel even in his genial moments. And one who would have fulfilled that part while tasting of shame and of unhappiness.

None believed in Art more than Wilde.

I will close this tribute by an allusion to his simplicity. Wilde, who suffered so much, suffered under his reputation of being affected. One evening Wilde, who was not usually fond of publicly deploring his lost treasures, lamented his paternity. After he had told me of his son Vivian's conversion to the Catholic faith, the boy having quite simply declared to his guardian, 'I am a Catholic,' Wilde said with a smile: 'And Vivian, twelve years old, lies down on a couch, and when they wish him to get up, says: "Leave me – I am thinking!" with a gesture, mind you, of my own – a gesture that people have jeered at and of which they have always declared it was affected!' This was the beginning of a rehabilitation among the mob.

And now the grandson of this Mathurin [sic]², who admired Balzac, from whom this unfortunate borrowed his fatal pseudonym of Sebastian Melmoth, sleeps; he sleeps, this son of a noble and learned father and mother, at whose christening stood a King of Sweden; sleeps, and sleeps badly, in a churchyard that is far enough away to choke the courage and the prayers of whoso might wish to venture there. Hardly will the echo of borrowed fables wake or lull him. Hardly will the occasional utterance of his name in scandal reach him, bringing its burden of insult.

He will, I hope, pardon me these words, uttered only for history, for sincerity and for justice, and to be the witnesses for one who was his friend in evil days, who is neither aesthetic nor cynic, and who in all humility sends greeting to him in his silence and his peace.

## NOTES

Ernest Harry La Jeunesse (1874–1917), French Littérateur. In a letter to Lord Alfred Douglas written from Berneval in 1897 Wilde said: I am greatly fascinated by the *Napoléon* [*L'Imitation de Notre-Mâitre Napoléon*] of La Jeunesse; and in a letter to Reginald Turner sent from Paris in 1898 he wrote: 'Kalisaya, the American Bar near the Credit Lyonnais, is now the literary resort of myself and my friends: and we all gather there at five o'clock – Moréas, and La Jeunesse, and all the young poets.'

1. Humbug.

2. Charles Robert Maturin (1782–1824), the Irish writer, was Wilde's greatuncle.

# *Appendix*:Additional Bibliography

*The references in this list – arranged alphabetically – comprise secondary material which may be of use in additional fields of biographical inquiry. A brief annotation has been supplied where necessary.*

Ainslie, Douglas, 'Swinburne, Wilde, and Pater', *Adventures, Social and Literary* (London: T. Fisher Unwin, 1922) pp. 92–7.

'All Sorts', *The Daily Saratogian* (7 June 1882) p. 1 [Wilde's visit to Longfellow during American lecture tour].

'Arrival of Oscar Wilde', *New York Daily Tribune* (3 Jan 1882) p. 5 [on American lecture tour].

'Artist Miles Visits Oscar Wilde', *Saint John Globe* (14 Oct 1882) p. 4 [during American lecture tour].

Asquith [Oxford], Margot, *More Memories* (London: Cassell, 1933) pp. 116–21.

Bain, James S., *A Bookseller Looks Back* (London: Macmillan, 1940) p. 132.

Bancroft, M. E., and S. B. Bancroft, *The Bancrofts: Recollections of Sixty Years* (London: John Murray, 1909) pp. 408–9.

Baring, Maurice, 'The Nineties', *Lost Lectures, or The Fruits of Experience* (London: Peter Davies, 1932) p. 102.

Beddington, Mrs Claude, 'Gladstone and Wilde', *All That I Have Met* (London: Cassell, 1929) pp. 33–41.

Birnbaum, Martin, *Oscar Wilde; Fragments and Memories* (London: Elkin Mathews; New York: James F. Drake, 1914).

Blanche, Jacques-Émile, 'Oscar Wilde', *La Pêche aux Souvenirs* (Paris: Flammarion, 1949) pp. 187–9.

Blei, Franz, 'Recollections', *Recollections of Oscar Wilde*, by Ernest La Jeunesse, André Gide, and Franz Blei, translation and introduction by Percival Pollard (Boston and London: John W. Luce, 1906) pp. 91–9.

Bristowe, Sybil, 'Mr. W. B. Yeats: Poet and Mystic', *T.P.'s Weekly* (London) (4 April 1913) 421 [Yeats on Wilde in an interview].

Champion, Pierre, *Marcel Schwob et son temps* (Paris: Bernard Grasset, 1927) pp. 98–9.

Chapman-Huston, Desmond, *The Lost Historian; A Memoir of Sir Sidney Low* (London: John Murray, 1936) pp. 68–74.

Cheiro [Count Louis Hamon], *Cheiro's Memoirs; The Reminiscences of a Society Palmist* (Philadelphia: J. B. Lippincott; London: William Rider, 1912) pp. 56–61 [meeting Wilde and reading his hand].

Claretie, Georges, 'L'Auteur de *Salomé*', *Le Figaro* (1 Apr 1907) p. 1.

Cooper-Prichard, A. H., 'Oscar Wilde at Lunch', *Cornhill Magazine*, LXXI (Aug 1931) 185–94.

—— 'Oscar Wilde at Afternoon Tea', *Cornhill Magazine*, LXIX (Nov 1930) 590–6.

Deghy, Guy, and Keith Waterhouse, *Café Royal: Ninety Years of Bohemia* (London: Hutchinson, 1955) pp. 58–64.

De Miomandre, Francis, *Figures d'Hier et d'Aujourd' hui* (Paris: Dorbon-Ainé, [1910]) pp. 37–44.

De Régnier, Henri, 'Oscar Wilde', *Les Annales Politiques et Littéraires*, LXXXV (29 Nov 1925) 563.

Dircks, Rudolf, 'Mr. Oscar Wilde', *Players of Today* (London: Simpkin, Marshall, Hamilton, Kent; Newcastle upon Tyne: Andrew Reid [1892]) pp. 100–2.

*Echoes of the 'Eighties; Leaves from the Diary of a Victorian Lady* (London: Eveleigh Nash, [1921]) pp. 213 21.

Ellis, Stewart M., *Mainly Victorian* (London: Hutchinson, [1925]) *passim*.

Fane, Lady Augusta, *Chit-Chat* (London: Thornton Butterworth, 1926) p. 103.

Field, Isobel, *This Life I've Loved* (London: Michael Joseph, 1937) pp. 130–40 [In San Francisco].

Flower, Newman (ed.), *The Journals of Arnold Bennett, 1911–1921* (London: Cassell, 1932) pp. 53–4 [Wilde and Frank Harris].

Ford, Ford Madox, *Ancient Lights and Certain New Reflections* (London: Chapman & Hall, 1911) pp. 150–4.

—— 'Memories of Oscar Wilde', *Saturday Review of Literature*, XX (27 May 1939) 3–4, 15–16.

Fox, Rev. Lawrence Charles Prideaux, 'People I have Met', *Donahoe's Magazine*, LIII, no. 4 (Apr 1905) 472 [Wilde's parents].

Fréchette, Louis, 'Oscar Wilde', *La Patrie* (Montreal) (20 Apr 1895) p. 1 [acrimonious recollections].

Germain, André, 'Wilde à Berneval', *La Revue Europèenne*, I (Dec 1923) 37–40.

—— 'Oscar Wilde', *Les Fous de 1900* (Paris: La Palatine, 1955) pp. 19–37.

Gide, André, *Si le Grain ne meurt* (Paris: Editions de la Nouvelle Revue, 1924). English translation by Dorothy Bussy entitled *If It Die* (London: Secker & Warburg, 1951) pp. 290–308.

Gower, Lord Ronald, *My Reminiscences* (London: Kegan Paul, Trench; Boston: Roberts Brothers, 1884).

Green, Roger Lancelyn, *A. E. W. Mason* (London: Max Parrish, 1952) *passim*.

Gregory, Lady [Isabella Augusta], *Journals 1916–1930*, ed. Lennox Robinson (London: G. P. Putnam, 1946; New York: Macmillan, 1947) p. 330.

Hartley, Harold, *Eighty-Eight Not Out: A Record of Happy Memories* (London: Frederick Muller, 1939) pp. 247–51.

Hodgetts, E. A. Brayley, *Moss from a Rolling Stone* (London: J. M. Dent; New York: E. P. Dutton, 1924) pp. 130–1.

Housman, Laurence, *The Unexpected Years* (London: Jonathan Cape, 1937) pp. 115–16.

—— 'The Causeur', *Adam International Review*, XXII, nos 241–3 (1954) ix.

Huddleston, Sisley, *Back to Montparnasse* (London: George G. Harrap; Philadelphia: J. B. Lippincott, 1931) pp. 261–4.

Ingleby. Leonard Cresswell, *Oscar Wilde; Some Reminiscences* (London: T. Werner Laurie, 1912).

Jaloux, Edmond, *Les Saisons Littéraires* (Fribourg: Éditions de la Librairie de l'Université, 1942) *passim*.

Jullian, Philippe, 'Fresh Remembrance of Oscar Wilde', *Vogue* (Boulder, Colorado), CLIV (1 Nov 1969) 176–9, 229–34.

Leslie, Shane, *The End of a Chapter* (London: Constable, 1916) *passim*.

——'Oscar Wilde – Frank Harris – Dr. Morrison', *Sir Evelyn Ruggles-Brise; A Memoir of the Founder of Borstal* (London: John Murray, 1938) pp. 128–36 [Wilde in prison].

'London Topics of the Day: Oscar Wilde Talking about America', *New York Times* (25 Nov 1883) p. 5.

Lorrain, Jean [Paul Alexandre Martin Duval], *Sensations et Souvenirs* (Paris: Bibliothèque-Charpentier, 1895) *passim*.

——, *La Ville Empoisonnée* (Paris: Éditions Jean Crès, 1936) pp. 303–9.

Lowndes, Mrs Belloc, *The Merry Wives of Westminster* (London: Macmillan, 1946) p. 174.

Lucas, E. V., *The Colvins and Their Friends* (London: Methuen; New York: Charles Scribner's Sons, 1928) *passim*.

Marlow, Louis, 'Oscar Wilde', *Seven Friends* (London: The Richards Press, 1953) pp. 1–25.

Maugham, W. Somerset (ed.), *The Truth at Last from Charles Hawtrey* (London: Thornton Butterworth, 1924) pp. 220–2 [on the skit, *The Poet and the Puppets*].

Millar, C. C. Hoyer, *George du Maurier and Others* (London: Cassell, 1937) pp. 60–1, 67–8, 74.

Mirbeau, Octave, *Diary of a Chambermaid* (New York: Didier; London: The Fortune Press, 1946) [contains a brief caricature of Wilde in the character of Sir Harry Kimberly].

'Mrs. Langtry on the Hudson', *New York Herald* (30 Oct 1882) p. 5 [meets Wilde during American lecture tour].

Nevill, Lady Dorothy, *The Reminiscences of Lady Dorothy Nevill*, ed. Ralph Nevill (London: Edward Arnold, 1906) p. 278 [letter on the death of Lord Lytton and on securing Zola's autograph].

Newbolt, Sir Henry, *My World as in My Time; Memoirs 1862–1932* (London: Faber & Faber, 1932) pp. 156–7.

'Oscar Interviewed', *Punch* (London) LXXXII (14 Jan 1882) 14 [fictitious].

Pearson, Hesketh, 'Oscar Wilde and His Actors', *Theatre Arts* (New York), XLV (Feb 1961), 63, 64, 75.

'A Poet's Day', *Punch* (London) LXXXII (4 Feb 1882) 58 [fictitious].

Ransome, Arthur, 'Oscar Wilde in Paris', *T. P. 's Magazine*, (June 1911) 427–35 (illustrated). Appeared without the illustrations in *The Bookman* (New York) XXXIII, no. 3 (May 1911) 268–73.

Raymond, Jean Paul [Charles Ricketts], *Beyond the Threshold* (Plaistow: Privately printed, 1929) pp. 18–23.

——, and Charles Ricketts. *Oscar Wilde: Recollections* (London: Nonesuch Press, 1932) [imaginary setting and conversations].

Raynaud, Ernest, 'Oscar Wilde à Paris', *La Mêlée Symboliste*, 2ᵉ partie: 1890–1900 (Paris: Renaissance du Livre, 1920) pp. 125–45.

Redesdale, Lord, *Memories* (London: Hutchinson, 1915) vol. II, pp. 647–8.

Richards, Grant, *Memories of a Misspent Youth*, 1872–1896 (London: Hutchinson, 1932) pp. 277–9.

Roberts, Arthur, *Fifty Years of Spoof* (London: John Lane, 1927) *passim*.

Robins, Elizabeth, 'Oscar Wilde to the Rescue', *Both Sides of the Curtain* (London: Heinemann, 1940) pp. 12–22.

Robinson, Lennox, 'Oscar Wilde', *I Sometimes Think* (Dublin: Talbot Press, 1956) pp. 105–9.

Ross, Margery (ed.), *Robert Ross; Friend of Friends* (London: Jonathan Cape, 1952) *passim*.

Salt, Henry S., *Seventy Years Among Savages* (London: George Allen & Unwin, 1921) pp. 86, 181–2.

Saltus, Mrs Edgar Evertson, 'Mrs. Saltus on Edgar', typescript (Item 1924 in the William Andrews Clark Memorial Library, California) [recollections of Oscar Wilde and Edgar Saltus].

Sitwell, Sir Osbert, 'Ada Leverson, Wilde & "Max"', *The National and English Review* (London) CXXXV (Sep 1950) 286–90.

*Soil: A Magazine of Art* (New York) I, no. 4 (Apr 1917) 149–56 [recollections by various hands].

*The Story of Oscar Wilde's Life and Experience in Reading Gaol by His Warder*, with a Tribute by Rose Freeman-Ishill (Berkeley Heights, New Jersey: The Oriole Press, 1963) [reprinted from *Bruno's Weekly* (22 Jan 1916)].

Stuart-Young, J. M. 'Oscar Wilde; A Memoir', *The Illustrated English Magazine*, XXXIII (Sep 1905) 573–6 [unauthentic].

Symons, A. J. A., 'Wilde at Oxford', *Horizon*, III, no. 16 (Apr 1941) 253–64; III, no. 17 (May 1941) 336–48.

'Ten Minutes with a Poet', *The New York Times* (3 Jan 1882) p. 5 [during American lecture tour].

Terry, Ellen, *The Story of My Life* (London: Hutchinson, 1909).

—— *Ellen Terry's Memoirs*, with preface, notes and additional biographical chapters by Edith Craig and Christopher St John (London: Victor Gollancz, 1933) pp. 140–1.

Troubridge, Laura, *Life Amongst the Troubridges*, ed. Jaqueline Hope-Nicholson (London: John Murray, 1966) *passim*.

Uzanne, Octave, *Visions de Notre Heure; Choses et Gens qui passent* (Paris: Librairie Henry Floury, 1899) pp. 13–15.

Vyver, Bertha, *Memoirs of Marie Corelli* (London: Alston Rivers, 1930) *passim*.

Ward, Edwin A., *Recollections of A Savage* (London: Herbert Jenkins, 1923) pp. 50–2, 108–11.

Whistler, James Abbott McNeill, *The Gentle Art of Making Enemies* (London: Heinemann, 1904) *passim*.

Wilder, Marshall P., *The People I've Smiled With* (London: Cassell [1889]) pp. 72–3.

# Index